Utilities'
Cost of Capital

by
Roger A. Morin, Ph.D.

Public Utilities Reports, Inc.
Arlington, Virginia

First Printing, June, 1984

Library of Congress Catalog Card No. 84-60531

ISBN 0-910325-03-0

Printed in the United States of America

ROGER A. MORIN

Dr. Morin is a graduate of the Wharton School's doctoral program, University of Pennsylvania, and is currently Professor of Finance at the College of Business Administration, Georgia State University. Prior to his doctoral studies in finance, Dr. Morin obtained an engineering degree in electrical engineering and an MBA in finance from McGill University in Canada.

Dr. Morin has combined his engineering background with his expertise in corporate finance to serve as financial and economic consultant to both private and public industries, including AT&T, Southern Bell, The Southern Co., GTE-Sylvania, General Public Utilities, Hydro-Quebec, the Canadian Radio-Television and Telecommunications Commission and numerous others. Dr. Morin served as director of the Financial Research Foundation of Canada for eight years, and was associated with the management consultant firm of Garmaise & Thomson in the area of investment management.

Dr. Morin serves as private financial consultant in corporate finance and in regulatory finance, and is a frequent expert witness on behalf of numerous regulated utility companies all across the U.S. and Canada. Dr. Morin has been a long-time faculty member for Advanced Management Research, Inc., and for The Management Exchange, Inc., developing and conducting national executive development seminars in all areas of corporate finance, including regulatory finance. Dr. Morin is the author of numerous academic publications in leading financial journals.

To Susan, Melanie, Marc

TABLE OF CONTENTS

APPENDICES

4-A	Call Option Valuation
6-A	Derivation of Extended DCF Model
6-B	The Cost of Equity and the Allowed Return on Book Equity
7-A	DCF Model Quarterly Timing Adjustment
10-A	Capital Asset Pricing Model
14-A	Derivation of Return on the Book Value of Equity

FIGURES

TABLES

PREFACE

The purpose of this monograph is to provide a complete, accurate, and easily understandable explanation of the contribution of financial theory toward solving the problem of estimating the allowed rate of return for regulated utilities. Modern financial theory is revolutinizing traditional approaches to cost of capital determination. This book explains the evolution, meaning, and practical significance of modern cost of capital theory.

The occasionally formidable mathematics is replaced by verbal intuitive explanations and easily understood diagrams and practical applications. Technical definitions and equations are kept to a minimum. Derivations and equations are relegated to appendices and footnotes whenever possible for the convenience of readers interested in such details. For the average reader, however, technical matters are reduced to a miminum, and no special knowledge or educational level is assumed. A rudimentary knowledge of basic accounting, algebra, and time value of money concepts is all that is necessary. Additional familiarity with statistics and economics and a first course in finance are helpful in certain portions of the book, although not requisite. The result is an accurate, yet easily understood presentation of the subject matter.

The book is not intended to serve as a textbook. It is directed at anyone professionally involved in cost of capital, particularly public utility cost of capital. The book is targeted at two broad groups of people - those who are involved in the regulatory process and those who counsel and provide services to regulatory commissions and to regulated utilities. The knowledge of cost of capital theory gained here should be helpful to public service commission staffs, utility attorneys, accountants, utility economists, cost of capital witnesses, utility financial analysts, academicians interested in rate of return regulation, and corporate staffs involved in Treasury, revenue requirements, and regulatory functions.

Although the content of this book is addressed to the specific problem of determining the cost of capital to a public utility, it has a broader interest. The alternative theories and models of security valuation and the cost of capital are analyzed at a level sufficiently broad so as to be valid for all industries. The book is intended to give cost of capital professionals in the unregulated arena a better understanding of rate of return theory. Moreover, the knowledge gained here should prove helpful to several professional groups outside the regulated arena. Anyone involved in business valuations or in ad valorem tax adjudication is inexorably involved with the cost of capital question.

The emphasis throughout the book is application rather than theoretical elegance. Cost of capital models are surveyed and evaluated on the basis of their conceptual consistency, applicability, and difficulty of implementation. The assumptions underlying the various theories are carefully spelled out. Numerous practical solutions to circumvent obstacles are offered, and the emphasis is clearly on decision-making rather than on academic excellence. A multitude of case studies and examples drawn from actual regulatory proceedings illustrate the text material. Several recurring controversies encountered in cost of capital regulatory proceedings are elucidated.

No attempt is made to differentiate between the various categories of utilities. The techniques and concepts described in the book are sufficiently broad as to apply to all types of investor-owned and publicly-owned regulated utilities, whether they be gas, electric, water, telecommunications, or others. The numerous examples and case studies are drawn from a wide spectrum of utilities and will capture to some extent the institutional differences between utilities.

Part One provides the conceptual and institutional background. The rudiments of rate of return regulation are reviewed and the central role of cost of capital is highlighted. The relationship between risk and return, crucial to cost of capital estimation, is thoroughly explained. Careful attention is paid to risk estimation in practical terms.

Part Two deals with the cost of equity capital, which is by far the most difficult and controversial element in cost of capital determination. Four chapters are devoted to Discounted Cash Flow techniques; the first two chapters provide the necessary conceptual background, as well as the major extensions and applications of the theory, and the next two chapters deal solely with the practical implementation of the theory. Contemporary techniques, including Risk Premium approaches, the Capital Asset Pricing Model, and Comparable Earnings are the subject of the next few chapters. A new theory, the Arbitrage Pricing Model, is explained in a separate chapter. Techniques based on Market-to-Book ratios, including Q-ratios and econometric cost of capital models, conclude Part Two of the book.

Part Three describes the broader questions of composite cost of capital and capital structure. The effect of capital structure on cost of capital, and the practical implications of the theory are explained. Interrelationships between rate base and invested capital, and the treatment of various components of the capital structure is analyzed. The related issues of intercorporate ownership and double leverage are raised.

Many people have contributed to the growth, interest, development, and practical use of modern cost of capital theory. Some of these contributors are acknowledged throughout the text, but references to several others are omitted because of space limitations.

This book is the culmination of a series of national cost of capital seminars offered on an ongoing basis since 1980, sponsored jointly by The Management Exchange Inc., and Public Utilities Reports Inc. I would like to express my deep appreciation to Tish Bliss of The Management Exchange and to James M. McInnis, President of Public Utilities Reports, who believed, supported, and implemented the idea of such seminars, and inspired me to undertake the writing of this book. My thanks also to Web Johnson and Gene Jackson for their assistance and support of this effort. Finally, I express my deep appreciation to my wife Susan, for her unfledging support of this endeavor.

I would like to extend special thanks to Victor Andrews, chairman of the Department of Finance at Georgia State University, for his intellectual leadership throughout the duration of the cost of capital seminars which we jointly taught, and from which this book culminated. He is responsible for several sections of this treatise, and his contributions are acknowledged throughout the text.

Where views and opinions are expressed in the book, they are my own and do not necessarily reflect the views of Public Utilities Reports, The Management Exchange, or Georgia State University. I assume responsibility for any errors likely to be found in an undertaking of this type, particularly a first edition.

Readers wishing to address comments, criticisms, inquiries, and suggestions beneficial in future editions are encouraged to do so. Of course, they will be acknowledged. Every effort will be made to reply to such letters. Correspondence should be addressed to:

Professor Roger A. Morin
Georgia State University
College of Business Administration
University Plaza
Atlanta, Ga. 30303

Part One

Introduction:
Rate of Return Regulation and the
Cost of Capital

CHAPTER 1

RATE OF RETURN REGULATION

1.1 THE RATIONALE OF REGULATION

While this book is not intended to cover all facets of rate of return regulation, but rather to cover the application of finance in regulatory rate hearings, it is nevertheless appropriate to preface the book with some brief comments on the general setting. More complete discussions are available in regulatory texts such as Phillips (1969), Kahn (1970), and Howe & Rasmussen (1982).

The capitalistic free-market system which normally sets prices, output levels, and general terms of trade in society, is generally unworkable in the case of services provided by public utilities since utilities act as monopolies, that is, they do not experience serious competition in a particular market area. As a result, public utility regulation replaces the free market system by establishing allowable prices for the rendering of public services[1].

Justifications for the breakdown of the competitive market system abound. Several economic and physical attributes of public utility markets rule out the usual competitive market system. Many public utility services are classified as natural monopolies, that is, decreasing cost service markets. Economies of large-scale production make it easier for one firm to supply the market at lower costs, hence prices, than if several smaller firms undertook to supply the same market. As output expands, decreasing average per unit costs ensue since the high fixed costs of capital intensive technologies are spread out over a progressively higher number of units of output. Public utilities can operate at substantially lower costs under monopolistic conditions than under competition by eliminating the duplication of costly plant facilities and distribution networks, or by facilitating the realization of optimal plant sizes. Economies of demand diversity from serving an entire market rather than serving a smaller fragmented market will also emerge under a regime of regulated monopoly.

The recent socio-political trend toward the free market and away from economic regulation has not escaped public utilities, with growing competition and deregulation in vast areas of communications and even power

3

generation. Economies of scale are becoming increasingly more difficult to locate in several public utility markets, with some markets even exhibiting increasing costs to scale. The natural monopoly argument for the existence of regulation, although necessary, is no longer sufficient to fully justify the institution of regulated monopoly.

Since public utilities are suppliers of essential and indispensable services to society and to other industries, they are clearly affected with the public interest. Closely allied with the bedrock industries of communication, transportation, and distribution, they constitute the essential infrastructure of the economy and the motor of economic growth. Moreover, public utilities are typically under legal obligation to serve all customers in their market area at reasonable rates and without undue discrimination, and the institution of regulated monopoly facilitates the fulfillment of these legal obligations.

To protect consumers from monopolistic prices and to preserve the public interest, the instrument of regulated monopoly has generally been adopted as a substitute for competition in markets served by public utilities, such as the production and distribution of gas and electricity, telecommunications, water, and cable television. The purpose of regulation is to duplicate the results that the competitive market system would achieve in the way of reasonable prices and profits.

Regulation achieves its aims by regulating output prices through the determination of a fair and reasonable rate of return which it allows utilities to earn. The output prices determined by the regulator will dictate the utility's profits. Given the amount of capital employed by the utility, the prices charged will in turn determine a rate of return. In determining the overall level of prices for the utility's products, the regulator must determine the rate of return on capital that should be earned. It is through the regulation of prices that the limitation on profit is achieved.

In a normally competitive industry, the forces of competition hold prices down to the costs of production, including a requisite expected return on invested capital. This expected rate of return is an average long-run concept and is not necessarily guaranteed at all times. Over the long-run, it will reflect the risks of the industry. The greater the risks confronted by the industry, the greater is the expected rate of return. The principal objective of regulation is to determine an allowed rate of return in such a way as to emulate the returns for industries in the competitive market. Regulatory commissions act as a substitute for the market place, setting allowed rates of return so as to satisfy consumer demand at non-monopolistic prices, and so as to ensure good performance. By controlling not only prices but also entry and service standards, the regulatory commission is the guarantor of acceptable performance.

In the next three sections, a brief overview of the regulatory process and of the issues generally involved is presented for the uninitiated, with special emphasis on the allowed rate of return[2].

1.2 OVERVIEW OF THE REGULATORY PROCESS

The regulation of output prices involves two major tasks[3]. The first is to set the proper level of rates in the aggregate, and the second is to develop the structure of rates. The level of rates, taken as a whole, ensures that total revenues will cover all operating expenses, including a fair return on the capital invested. The structure of rates, or "rate design" as it is commonly referred to, determines the apportionment of total costs among different customer classes and categories of service. Rate design will not be discussed in this book, as it lies outside the province of finance.

In a nutshell, the determination of rates is implemented by defining a total "revenue requirements", also referred to as the total "cost of service", then by adjusting the rates so as to achieve these totals. More specifically, the rates set by the regulators should be sufficient to cover the utility's costs, including taxes and depreciation, plus an adequate dollar return on the capital invested. The expected return in dollars, or profit, is obtained by multiplying the allowed rate of return set by the regulator by the "rate base". The rate base is essentially the net book value of the utility's plant considered used and useful in dispensing service plus some reasonable allowance for working capital requirement, and may include any new investment to be undertaken by the utility. An estimate of revenue requirements is derived from a thorough scrutiny of total company costs during a "test year", adjusted for known changes between the test year and the period for which the rates will be in effect.

The test year can be historical, current, or forward. In the past, most utility commissions have employed an historical test year. In recent periods of rapid cost inflation, the use of a current or forward test year has become more prevalent, in an attempt to temper the eroding effects of inflation on earnings and to offset to some extent the attrition of earnings due to regulatory lag[4]. Those who favor the use of an historical test year contend that ratemaking should be based on verifiable actual costs, rather than on arbitrary and speculative estimates. Moreover, in times of inflationary adversity, the use of the historical test year constitutes an incentive for efficiency in utility operations. Those who favor a forward test year point to the deleterious effects of regulatory lag during inflationary periods, exarcebated by adherence to an historical test period. More frequent rate filings, deterioration of financial condition, downgrading of bonds, and difficulty in attracting capital are the inevitable consequences of reliance on antiquated historical data.

The process of determining revenue requirements can be capsulated by the following equation:

$$\text{Revenue Requirements} = \text{Cost of Service}$$
$$R = O + D + T + kB \qquad\qquad (1\text{-}1)$$

where R = total revenue requirements
O = total operating expenses
D = annual depreciation charges
T = income taxes
k = allowed rate of return
B = rate base

In words, revenue requirements must be sufficient to cover the costs of service, which are comprised of operating expenses, including taxes and depreciation, and a fair return on the net plant employed by the utility. The average revenue per unit of output, or product price, is in turn obtained by dividing the revenue requirements by the quantity of output demanded, denoted by the letter Q:

$$\text{Price} \;=\; \frac{\text{Revenue Requirement}}{\text{Quantity Demanded}} \;=\; R/Q$$

Two simplistic numerical examples will serve to illustrate the calculation of revenue requirements and to highlight the issues involved.

EXAMPLE 1

North American Utility has a rate base (B) of $10 million, and expects to produce and sell 1 million units (Q). These can be kilowatt-hours, cubic feet of gas, number of residential telephones, etc. The rate of return (k) allowed by the public service commission is 12%. The operating expenses (O) of production are expected to be $6 million, and depreciation and taxes ($D + T$) will amount to $2.8 million.

The price per unit of output can be derived by dividing the revenue requirement by the quantity of output as follows:

$$\begin{aligned}
\text{price per unit} &= \text{revenue requirement } / \text{ output} \\
&= (O + D + T + kB) \,/\, Q \\
&= [\$6 + \$2.8 + 0.12\,(\$10)] \,/\, 1{,}000{,}000 \\
&= \$10{,}000{,}000 \,/\, 1{,}000{,}000 \\
&= \$10.00 \text{ per unit}
\end{aligned}$$

The regulator sets a price of $10.00 per unit so as to enable the utility to earn a 12% return on its capital. This return is only an expectation however, and is not guaranteed by the regulator. The actual return earned may very well deviate from what was anticipated, due perhaps to a shortfall in demand or to an understatement of costs. Or perhaps, as is likely, the regulator does not react instantaneously to the deviations from expected revenues and costs, and will only reset the prices after a lag period. This delayed reaction to outcomes which differ from expectations is referred to as "regulatory lag".

In the absence of regulatory lag, if the utility's revenues exceed the sum of operating costs and 12% of the rate base, product prices are reduced until the return is reduced to 12%. If on the other hand, the utility's investments are unable to yield a 12% return, and the utility's investments are considered desirable by the regulator, product prices are increased until the return reaches 12%.

To anticipate the material of subsequent chapters, the $1,200,000 of dollar returns generated by the revenues in excess of operating expenses will serve to service the $10,000,000 of capital supplied by investors, including both bondholders and shareholders. These investors as a group have certain return requirements, in our example 12%, in much the same way that suppliers of materials or labor services expect a certain wage based on supply and demand conditions in those markets. The return required by investors is set in capital markets by the forces of competition, and is the cost of capital, or the opportunity cost of the total funds employed by the utility.

The next example is a slightly more complex illustration and places more emphasis on the actual determination of the allowed rate of return.

EXAMPLE 2

Referring to a utility's balance sheet and income statement, the upper portion of Figure 1-1 shows North American Utility's total assets of $900 million, financed 60% by debt and 40% by equity capital[5]. The lower portion of Figure 1-1 depicts the process used to compute revenue requirements. Operating expenses including depreciation are assumed to be $350 million. Figure 1-2 sketches the method of computing the allowed return.

The first and pivotal step is to determine the dollars necessary to service the capital invested. As shown in Figure 1-2, earnings of $115,200,000 are required to service both the debt and equity capital of the company. This latter figure is arrived at by multiplying the allowed rate of return of 12.8% by the rate base of $900 million. To develop the allowed rate of return of 12.8%, the regulator determines the fair and reasonable return to debt capital and to equity capital, in our example 10% and 17%, respectively. These rates are in turn multiplied, or weighted, by the relative proportions of debt and equity in the firm, here 60% and 40% respectively, to produce the 12.8% allowed return as follows:

**FIGURE 1-1   CALCULATIONS TO DETERMINE TOTAL
REVENUE REQUIREMENTS**

			%
Assume:	Debt	$540,000,000	60%
	Equity	360,000,000	40%
	Total Capital	$900,000,000	100%

Fair Return on Equity (17% × 360,000,000)	$61,200,000
+ Income Taxes (50% of Profit Before Taxes)	61,200,000
Required Profit Before Taxes	$122,400,000
+ Interest (10% × 540,000,000)	54,000,000
Required Profit Before Interest and Taxes	$176,400,000
+ Operating Expenses (including depreciation, assumed)	350,000,000
= Total Required Revenue	$526,400,000

MEMO: Cost Rate to Service Capital and Taxes = (Required Profit Before Interest and Taxes)/Capital Base

Cost of capital including tax = 176,400,000/900,000,000
= 19.6%

Source: Adapted from an example in Robichek (1978).

TYPE OF CAPITAL	AMOUNT	ALLOWED RETURN	% PROPORTION	WEIGHTED RETURN (COST)
Debt	$540	10%	.60	6.0%
Equity	$360	17%	.40	6.8%
			ALLOWED RETURN	12.8%

The overall allowed return of 12.8% is the weighted average return on the pool of funds assembled by the utility in the proportions assumed.

Figure 1-2

CALCULATIONS TO DETERMINE THE ALLOWED RATE OF RETURN

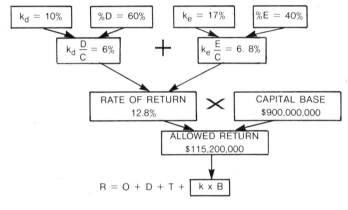

Definitions:

k_d = interest rate on debt capital
k_e = allowed return on equity capital
D = debt
E = equity
C = total capital = D+E
$k_d D/C$ = weighted cost of debt
$k_e E/C$ = weighted cost of equity

SOURCE: ADAPTED FROM ROBICHEK (1978)

In the second step, the revenue requirements are calculated, following a procedure which has evolved in practice, often referred to as the embedded cost approach. The computation is shown in the lower portion of Figure 1-1, based on the information of Figure 1-2. The method of calculation follows directly from the seminal ratemaking formula in Equation 1-1:

$$B = \$900 \text{ (given)}$$
$$k = 12.8\% \text{ (Fig. 1-2)}$$
$$O + D = \$350 \text{ (given)}$$
$$T = \$61.2 \text{ (Fig. 1-1)}$$

$$R = O + D + T + kB$$
$$= 350 + 61.2 + 0.128 \times 900$$
$$= \underline{\$526.4}$$

A sum of $61,200,000 is required to service the requirements of common stockholders. But in order to provide one dollar of return to the stockholders, the utility must earn two dollars on a pre-tax basis, if the tax rate is 50%. As seen from Figure 1-1, to provide $61,200,000 to equity owners, the regulator must allow twice that amount, or $122,400,000 of before tax profits.

An additional sum of $54,000,000 is necessary to service the requirements of bondholders. But since interest payments are deductible before computing taxable income, only one dollar of revenue is required to service one dollar of interest money. The total amount of revenues required to service total capital and the attendant taxes is the required profit before interest and taxes of $176,400,000 shown on Figure 1-1, which is 19.6% of the total capital. Based on a rate base of $900 million and an allowed return of 19.6% including taxes, the expected earnings of the utility will be $176.4 million (i.e. 0.196 x $900), sufficient to pay the company's contractual obligation to its bondholders of $54 million (0.10 x $540), and to service the after-tax requirements to shareholders of $61.2 million (0.17 x $360), or $122.4 million before taxes. Adding the operating expenses of $350 million to the amount of $176.4 million required to service capital, total revenue requirements of $576,400,000 are obtained.

As the two examples make abundantly clear, the utility's allowed rate of return is of paramount importance in determining rates.

1.3   THE ALLOWED RATE OF RETURN

The heart of utility regulation is the setting of just and reasonable rates by way of a fair and reasonable return. How then does a regulatory commission determine a rate of return that is fair and reasonable? Although there are no hard-and-fast rules, no mathematical formula nor scientific panacea which can be mechanically applied, two landmark Supreme Court cases define the legal principles underlying the regulation of a public utility's rate of return and provide the foundations for the notion of a fair return:

1. *Bluefield Water Works & Improvement Co. v. Public Service Commission of West Virginia* (262 U.S. 679, 1923).

2. *Federal Power Commission v. Hope Natural Gas Company* (320 U.S. 391, 1944).

The *Bluefield* case set the standard against which just reasonable rates are measured[6]:

"A public utility is entitled to such rates as will permit it to earn a return on the value of the property which it employs for the convenience of the public equal to that generally being made at the same time and in the same general part of the country on investments in other business undertakings which are attended by corresponding risks and uncertainties . . . The return should be reasonable, sufficient to *assure confidence* in the financial soundness of the utility, and should be adequate, under efficient and economical management, to *maintain and support its credit and enable it to raise money* necessary for the proper discharge of its public duties."

The *Hope* case expanded on the guidelines to be used to assess the reasonableness of the allowed return. The Court reemphasized its statements in the *Bluefield* case and recognized that revenues must also cover "capital costs". The Court stated:

"From the investor or company point of view it is important that there be enough revenue not only for operating expenses but also for the capital costs of the business. These include service on the debt and dividends on the stock . . . By that standard the return to the equity owner should be *commensurate with returns on investments in other enterprises having corresponding risks.* That return, moreover, should be sufficient to assure confidence in the financial integrity of the enterprise, so as to *maintain its credit and attract capital.*"

The U.S. Supreme Court reiterated the criteria set forth in *Hope* in the *Federal Power Commission v. Memphis Light, Gas & Water Division*, 411 U.S. 458 (1973), and *Permian Basin Rate Cases*, 390 U.S. 747 (1968) cases. In the latter case, the U.S. Supreme Court stressed that a regulatory agency's rate of return order should " ... reasonably be expected to maintain financial integrity, attract necessary capital, and fairly compensate investors for the risks they have assumed ... "

Two standards of fairness and reasonableness of the allowed rate of return for a public utility emerge from the statements of the Court in these two cases[7]:

1. A standard of capital attraction, and

2. A standard of comparable earnings

The economic logic underlying the notion of a fair return is straightforward. There is an opportunity cost associated with the funds that capital suppliers provide a public utility. That cost is the expected return foregone by not investing in other enterprises of corresponding risks. Thus, the expected rate of return on a public utility's debt and equity capital should equal the expected rate of return on the debt and equity of other firms having comparable risks. Moreover, a utility should maintain its credit so that it continues to have access to the capital markets to raise the funds required for investment. The allowed return should therefore be sufficient to assure confidence in its financial health so it is able to maintain its credit and continue to attract funds on reasonable terms.

In contrast to the transparency of the legal and economic concepts of a fair return, the actual implementation of the concept is more controversial. The fair return to the equity holder of a public utility's common stock has been typically derived from two main approaches:

1. Comparable earnings, and

2. Discounted Cash Flow (DCF) Techniques

Both of these approaches are treated extensively in subsequent chapters. Briefly, the comparable earnings standard uses as the measure of fair return the returns earned on book equity investments in firms having comparable risks. In application, the rates of earnings experienced on common equity by firms comparable in risk to the utility in question are considered. The attraction of capital standard, which focuses on investors' return requirements, is applied through the Discounted Cash Flow or market value method. This test defines fair return as the return investors anticipate when they purchase equity shares of comparable risk companies in the financial marketplace; this is a market-based rate of return, defined in terms of anticipated dividends and capital gains relative to stock prices.

Recent developments in financial theory have given considerable impetus to the determination of fair return based on formal risk-return models. Risk Premium approaches, which make use of information on the relative risk premium between stocks and bonds, are often used as complementary techniques to provide an additional check on the results provided by the aforementioned techniques. More refined market-based techniques, such as the Capital Asset Pricing Model (CAPM) and Arbitrage

Pricing Theory (APT), have recently appeared in the regulatory process. These techniques are analysed in subsequent chapters.

The Hope case was also responsible for the so-called "end-result" doctrine, suggesting that the regulatory methods employed are immaterial so long as the end result is reasonable to the consumer and investor. In other words, a regulator is not bound to use any single formula in determining rates. It is the result reached and the impact of the rate order rather than the method or the theory employed which is controlling. Potential infirmities inherent in the methods used are of secondary importance. This is a reassuring assertion, given the stringency and surrealism of the assumptions which frequently characterize the models and theories employed in the determination of a fair return. The end-result doctrine is reminiscent of the philosophy of economic positivism, which states that the value of a model or theory should not be assessed by the severity or realism of its assumptions, but rather by its ability to explain or predict economic phenomena.

1.4 REGULATORY ISSUES

There are numerous issues, points of contention, and controversies in regulatory proceedings[8]. Discussion of these issues can best be structured on a sequential term-by-term analysis of the seminal cost of service formula:

$$R = O + D + T + kB \qquad (1\text{-}2)$$

The allowed rate of return 'k', or cost of capital, can be expressed as the weighted sum of debt cost, k_d, and equity cost, k_e, with the ratios of debt, D, and equity, E, to the total capital, C, serving as weights:

$$k = k_d\, D/C + k_e\, E/C \qquad (1\text{-}3)$$

Substituting Equation 1-3 into Equation 1-2, an expanded cost of service formula is obtained:

$$R = O + D + T + (k_d\, D/C + k_e\, E/C)\, B \qquad (1\text{-}4)$$

Following each term of Equation 1-4, the dominant issues arising in practice are as follows:

(1) The appropriate level of operating expenses. Operating costs, acceptable for ratemaking, are monitored and subject to scrutiny by the regulator. Public Service Commissions make judgments with respect to which cost items are authorized for inclusion in the cost of service

computation. Controversies over the disallowance of certain expense categories are frequent, for example, advertising expenses, charitable donations, and executive salaries.

The distinction between outlays to be charged directly as operating expenses and outlays to be capitalized, that is, entered in revenue requirements in the form of annual depreciation charges, is also scrutinized closely.

It is interesting to note that while the operating expenses and capital outlays of public utilities constitute the major component of revenue requirements, and directly involve the efficiency with which society's resources are used, regulators devote relatively less attention to these items in sharp contrast to the major attention given to controlling the rate of return. Perhaps this is not so surprising, given the political visibility of profit levels and the administrative infeasibility of monitoring company expenses.

(2) The method of depreciating capital outlays, and the appropriate accounting treatment of depreciation tax savings to be used for ratemaking are contentious issues. Several options are available for depreciating utility plant, including straight-line, double-declining, and sum-of-the-digits methods. Tax savings are generated if a utility is allowed a more rapid rate of depreciation in the early years of an asset's life for tax purposes than for ratemaking purposes. Tax savings also occur if investment tax credits are available to the utility. Some regulatory commissions require that these savings be "flowed-through" to customers in the years in which they are earned, thereby reducing revenue requirements in those years relative to what it would otherwise be. Other regulatory commissions require that these savings be "normalized", and that the rate base be reduced each year by the amount of the reduction in the normalization reserve for that year. This issue is explored in more detail in Chapter 4, insofar as it influences the quality of the utility's earnings, its riskiness, and hence its cost of capital.

(3) The appropriate level of the capital base raises controversies as to what should be included or excluded from the rate base, the test period to use, and the valuation basis.

With regards to the proper inclusions and exclusions, traditional practice is to include all assets which are "used and useful". This is notably ambiguous in the case of construction work in progress (CWIP). Can CWIP be classified as used and useful, and is it not essential for continuing service for current ratepayers and for the going concern value of the enterprise? The issue of CWIP and the attendant allowance for funds used during construction (AFUDC) is addressed in Chapter 4, insofar as it affects the quality of earnings, cash flows, risk, and the utility's cost of capital.

Two general concepts of rate base valuation prevail: original cost and fair value. Reproduction cost and current cost concepts are variants of the fair value concept. All three concepts attempt to measure changes in the value of utility plant and facilities since their original inception. Because of its administrative tractability and verifiability, the original (historical or book) cost approach is preferred in practice by a majority of commissions.

Valuation of the rate base was highly controversial prior to the landmark *Hope* decision in 1944. The *Smith v. Ames* judgment by the Supreme Court in 1898 had set the stage for fair value, embroiling regulators and courts in endless battles over the definition and measurement of fair value and sunk capital. In *Smith v. Ames* (1969 U.S. 467), the court stated:

> "What the company is entitled to ask is a fair return upon the value of that which it employs for the public convenience . . . And, in order to ascertain that value . . . the amount and market value of its bonds and stock . . . are to be given such weight as may be just and right in each case."

In the *Hope* decision, the Court eliminated the necessity for regulatory commissions to rely on reproduction cost exclusively in determining rates. The "end-result" doctrine was promulgated, and as long as investors are fairly treated and as long as rates are fair to consumers, the Court would not dictate any particular rate base. In the *Hope* decision, the Court dealt a major blow to the notion of a fair value rate base. The inherent circularity of a fair value rate base whereby rates are made to depend upon fair value when fair value of the utility itself depends on earnings under whatever rates are anticipated, was recognized by the Court.

Attention then shifted from the rate base to the fair rate of return, although controversy over the rate base still remains.

It should be mentioned that there are welfare implications, depending on the rate base valuation method used. Gordon (1977) has shown that the risk and thus shareholders' required rate of return is higher under the replacement than under the historical cost method. Moreover, the risk to ratepayers is higher with a replacement cost rate base because any unanticipated changes in costs of production are reflected immediately in the rates. With an historical rate base on the other hand, the rates are adjusted only when the physical plant and facilities are actually replaced.

The most controversial step in the determination of revenue requirements, and the principal concern of this monograph, is the determination of a fair rate of return. Both the specific return on each type of capital, debt and equity, and the relative mix of debt and equity employed, must be addressed.

Return on Debt Capital. The return on debt is the least controversial element. Payments on bonds and on preferred stock are embedded costs, clearly stated on the bond and preferred stock certificate. The embedded cost of debt and preferred stock is simply the total interest payments divided by the book value of the outstanding debt, and preferred dividends divided by the amount of preferred outstanding, respectively. The only problem in determining the cost rate is in a period where future interest rates are expected to differ from the interest rates on the existing debt, and the utility is expected to issue fixed-cost financing in the near future.

Return on Common Equity Capital. The cost of common equity capital is controversial, and a major share of regulatory proceedings is devoted to the determination of a fair rate of return on commony equity. A large portion of this monograph is in fact aimed at estimating the allowed return on common equity.

Unlike the fixed and known contractual payments on bonds, earnings on common stock are residual in nature, available only after prior legitimate claims on earnings have been met. It is difficult to specify what these residual earnings will be in advance. Application of the standards laid down in the Bluefield and Hope decisions presents a number of problems, which this monograph will attempt to solve. One major roadblock in applying the comparable risk standard of Hope is the measurement of risk, so that comparable risk investments can be used as a guide in establishing a fair return. The basic questions of how the return to the equity owner is to be measured, whether it should be on the basis of book or market value, and over what time period present problems as well.

Prior to the mid 1960's, regulators placed almost exclusive reliance on the Comparable Earnings approach. Because of several problems encountered in implementing the approach, the Discounted Cash Flow approach has supplanted the Comparable Earnings in popularity. Following major theoretical developments in finance, the Capital Asset Pricing Theory has achieved some notoriety in regulatory proceedings. More recently, contemporary advances in finance and economics have spawned the Q-ratio, the Arbitrage Pricing Theory, and more elaborate Risk Premium approaches, all of which are likely to gain prominence in future regulatory proceedings. The return on equity is inevitably arrived at by judgment, enlightened by the implementation of a vast arsenal of techniques, models, and theories, each with its own set of assumptions, simplifications, premises and problems. These methodologies will be surveyed and analyzed in subsequent chapters.

Capital Structure. The existence of an optimal proportion of debt and equity capital is occasionally a contentious issue. Sometimes, the regulator will impute debt/equity proportions other than those actually employed by the utility, if the capital structure is deemed non-optimal by the regulator. The correct mix of debt and equity capital is particularly relevant for ratepayers, since equity costs approximately twice as much as debt owing to the tax deductibility of interest payments on debt. Another issue in determining the capital structure is whether book value weights or market value weights should be employed in computing the weighted average cost of capital. These topics will be covered in Chapters 14 and 15.

1.5 LIMITATIONS OF RATE OF RETURN REGULATION

In this monograph, the framework of rate of return regulation is taken as given, along with the existing legal and procedural context, although it may not necessarily be the best. The purpose of this book is not to review the critiques and condemnations of rate of return regulation. Adequate treatment of this subject exists elsewhere[9]. Nevertheless, some caveats and reservations are worthy of mention.

Even if the rate base and the allowed rate of return can be correctly identified, rate of return regulation as an institution has potential shortcomings.

With the spirit and spur of competition removed, what incentives does the utility have to be efficient and produce at least cost? Under the umbrella of rate of return regulation where ideally the allowed return is continuously adjusted downward if the utility becomes more cost efficient, and upwards otherwise, will the firm strive for efficiency? Some incentives for efficiency within the framework of rate of return regulation have been proposed. Allowing a range of permissible returns instead of a specific number, within which the utility's return could fluctuate, reaping some reward for success, and penalty for failure, could provide utility management some incentive for efficiency. An allowance over and above the cost of capital has been proposed to provide the same incentives to management that competition provides in the unregulated sector of the economy. But as Averch-Johnson (1962) have shown, there is an incentive to overcapitalize when the allowed return exceeds the cost of capital, and the stock price increases with the quantity of capital employed by the utility; investment projects that would not be accepted by a profit maximizing firm may be acceptable to a regulated utility due to the associated increase in the rate base. Myers (1972) has advocated the conscious use of regulatory lag as an incentive device. But are the benefits obtained with such a scheme sufficient to offset the resulting increase in the risk of the return to be realized?

As pointed out by Kahn (1970), control over the allowed return may not be sufficient to protect the consumer against monopoly pricing for a utility operating in more than one market. A utility with two markets for example, where demand is more price elastic in one is motivated to lower the price in that market below cost in order to increase demand. Not only may an increase in capacity be required, but losses in that market fall on the consumer, and the price in the other market is raised toward the monopoly price.

Finally, non-price dimensions of utility products may be ignored by strict adherence to the limitation of profits. Quality of service, reliability, and safety of service may be compromised according to this argument. But the fact that utilities are greatly exposed to public criticism for inadequate service tempers this argument. If anything, there is an inclination to expand the rate base and improve service in rate-of-return regulation. Besides, additional costs of improving service can always be included in the cost of service. A thorough reading of the literature leaves one with the feeling that in spite of its failings, rate of return regulation remains the best overall regulatory framework.

This book focuses on the rate of return component of regulation. The first few chapters establish the conceptual foundations of rate of return and cost of capital. The relationship between return and risk which underlies the cost of capital concept is emphasized. The next several chapters survey the techniques available to estimate the cost of equity capital, pointing out the assumptions, strengths and weaknesses, and applicability of each technique. The last few chapters discuss the composite cost of capital and the related capital structure effects.

Notes

[1] For an excellent exposition of the rationale of regulation, see Kahn (1970), Chapter 1.

[2] For a recent and comprehensive overview of the regulatory process and of the issues involved, see Howe & Rasmussen (1982), Chapter 4. Classic treatments of the same subject are also found in Garfield & Lovejoy (1964), Phillips (1969), and Kahn (1970).

[3] See Kahn (1970), Chapter 2.

[4] For an analysis of regulatory lag and possible remedies, see Kolb, Morin & Gay (1983).

[5] This example and the accompanying figures are adapted from Robichek (1978).

[6] Emphasis in the quotes is provided by the author.

[7] Similar legal principles underlying the notion of a fair return were enunciated in several landmark court cases in Canada. See for example *Northern Alberta Natural Gas v. Board of Public Utilities Commissioners of Alberta* (1926), *Northwestern Utilities v. City of Edmonton* (1929), 2 D.L.R. 4, p. 8, and *British Columbia Electric Railway v. Public Utilities Commission of British Columbia et al,* (1960), 45 D.L.R. (2nd), pp. 697-8.

[8] It is obviously impossible to do justice to all aspects of regulation in such a limited space; only a brief outline of the issues that play a role of particular importance when financial theory is introduced into regulatory proceedings is reported. See Howe & Rasmussen (1982), Chapter 4, and Kahn (1970) for a more comprehensive treatment of regulatory issues.

[9] A critique of public utility regulation is available in Howe & Rasmussen (1982), Chapter 6. See also Gordon (1977), Averch-Johnson (1962), Myers (1972), and Kahn (1970).

CHAPTER 2

THE CONCEPT OF COST OF CAPITAL

2.1 THE CONCEPT OF COST OF CAPITAL

As discussed in the previous chapter, the revenues generated when the allowed rate of return is applied to the rate base are used to service the capital supplied by investors to the utility. The aggregate return required by these investors is called "cost of capital". The cost of capital is the opportunity cost, expressed in percentage terms, of the total pool of capital employed by the utility. It is the composite weighted cost of the various classes of capital (bonds, preferred stock, common stock) used by the utility, with the weights reflecting the proportions of the total which each class of capital represents.

While utilities enjoy varying degrees of monopoly in the sale of public utility services, they must compete with every one else in the free open market for the input factors of production, whether it be labor, materials, machines, or capital. The prices of these inputs are set in the competitive marketplace by supply and demand, and it is these input prices which are incorporated in the cost of service computation. This is just as true for capital as for any other factor of production. Since utilities must go to the open capital market and sell their securities in competition with every other issuer, there is obviously a market price to pay for the capital they require, for example, the interest on debt capital, or the expected return on equity.

The Price of Capital and Opportunity Cost

While the market price of labor, materials, and machines is easily verifiable, the price of the capital input is more complex to determine. When investors supply funds to a utility by buying its stocks or bonds, not only are they postponing consumption, giving up the alternative of spending their dollars in some other way, but they are also exposing their funds to risk. Investors are willing to incur this double penalty only if they are adequately compensated. The compensation they require is the price of capital. If there are differences in the risk of the investments, competition among firms for a limited supply of capital will bring different prices. These differences in risk are translated into price differences by the capital markets in much the same way that commodities which differ in characteristics will trade at different prices.

The important point is that the prices of debt capital and equity capital are set by supply and demand, and both are influenced by the relationship between the risk and return expected for those securities and the risks expected from the overall menu of available securities.

The concepts underlying the cost of capital are firmly anchored in the opportunity cost notion of economics. The cost of a specific source of capital is basically determined by the riskiness of that investment in light of alternate opportunities, and equals the investor's current opportunity cost of investing in the securities of that utility. A rational investor is maximizing the performance of his portfolio only if returns expected on investments of comparable risk are the same. If not, the investor will switch out of those investments yielding low returns at a given risk level in favor of those investments offering higher returns for the same degree of risk. This implies that a utility will be unable to attract capital unless it can offer returns to capital suppliers comparable to those achieved on alternate competing investments of similar risk.

The price of capital is expressed as a percentage rate per dollar of capital supplied, referred to as the investor's "required rate of return". Cost of capital is synonymous with required return (market yield). The duality between cost and return can be demonstrated as follows[1]. A utility issues a financial security to investors, and receives an immediate inflow of cash, to be followed by periodic cash outflows required to service the security issued. The initial cash inflow to the utility corresponds to an equivalent cash outflow for the investors who purchase the security. The sequence of periodic cash outflows servicing the security corresponds to a sequence of cash receipts for the investors. The cash flows from the utility's point of view and from that of investors are exact counterparts, mirror images of one another. In the case of a bond for example, the compensation received by bondholders is the expected stream of coupon payments over the life of the bond plus the expected proceeds from either the sale or redemption of the bond. In the case of common stock, it is the stream of future dividends and the expected proceeds upon resale at some future date.

Based on orthodox time value of money concepts, the investor's return is that rate of return which makes the present value of the expected cash receipts equal to the current price, or outflow. The cost of the funds raised to the utility is that rate which makes the present value of the cash outflows required to service the security equal to the cash received initially. But since the cash flow stream to the investor is identical to that of the utility, these two rates must be identical[2]. In other words, the cost of capital to the utility is synonymous with the investor's return, and the cost of capital is the earnings which must be generated by the investment of that capital in order to pay its price, that is, in order to meet the investor's required rate of return.

Cost of Capital and Rational Investment Behavior

The concept of cost of capital can be approached not only by reference to the fundamental economic concept of opportunity cost which pertains to the supply side of capital markets but also by reference to the demand side of the capital markets.

The demand side viewpoint recognizes that regulated utilities are private corporations with shareholders-owners, and that management's principal responsibility is to maximize their well-being, as measured by stock price. Thus, only those investment decisions which maximize the price of the stock should be undertaken. A utility will continue to invest in real physical assets if the return on these investments exceeds or equals its cost of capital. The cost of capital is the minimum rate of return which must be earned on assets to justify their acquisition, and the regulator must set the allowed return such that optimal investment rates are obtained, and that no other investment rate would result in a higher share price.

In this context, the cost of capital is the expected earnings on the utility's investments which are required to leave unchanged the value of the previously invested capital. If new capital does not earn its price or required rate of return, the value of existing equity has to make up the difference. If the new capital earns a return greater than its price, existing shareholders will participate in the difference. If earnings on the investment of capital meet the required rate of return, existing shareholders will neither gain nor lose.

$$\text{Cost of Capital} = \text{Required Rate of Return} = \frac{\text{Required Earnings}}{\text{Capital Invested}}$$

2.2 THE ALLOWED RATE OF RETURN AND COST OF CAPITAL

The regulator should set the allowed rate of return equal to the cost of capital so that the utility can achieve the optimal rate of investment at the minimum price to the ratepayers. This can be demonstrated as follows.

In Example No. 2 of Chapter 1, a utility with a rate base of $900 million was considered, financed 60% by debt and 40% by equity. The cost of capital was estimated at 12.8%. Now suppose that the regulator sets the allowed return at 10% instead. To service the claims of both the bondholders and shareholders, earnings over costs should amount to $115,200,000 (12.8% x $900,000,000).

If the utility is allowed a return of only 10% on a rate base of $900 million, earnings of only $90,000,000 are produced, that is 10% of $900 million. While the earnings are sufficient to cover the interest payments of $54 million to the bondholders who have a prior claim on earnings, they are not enough to cover the claims of shareholders in the amount of $61.2 million. The stock price has to fall to a level such that an investor who purchases the stock after the price reduction will just obtain his opportunity cost. If the utility nevertheless undertakes capital investments which are allowed to earn 10% while the cost of the funds is 12.8% because they are mandatory, the inevitable result is a reduction in stock price and a wealth transfer from shareholders to ratepayers.

Conversely, if the allowed rate of return is greater than the cost of capital, capital investments are undertaken and investors' opportunity costs are more than achieved. Any excess earnings over and above those required to service debt capital accrue to the equity holders, and the stock price increases. In this case, the wealth transfer occurs from ratepayers to shareholders.

Investments are undertaken by the utility with no wealth transfer between ratepayers and shareholders only if the allowed rate of return is set equal to the cost of capital. In this case, the expected earnings generated from investments are just sufficient to service the claims of the debt and equity holders, no more no less. Setting the allowed return equal to the cost of capital is the only policy which will produce optimal investment rates at the minimum price to the ratepayer.

The implication of such a policy for the relationship between stock price and book value per share will be spelled out in Chapter 13. Essentially, if the allowed return is equal to the cost of capital, stock price is driven to book value per share.

2.3   DETERMINATION OF THE COST OF CAPITAL

The standard procedure which has evolved in practice for the determination of the allowed rate of return is now described. As demonstrated in the previous section, the allowed return should be set such that the opportunity costs of bond holders and stockholders are covered. The general procedure is schematically depicted in Figure 2-1[3]. The cost of debt and common equity are first determined separately, then weighted by the proportions of debt and equity in the capital structure to arrive at the weighted average cost of capital, which is finally translated into an overall allowed rate of return.

As an example, Table 2-1 below illustrates the computation of the overall rate of return requested from the Federal Energy Regulatory Commission by the Georgia Power Company in a 1981 filing for rate relief[4]. The overall return of 11.22% is obtained by multiplying the embedded cost of debt and the embedded cost of preferred stock by their respective proportion in the capital structure, and adding to this the product of the cost of common equity and the proportion of equity in the capital structure.

Two feedback effects on the cost of capital are shown on Figure 2-1. The mix of debt and equity employed in computing the weighted average cost of capital influences the return required by debt and equity capital suppliers. For example, increasing the proportion of low-cost debt financing lowers the overall cost of capital but increases the financial risk of the company to the detriment of the shareholders who require a higher return in compensation for the increased risk. As the utility employs relatively more

Figure 2-1

SCHEMATIC REPRESENTATION OF COST OF
CAPITAL DETERMINATION

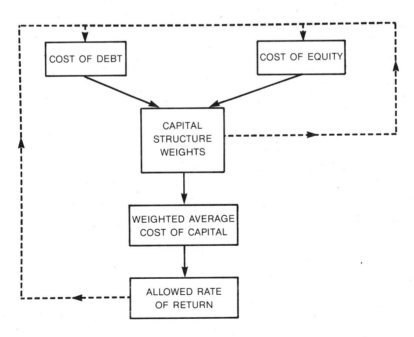

SOURCE: ADAPTED FROM LERNER (1973)

debt capital, the low cost advantage of debt may be more than offset by the increased cost of equity. Capital structure effects are discussed more extensively in Chapter 14.

The second feedback loop in Figure 2-1 stems from the impact of the return allowed by the regulator on the cost of debt and equity. If the regulator systematically awards inadequate returns or if the utility is not provided with a fair opportunity to earn its allowed rate of return, investors will demand higher returns in compensation for the increased "regulatory" risk[5].

While the procedure for computing the cost of capital is clear from the table above, the origin of the required input numbers is not so apparent. The cost of debt and preferred stock, the cost of common equity, and the capital structure proportions are required ingredients.

The Cost of Debt and Preferred Stock

From Table 2-1, the 8.81% and 9.02% figures for the cost of debt and preferred capital are "embedded" cost figures. Under standard regulatory practices which use book value rate bases, the embedded cost of debt is the actual interest obligation, including amortization of discount, premium and expense, of the utility's embedded debt outstanding related to the principal amount outstanding as of a particular date, expressed as a percent. Similarly, the cost of preferred stock is the actual dividend obligation of the stock outstanding, related to the net proceeds from the sale of that stock. Frequently, the utility is allowed to include the amount of interest or dividend forecast for an impending debt or preferred stock issue. While the inclusion of the embedded cost of debt and preferred cost in the overall cost of capital assures that the actual costs associated with the current amounts of outstanding are taken into account in the computation of revenue requirements, the company's current borrowing rate can be much higher or lower than its embedded rate.

It is sometimes proposed that the current rather than the embedded cost of debt and preferred should be used[6]. The use of incremental, or current, yields would reflect more adequately the opportunity cost of the funds invested in the utility and the returns foregone by investors. Moreover, the cost of capital number utilized routinely in capital expenditures analysis requires the use of current market yields.

TABLE 2-1 ILLUSTRATIVE COST OF CAPITAL CALCULATION

Component	Estimated Balance 7/31/81	Adjustments	Adjusted Estimated Balance 7/31/81	Estimated Proportion	Estimated Cost	Estimated Component (5×6)
(1)	(2) (000)	(3) (000)	(4) (000)	(5)	(6)	(7)
Long-Term Debt	$2,511,109	$ –	$2,511,109	59.53%	8.81%	5.24%
Preferred Stock	479,094	–	479,094	11.36	9.02	1.03
Common Equity	1,215,635	12,140	1,227,775	29.11	17.00	4.95
TOTAL	$4,205,838	$12,140	$4,217,978	100.00%		11.22%

SOURCE: MORIN (1981A)

The counter-argument is that the application of current yields to their respective book values would not provide bond holders and preferred stockholders with their opportunity cost. They receive the same interest and dividend payments, irrespective of the utility's earnings. The difference between the embedded and the current yields would accrue to common shareholders, conferring upon them a windfall gain or loss over and above their return requirement which is already being covered. In other words, it is impossible to flow the difference between embedded and current yields to bondholders and preferred shareholders without altering the common stockholder's return.

Moreover, why should regulation excnerate bondholders and preferred stockholders from the risk of mistaken expectations. When the investor initially purchased the security, the risk of interest rate changes and the risk of inflation were incorporated into the investor's required return. Should regulation exempt investors from the risk of erroneous anticipations? Finally, the use of book value regulation preempts the use of current yield instead of embedded yield. Since the time the investor purchased the securities, changes in interest rates are reflected in changes in the market value of the securities, not in the book value. Only when the securities were initially purchased did book value represent opportunity cost. After that, it is market price which captures opportunity cost, not book value. If the use of current yield is advocated as an alternative to embedded yield, consistency and logic require the use of market value weights.

Capital Structure Weights

The numbers listed under "% proportions" in Table 2-1 refer to the proportions of debt, preferred, and common equity actually employed, and not to the proportions to be employed in the future. Moreover, the weights are book value and not market value weights. The pros and cons and implications of book versus market weights are explored in Chapter 14.

The Cost of Equity Capital

The percentage cost of equity is arrived at by judgment, supported by a wide array of models, concepts, and methodologies which make up the remainder of this book. Broadly speaking, the techniques for estimating the cost of common equity fall into two general families: accounting-based and market-based techniques. Accounting-based techniques are associated with the Comparable Earnings standard, while market-based approaches such as DCF, Capital Asset Pricing Model, Arbitrage Pricing Theory are directly consistent with the market-based standards of a fair return enunciated in the *Bluefield* and *Hope* cases.

The concept of cost of capital described in this chapter can be succintly summarized as follows: A regulated utility should be entitled to a return that allows it to raise the necessary capital to meet service demand without cost to existing shareholders. This return is the weighted average of the embedded cost of debt and preferred capital, and a return on the common equity capital equal to the currently required return on equity. The two principal problems in implementing the approach are the determination of the appropriate set of capital structure weights and the estimation of the required return on equity. The optimal capital structure issue is treated in Chapter 14.

In the next chapter, the factors which impinge upon the required return are identified. Since all such factors can be subsumed under the broad heading of "risk", the concept of risk and the measurement of risk are examined.

Notes
[1] For an excellent exposition of the relationship between yield and capital cost, see Lusztig & Schwab (1977), Chapter 13.

[2] This statement abstracts from the effects of flotation costs. In fact, costs to the issuer exceed the return required by investors to the extent that flotation costs decrease the net amount of funds actually available to the issuer. More on this in Chapter 6.

[3] The schematic cost of capital diagram shown in Figure 2-1 is proposed by Lerner (1973).

[4] See Morin (1981A).

[5] Regulatory risk and its impact on cost of capital is discussed in Chapter 5.

[6] The issue of book value weights versus market value weights is explored more fully in Chapters 14 and 15.

CHAPTER **3**

RISK AND RETURN

Regulated public utilities are entitled to recover through the rates charged to their customers all costs of providing service, including a fair return on capital. The landmark *Bluefield* and *Hope* cases established the criterion that the fair return be commensurate with those available on alternate investments of comparable risk. Implementation of this criterion requires a firm and comprehensive conceptualization of the relationship between return and risk. The previous chapter established the link between the allowed rate of return and the cost of capital. This chapter links the cost of capital to risk. The determinants of required return under the general heading of risk are described in the first section, and the nature and measurement of risk are explored from two distinct conceptual frameworks in the second section. The next chapter discusses the practical aspects of risk estimation.

3.1 THE DETERMINANTS OF REQUIRED RETURN

It is useful to conceptualize the required return on any security, such as a share of common stock, as the sum of the riskless rate of interest and a risk premium as follows:

Required Return = Risk-Free Rate + Risk Premium

$$k = R_f + RP \qquad (3\text{-}1)$$

where,

$$k = \text{required return}$$
$$R_f = \text{risk-free rate}$$
$$RP = \text{risk premium}$$

The risk-free rate, R_f, can be disaggregated into a "real" risk-free rate of interest, r, and an inflation premium, π. The risk premium, RP, can be decomposed into a subset of four elements: interest-rate risk, business risk, financial risk, and liquidity risk, denoted by the symbols i, b, f, and l, respectively. Hence, the required return is the sum of the following six elements, each of which exerts an influence on its magnitude:

$$k = r + \pi + i + b + f + l \qquad (3\text{-}2)$$

Each risk component of required return (cost of capital) is now discussed separately.

Real Risk-free Rate of Return

The risk-free rate is the return that would be required by investors in the absence of inflation and risk. The amount and timing of all the cash flows generated by the risk-free security are known with certainty and are unaffected by inflation. Hence, the real risk-free rate reflects the pure time value of money to an investor, which can be regarded as the price of postponing consumption by one year, and is determined by the supply and demand for funds in the economy. The supply of funds reflects the time preference of individuals for consumption of income, and the basic thriftiness and saving propensity of the population, and is influenced by the relative ease or tightness of the government's monetary policy. The demand for funds is largely dictated by the availability of investment opportunities in the economy and by the government's fiscal policies.

Inflation Premium

To the real risk-free interest rate is added a premium equal to the rate of inflation expected by investors. Lenders seek compensation for the expected erosion in the purchasing power of their investment holdings. If, for example, investors require a real return of 4%, but expect the purchasing power of the interest or dividend payment flows to decline by 8% per year in the future, then they will demand an additional compensation of 8%. If they do not include an 8% inflation premium, the return they receive in real terms will be negative at -4%. By raising the required return to 12% to include an inflation protection premium of 8%, investors actually receive 4% in real terms. Of course, investors will only receive compensation for expected inflation, and not for unanticipated inflation. If the actual inflation deviates from the expected rate, the real return will be correspondingly higher or lower than 4%. The sum of the real rate of interest and the inflation premium is known as the "nominal" risk-free rate, and is readily observable in the market for government securities. The risk-free rate can be specified for a given holding period as the yield on a U.S. government bond of comparable maturity.

Interest Rate Risk

To the nominal rate is added a risk premium to compensate investors for uncertainty about future real rates of return and inflation rates. Interest rate risk refers to the variability in return caused by subsequent changes in the level of interest rates. It stems from two sources. The first source is the uncertainty regarding the rate at which interest of dividend receipts can be reinvested. In the case of a bond, for example, the holding period return will be largely dictated by the rate at which the periodic interest coupons can be reinvested, and the greater the uncertainty of future interest rates, the greater is the reinvestment risk.

The second source of interest rate risk stems from the negative relationship between interest rates and value. When interest rates rise, a previously issued bond paying a fixed contractual return will become a less desirable investment, falling in price. This is because any change in the bond's required return can only be accomplished through a capital loss, since the bond's contractually fixed interest payments do not vary over its life. If an investor decides to sell the bond prior to maturity, the price that someone else is willing to pay will depend on prevailing interest rates at that time. If, for example, prevailing interest rates are at 15%, a bond yielding 12% on its face value will be worth less than the 15% bonds currently available in the market. The entire process works in reverse as well. Fixed-income contracts increase in value as interest rates decline.

Stock prices, and particularly those of high-yielding public utilities, are also influenced by fluctuations in prevailing interest rates on alternative competing investments, since the dividends derived from ownership of stocks compete with the coupon interest payments from bonds.

The first three components of required return discussed thus far reflect broad economic forces outside a firm's control, and systematically affect all firms. The remaining components of risk are specific to a particular company.

Business Risk

The fourth component of return is the business risk perceived by investors. Business risk encompasses all the operating factors which collectively increase the probability that expected future income flows accruing to investors may not be realized, because of the fundamental nature of the firm's business.

Business risk is due to sales volatility and operating leverage. Sales volatility refers to the uncertainty in the demand for the firm's products due in part to external non-controllable factors, such as the basic cyclicality of the firm's products, the products' income and price elasticity, the amount of competition, the availability of product substitutes, the risk of technological obsolescence, the degree of regulation, and the conditions of the labor and raw materials markets.

The business risk of utilities is assessed by examining the strength of long-term demand for utility products and services. The size and growth rate of the market, the diversity of customer base and its economic solidity, the availability of substitutes and degree of competition, the utility's relative competitive standing in its major markets, including residential, industrial, and commercial markets all impact business risk.

Sales volatility is also related to internal or controllable factors. The reactions of a firm's management to the business environment, such as the adoption of a particular cost structure, are important dimensions of business risk. If all production costs are variable, then operating income varies proportionately to sales variability. If, as is the case for utilities, a large portion of costs are fixed, then operating income will be far more volatile than sales. This magnification effect of fixed costs on the variability of operating income is referred to as "operating leverage".

Diversification and flexibility in the fuel mix, and the dependability of fuel deliveries are examples of internal risk factors for electric utilities. Operating efficiency from the standpoint of cost and quality of service is another factor which may influence a utility's competitive risk exposure. Other examples of internal risk factors include the degree of diversification in the firm's asset structure, managerial efficiency, growth strategy, research and development policies, and competitive posture.

The impact of inflation on a specific company's sales, costs, profits, cash flows, prices, and the firm's response to such inflationary conditions are also part of the firm's business risk. The size of a utility's construction program is also a source of business risk, to the extent that new construction is to meet projected demand, and that the latter is more difficult to forecast than existing demand. This forecasting risk is compounded by regulatory lag and attrition.

Regulatory Risk

An important component of business risk for utilities is "regulatory risk". Regulation can compound the business risk premium if it is unpredictable in reacting to rate hike requests both in terms of the time lag of its response and its magnitude. For example, if the regulatory response to rising operating costs and higher capital costs because of high unanticipated inflation is inadequate or untimely, or if the utility is not given the opportunity to cover the higher costs because of political factors or inadequate regulation, the business risk premium rises further, along with capital costs. Regulation can also diminish business risk. Bonded rate increases, adoption of forward test years, and automatic adjustment mechanisms such as fuel adjustment clauses are examples of attempts to lower regulatory risk.

Any factor which complicates the investor's ability to assess future prospects will accentuate business risk and regulatory risk. Accounting gimmickry which conceals true earnings and unclear or irrational regulatory decisions accentuate the investor's forecasting risk.

Regulatory jurisdictions are evaluated on the basis of three major headings: earnable return on equity, regulatory quality, and regulatory technique. To assess these three factors, the length of regulatory lag, the inclusion or exclusion of construction work in process, the type of test year employed, whether historical or forward, the normalization of tax timing differences versus flow-through techniques, the proportion of earnings represented by the allowance for funds used during construction (AFUDC), environmental issues, and judicial and legislative mandates are the major factors considered.

Financial Risk

Financial risk stems from the method used by the firm to finance its investments and is reflected in its capital structure. It refers to the additional variability imparted to income available to common shareholders by the employment of fixed cost financing, that is, debt and preferred stock capital. Although the use of fixed cost capital can offer financial advantages through the possibility of leverage of earnings, it creates additional risk due to the fixed contractual obligations associated with such capital. Debt and pre-ferred stock carry fixed charge burdens which must be supported by the company's earnings before any return can be made available to the common shareholder. The greater the percentage of fixed charges to the total income of the company, the greater the financial risk. The use of fixed cost financing introduces additional variability into the pattern of net earnings over and above that already conferred by business risk, and may even introduce the possibility of default and bankruptcy in unusual cases.

ILLUSTRATION

The idea that financial risk increases with leverage and that the greater the leverage, the greater the cost of equity is one of the most important in finance. For example, consider a company with a total capitalization of $600,000. The company can be either financed entirely through common

equity contributed by the shareholders, or by issuing $300,000 of debt at a
10% rate of interest and having an equity investment of just $300,000. The
expected earnings before interest and taxes (EBIT) are $100,000. The
financial results obtained for the two alternative capital structures are shown
in Table 3-1 below for three assumed levels of EBIT, $80,000, $100,000,
and $120,000.

TABLE 3-1 DEMONSTRATION OF THE IMPACT OF LEVERAGE ON EQUITY RETURNS

	ALL EQUITY (000$)			50% DEBT (000$)		
EBIT	$80	$100	$120	$80	$100	$120
Interest	0	0	0	30	30	30
Profit Before Tax	80	100	120	50	70	90
Taxes (50%)	40	50	60	25	35	45
Profits After Tax	40	50	60	25	35	45
Return on Equity	40/600	50/600	60/600	25/300	35/300	45/300
	6.7%	8.3%	10%	8.3%	11.7%	15%

At a EBIT level of $100,000, the use of debt financing has increased the
return on equity from 8.3% to 11.7%. The shareholders' gain is the result of
raising funds on the debt market at an after-tax cost of 5% and investing
these funds to yield a return well in excess of that cost. But the risk to the
shareholders has increased. The earnings available to common shareholders
are more volatile, the greater the relative amount of debt used. Leverage is a
two-edged sword; just as shareholders gains are magnified in the case of
favorable operating results, potential losses are also magnified in the case of
unfavorable results. In the example of Table 3-1, the consequences to the
shareholders of a 20% variation in Earnings before Interest and Taxes in
either direction are calculated. The return on equity figures of Table 3-1 can
be summarized as follows:

Operating Results	Equity Financing	50% Debt Financing
$80,000	6.7%	8.3%
$100,000	8.3%	11.7%
$120,000	10.0%	15.0%

It is clear from these results that variations in operating earnings cause
amplified variations in equity returns when debt financing is used. The
spread in equity returns is wider in the case of debt financing, and the

greater the leverage, the greater the spread and the greater the cost of common equity.

More generally, a financial risk premium is required by both bond-holders and common shareholders. Common equity holders require compensation for the additional magnification induced in their future earnings, while bondholders require compensation for the greater risk of default. A formal analytical expression for the required return on levered common equity is derived in Chapter 14, showing the profound effect of the variability introduced to the firm's income stream by senior fixed charges on the market valuation of common stock. The expression linking equity returns and capital structure is as follows:

$$r = [R + (R - K_d) \, D/E](1 - t) \tag{3-3}$$

where,

r = rate of return on common equity
R = rate of return on total assets
K_d = interest rate on debt
D/E = debt to common equity proportion
t = income tax rate

In words, this expression states that the return on the book value of equity is directly proportional to the rate of return on assets, plus a risk premium equal to the excess of the asset rate over the debt rate levered by the debt/equity ratio in book value terms. A given variation in R due to business risk is magnified into a larger variation in the return on equity, r; the greater the relative proportion of debt, D/E, the greater is the magnification effect.

Although financial risk is unique to a specific firm and is distinct from the firm's business risk, business and financial risk are interrelated. The overall risk to the common stock investor is a composite of the business and financial risk. The overall risk of two firms may be similar when a high business risk firm has assumed less financial risk while a low business risk firm has assumed greater financial risk. In general, unregulated companies have greater business risk than regulated utilities, and because of these differences in business risk, utilities have adopted a correspondingly higher amount of financial risk in their capital structures.

Finally, it should be noted that financial risk can arise not only because of variations in capital structure, but also because of resort to financing methods which impart some unpredictability to future earnings. The presence of convertible bonds or convertible preferred shares, or the presence of securities issued with warrants attached create uncertainty as to the exact time at which the rights of those securities will be exercised and as to the impending dilution in earnings per share.

Liquidity Risk

The ability to buy or sell an investment quickly and without a substantial price concession is referred to as liquidity. Liquidity risk represents the possibility of sustaining a loss from current value when converting an asset into cash. Securities listed on the New York Stock Exchange are highly liquid, whereas the shares of over-the-counter companies are less marketable. Closely-held securities possess very little liquidity.

In summary, required return on investment is determined by the nominal risk-free rate and a risk premium. The risk-free rate is driven by expected inflation and by variations in the real rate of interest. The latter is determined by investors' time preference for consumption, by the availability of investment opportunities in the economy, and by the demand and supply for funds, largely influenced by fiscal and monetary policy. These factors are systematic in that they affect all securities. The risk premium is affected by business, financial, and liquidity risk. The role of regulatory risk is in turn crucial in determining the level of business risk. The determinants of required return are summarized schematically in Figure 3-1.

3.2 THE CONCEPT OF RISK

The *Hope* case strongly suggested that a fair return should be commensurate with the returns earned by other firms with corresponding risks. Hence, the proper measure(s) of risk to be used in regulatory proceedings is crucial in setting a fair return for public utilities. The previous section identified the various risk components which determine the required return on a security. This section addresses the actual measurement of risk by investors.

The appropriate measure of risk in regulatory proceedings depends on the framework in which investors view risk. There are two general frameworks within which the measurement of risk can be approached:

1. Firm-specific risk

2. Portfolio risk

The firm-specific viewpoint considers the risk of a security as if that security was viewed in isolation by the investor, and envisages risk as the total variability of its returns. In contrast, the portfolio viewpoint considers the

Figure 3-1

THE DETERMINANTS OF REQUIRED RETURN

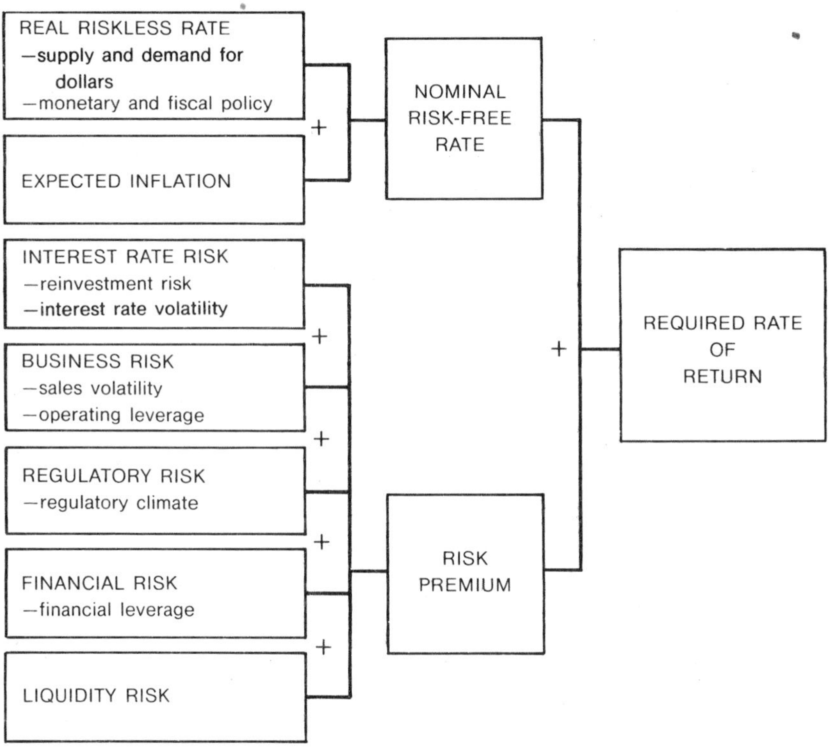

risk of a security in the context of a diversified portfolio, and envisages risk as only that portion of the security's total risk which cannot be diversified away by the investor. Which is the predominant viewpoint is an empirical question.

In a comprehensive study of individual investors' behavior, Blume & Friend (1978) found that when purchasing stock, 82% of all stockholders evaluate both the risk involved and the potential return. The three most commonly used measures of risk by these investors are price volatility (standard deviation), earnings volatility, and published beta coefficients. The first two measures of risk are consistent with the total variability framework, and the third measure is consistent with the portfolio framework. In a survey of 210 investment bankers regarding methods employed by them to assess utility risk, Chandresekaran & Dukes (1981) found that beta was the most popular, followed by standard deviation, coefficient of variation, and skewness. In a 1983 study of 165 public utility firms and 51 public utility commissions, Dukes & Chandy (1983) found that the risk measure most used was beta with 65% of the utilities and 82% of the commissions. The standard deviation was used by 14% of the utilities and 42% of the commissions. Both frameworks are thus relevant. The first section of this chapter approaches risk from the total variability viewpoint, and the second section from the portfolio viewpoint.

Firm-specific Risk

The objective of any investor is to realize a given rate of return on the funds he manages. The realization of this return is not guaranteed in advance, however. The realized return, in the form of income and capital gains from holding a particular security, may differ from the expected return. The risk of an investment is therefore related to the potential variability of its return. Measuring risk is thus equivalent to measuring variability of market returns[1]. The classic measure of variability employed by statisticians is variance, σ^2, or more commonly its square root: the standard deviation, σ. Both of these measures are essentially measures of dispersion around an average.

Variance is simply the average deviation from the mean and is calculated by estimating the squared deviation of the realized return from its average value, summing the squared deviations and dividing by the number of observations. The variance is written as:

$$\sigma^2 = \sum_{t=1}^{n} \frac{(R_{it} - \overline{R})^2}{n} \tag{3-4}$$

where 'n' is the number of observations, $\overline{R}$ is the average realized return for security 'i', and R_{it} are the individual period returns. The standard deviation is obtained by taking the square root of the variance. The average realized return, $\overline{R}$, is calculated by summing the realized returns and dividing by the number of observations, that is,

$$\overline{R} = \sum_{t=1}^{n} \frac{R_{it}}{n} \tag{3-5}$$

The individual security returns for a given period, R_{it} include not only the dividend or interest income from the security but also any appreciation in value of the security during the period in question. More formally, the return for a given period can be written as:

$$R_{it} = \frac{D_t + (P_t - P_{t-1})}{P_t}$$

(3-6)

where,

R_{it} = return of security 'i' during period 't'

D_t = dividends received during period 't'

P_t = price of security 'i' at the end of the period

P_{t-1} = price of security 'i' at the beginning of the period

Table 3-2 below illustrates the computations of standard deviation. Column 2 shows the four quarterly returns of the security in the last year. The average return per period is 4%, and the variance is 242/4 = 60.5, and the standard deviation is the square root of 60.5, or 7.78%. In other words, the average realized return for the security over the four quarters was 4%, with an average deviation of 7.78% around this mean return. Basically, the standard deviation measures the size and frequency of the deviations of the realized returns from the average, and places a heavy weight on large deviations, since it is computed by squaring all the deviations. The standard deviation of the security's returns over the one-year interval can be assessed in a similar manner from the past observations of 52 weekly returns, or 12 monthly returns, instead of four quarterly returns.

TABLE 3-2   CALCULATION OF STANDARD DEVIATION

Period	Return	$R - \overline{R}$	$(R - \overline{R})^2$
Quarter 1	+ 8%	4%	16
Quarter 2	+ 13%	9%	81
Quarter 3	+ 3%	−1%	1
Quarter 4	−8%	−12%	144
	$\overline{R} = 4\%$		242

R = return per sub-period

$\overline{R}$ = average return for the overall period

Figure 3-2 shows the probability distribution of returns for the company in the example of Table 3-2. Probability distributions depict the distribution of possible return outcomes with an indication of the subjective or objective probability of each occurrence. Empirical research has shown these distributions to be normally (bell-shaped) distributed. These distributions are essential for investors who want to know the average return they can expect from each potential investment and the risk associated with that investment.

Of course, the investor is interested in future variability, and not in historical variability per se. The variability of realized returns is only a surrogate for the future variability, and is valid only if the historical standard deviation remains reasonably stable over time. The next chapter will elaborate on this point.

Figure 3-2

THE PROBABILITY DISTRIBUTION OF RATE OF RETURN

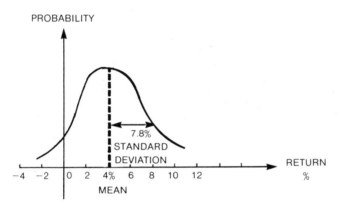

In summary, for the investor who views a security in isolation, a good estimate of its risk is a sample standard deviation of realized rates of return.

Risk from a Portfolio Viewpoint

Prior to recent theoretical development, it was generally believed that the correct measure of a security's risk was the standard deviation of realized rates of return. Progress in portfolio theory over the last decade has provided the theoretical basis for measuring investor risk on a share in a new light. What portfolio theory has made clear is that the only risk of concern to an investor is the risk that he cannot diversify away by holding a large number of shares directly or indirectly through investment in a mutual fund or other financial institution. For investors who hold only the securities of one firm, the total risk of that security, as measured by the standard deviation, is most relevant. But for investors who diversify by investing in several other securities, it is the contribution of a security to the risk of the portfolio as a whole rather than the security's own total risk which is relevant.

To illustrate this point intuitively, consider two equity investments in isolation, both of whom have a large standard deviation of return. One investment is in gold mining, a highly volatile but counter-cyclical sector, and the other is in heavy capital equipment, a volatile cyclical sector. If when the first stock goes up the other one goes down, and conversely, then the return on a combination of these two securities is relatively stable. The price movements in the gold stock are offset by equal but opposite price movements in the cyclical stock. Accordingly, the portfolio is almost risk-free, although its component securities have very risky returns. This example suggests that the measurement of risk should be more appropriately directed at measuring the extent to which an individual security contributes to the overall risk of a portfolio. It can be shown that the risk of a security is proportional to the covariance of its returns with the portfolio's overall return[2].

The fundamental idea underlying the modern view of risk is that security price fluctuations are attributable to both the general influence of the market and to factors specific to the company, such as new products, mergers, rate hearings, financing practices, and reorganizations. The general market movement in turn reflects economic events which affect all firms, such as inflation, politics, interest rates, monetary and fiscal policy. The partitioning of total variability into a market-related component and a company-specific component can be conceptualized graphically as in Figure 3-3. The individual security's returns are shown on the vertical axis, and the corresponding returns on the overall market on the horizontal axis. To each past time period corresponds a point on the graph: the security's observed return for the period, and the market's corresponding return observed for the same period. The observations are seen to scatter around a straight line. The linear relationship can be expressed as follows:

$$R_{it} = a_i + \beta_i R_{Mt} + \epsilon_{it} \qquad (3\text{-}7)$$

where,

R_{it} = **return of security 'i' for a given period 't'**

R_{Mt} = **return on a market index during period 't'**

β_i = **beta, or slope of the line indicating the relationship between the security's price fluctuations and those of the general market**

a_i = **alpha, or intercept of the line, or again the expected value of R_{it} when R_{Mt} is zero**

ϵ_i = **residual error term**

This relationship hypothesizes that the return on a security is related

Figure 3-3

THE RELATIONSHIP BETWEEN SECURITY RETURNS
AND MARKET RETURNS

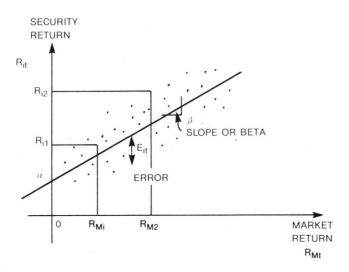

to a market return component, $B_i R_{Mt}$, and to a firm specific component, $(a_i + \epsilon_{it})$. By taking the variance on both sides of Equation 3-7, it can be demonstrated that the variance of the rate of return on a security can be partitioned into a risk component due to the general variability in the overall market and a risk component due to factors peculiar to the company[3]:

Total Risk = Market Risk + Specific Risk

$$\sigma_i^2 = \beta_i^2 \sigma_M^2 + \sigma^2(\epsilon_i) \qquad (3\text{-}8)$$

where,

$\sigma_i^2 =$ **total risk of a security measured by its variance**

$\sigma_M^2 =$ **variance of return of the market index**

$\beta_i =$ **beta of the security, measuring the sensitivity of R_{it} to R_{Mt}**

$\sigma^2(\epsilon_i) =$ **portion of total risk attributable to specific factors**

The first element of risk is the systematic component, $B_i \sigma_M^2$, and is related to the variance of the overall market, σ_M^2. The second element is the specific, or diversifiable risk, $\sigma^2(\epsilon_i)$.

Since investors are risk averse, they will diversify their portfolios by purchasing a large number of shares directly or through a mutual fund. The diversification efforts of investors will reduce in importance the specific risk component, and as a result, the risk of the stock will be proportional to its beta. As long as the firm-specific factors are uncorrelated with one another, they can be eliminated by diversification by virtue of the law of large numbers; the ups and downs of one firm are offset by that of another.

If the specific risk, $\sigma^2(\epsilon_i)$, can be eliminated by adequate diversification, the only relevant risk left to the investor is the market risk component, $B_i\sigma_M^2$. In other words, the portfolio's total risk approximates the variance of the market return, σ_M^2 times the average beta coefficients of the component securities squared. Since the market's variance risk is constant for all securities, the average beta becomes a measure of portfolio risk. And so an individual security's beta, to the extent that it contributes to the average beta of the portfolio, is a measure of risk for that security. The beta coefficient allows us in essence to distinguish between two components of total risk: one component which can be eliminated by diversification, and another which is market-related, and thus unavoidable.

This can also be seen from the graph of Figure 3-3, which plots an individual security's historical returns against the corresponding returns on the market. Not all observations of Figure 3-3 fall on the straight line, however, implying that the security's return is not totally explained by the overall market's behavior. The proportion of fluctuations not explained by the market is referred to as the specific risk of the security. The degree of scatter of the observations around the regression line is a reflection of the security's specific risk, $\sigma^2(e_i)$.

Modern theory of investment behavior rests on the notion that the specific risk component not explained by the market can be diversified away by the investor. As the portfolio becomes progressively more diversified by the addition of securities, the specific risk component declines sharply, as shown in Figure 3-4. Thus, for a diversified investor, the relevant risk of a security is reduced to its market risk, or beta, the risk that cannot be eliminated by diversification.[4]

The calculation of systematic or market risk proceeds directly from Equation 3-7, which is a standard linear regression equation. Market risk, or beta, is the slope of that regression line. Securities with slope (beta) values of less than 1.00 are said to be less risky than the market, and stocks with beta values greater than 1.00 are said to be riskier than the market. Beta can be thought of as the sensitivity of a given security to the market as a whole or as a measure of the extent to which the return on the security tracks the trend of the market. Beta is a widely disseminated risk measure, and beta estimates are published regularly by such firms as Value Line, Merrill Lynch,

Figure 3-4

PORTFOLIO RISK AND DIVERSIFICATION

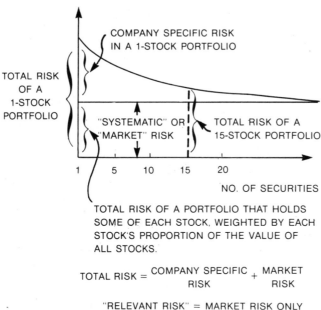

TOTAL RISK OF A PORTFOLIO THAT HOLDS
SOME OF EACH STOCK, WEIGHTED BY EACH
STOCK'S PROPORTION OF THE VALUE OF
ALL STOCKS.

$$\text{TOTAL RISK} = \frac{\text{COMPANY SPECIFIC}}{\text{RISK}} + \frac{\text{MARKET}}{\text{RISK}}$$

"RELEVANT RISK" = MARKET RISK ONLY

and Barr Rosenberg & Associates. Utilities generally have betas ranging from 0.50 to 0.80.

In summary, there are two fundamental objective scientific measures of risk: the standard deviation of the rate of return to investors, and the beta coefficient. These risk measures are readily available from investment services, and are in wide use by the investment community. Both measures aim at assessing the volatility of a security's return, but each in a different context. For undiversified investors, the standard deviation is the relevant measure of risk while for large diversified portfolios, the portfolio's volatility is more closely related to the beta coefficient of the constituent stocks than to their standard deviations.

Notes

[1] The most widely used measure of variability is the standard deviation of return. The quantification of risk in the standard deviation framework owes its origins to Markowitz (1952), and can be found in any corporate finance or investments

textbook. See for example, Brealey & Myers (1984), Brigham (1982A), and Reilly (1979).

[2] Let R_p represent the return on a portfolio of securities, σ_p^2, the variance of R_p, and x_i the proportion of funds allocated to each security in the portfolio. Then the portfolio's return is the weighted sum of the returns of its component securities, and the portfolio's risk is the weighted sum of the individual securities' risks and pairwise covariances:

$$R_p = \sum_{i=1}^{n} X_i \, R_i \tag{1}$$

$$\sigma_p^2 = \sum_{i=1}^{n} \sum_{j=1}^{n} X_i \, X_j \, \sigma_{ij} \tag{2}$$

where σ_{ij} is the covariance between R_i and R_j and $\sigma_{ii} = \sigma_i^2$. For a portfolio which consists of only one security, then clearly the relevant risk of security 'i' is simply σ_i. To analyse the contribution of security 'i' to portfolio risk, σ_{ip}, take the first derivative of Equation 2 with respect to x_i:

$$\frac{d\sigma_p^2}{d\,X_i} = 2X_i\sigma_i^2 + 2 \sum_{k\neq1}^{n} X_k\sigma_{ik} = 2 \sum_{k=1}^{n} X_k\sigma_{ik} = 2\sigma_{ip}$$

Thus, the risk of security 'i' is proportional to its covariance with the portfolio's return, R_p. This is shown in Myers (1972).

[3] Total risk as measured by the variance of returns, may be partitioned into the market and company-specific component as follows:

$$\sigma^2(R_i) = \textbf{total risk of security 'i'}$$

$$= \sigma^2 \, (\alpha_i + \beta_i \, R_M + \epsilon_i) \qquad \text{substituting Eq. 3 – 7}$$

$$= \beta_i^2 \, \sigma_M^2 + \sigma^2 \, (\epsilon_i) \qquad \text{since } \sigma^2(\alpha) = 0$$

$$= \textbf{MARKET RISK} + \textbf{SPECIFIC RISK}$$

[4] Continuing the line of thought of Footnote 2, as the number of securities in a portfolio increases, R_p becomes progressively more correlated with R_M, the return on the market. This suggests that σ_{iM} is the only relevant measure of risk of security 'i'. σ_{iM} is proportional to the coefficient β_i in the linear regression equation of Equation 3-7 since β_i is given by σ_{iM}/σ_M^2.

CHAPTER 4

RISK ESTIMATION IN PRACTICE

A plethora of empirical evidence supports the notion that investors expect and realize on average higher returns for assuming higher risks. This result holds true across bond quality differences, between corporate bonds and stocks, and across differences in stocks' standard deviations. The seminal Ibbotson-Sinquefield (1982) study supports the conclusion that on average stocks are riskier than corporate bonds in terms of standard deviations. Melicher (1979) reviews the empirical evidence on the positive relationship between risk and return for both stocks and bonds in the context of regulated utilities. The positive relationship between return and both standard deviation and beta is well documented in the financial literature. Summaries of the empirical evidence are available in numerous investment textbooks, such as Reilly (1979), Sharpe (1981), and Elton & Gruber (1981).

This chapter discusses the practical and conceptual difficulties encountered in applying risk measures in the context of regulatory ratemaking. The first two sections concentrate on standard deviation and beta, respectively. The third section explores the relationship between these risk measures and company accounting data, and the fourth section reviews alternate risk measures largely based on accounting quantities. The fifth section presents a comprehensive example of a risk filter designed to identify companies of comparable risk. The last section describes a new risk estimation technique, based on call option pricing concepts.

4.1 STANDARD DEVIATION AS A RISK MEASURE

Variability of market return as measured by the standard deviation of realized market returns over some given time period is one of the most widely used measure of risk by investors[1]. All that is required for its computation is a time series of market prices and dividends at regular intervals of time over a given time period, from which holding period returns can be computed. From the return data, the calculation of mean return and standard deviation follows routinely from the formulas supplied in Equations 3-4 and 3-5. Alternately, the standard deviation can be computed directly from the return data by using the standard deviation function available on most business electronic calculators.

Raw monthly and daily market return data from 1928 to the most recent year are available for over 1300 stocks listed on the NYSE from the University of Chicago's Center for Research in Security Prices (CRISP) computerized data bases. Standard deviations and betas can be readily computed from these data sources over any desired period. Earnings, dividends, volume data and extensive information on market indices are also available. Value Line Investment Service provides direct estimates of standard deviation for 1700 stocks on the Value Line Data Base. Value Line computes standard deviation using weekly market returns over the most recent five-year period.

Practical and Conceptual Difficulties

(1) Choice of Time Period. When computing the standard deviation, the choice of time period should be governed by the need for statistical significance and economic relevance. The period should be long enough to avoid undue distortion by short-term random influences, yet short enough to encompass current conditions relevant for investors' assessment of the future. Three to five years of monthly returns, or ten years of quarterly data are frequently employed.

(2) Stability. One potential limitation of the standard deviation computed from historical data is that it may be sensitive to the time period and choice of time interval. The sensitivity of the measure to the choice of time period, and the stability of the measure for a particular utility relative to other utilities and to other unregulated industrials should be checked. This is an unavoidable problem encountered in any statistical estimation and is not peculiar to the standard deviation. No risk measure is immune to instability and complete insensitivity to computational procedures[2]. None of the risk measures discussed in this chapter measure risk in a pure absolute sense. All are proxies for future risks, based on historical data. Future risk is something which lies in the minds of investors, and there is no infallible method to ascertain it. Nevertheless, historical risk measures are relevant to the extent that they are used by investors to assess the future and to formulate their anticipations.

(3) Absence of Market Data. Frequently, there is no public market for the utility's stock, as in the case of a subsidiary of a diversified parent, a wholly-owned subsidiary of a utility holding company, or a privately-held company. Or sometimes, one wishes to compare the relative riskiness of a constellation of subsidiaries, both regulated and unregulated. The standard

deviation of market return cannot be estimated under these circumstances, and substitute measures of risk must be computed, usually based on accounting data. Several accounting-based risk measures correlated with the standard deviation of market returns are discussed in the fourth section of this chapter. To anticipate, the volatility of earnings per share around trend, the average absolute percent change in earnings per share, and the standard deviation of book returns on equity are suitable risk estimators.

(4) Lack of Comparability. A frequent criticism voiced at the standard deviation is that when it is used as a device to screen comparable risk firms, the end result is usually a list of companies quite dissimilar to utilities in terms of nature of business. It should be emphasized that the definition of a comparable risk class of companies does not entail similarity of operation, product lines, or environmental conditions, but rather similarity of experienced business risk and financial risk. When the standard deviation is used as a screening device, the selected reference group of companies includes companies with similar business and financial risk, rather than companies with similar output or operations.

Total risk may be similar even though the business risk component of the reference companies is different. As discussed in Chapter 3, Section 2, a firm with low business risk can assume larger financial risks by a greater reliance on debt capital, while a volatile cyclical business can attenuate its total risk by a lower financial risk and using less debt capital. Moreover, when designing a reference group of comparable risk companies, a diversified list of companies has a built-in element of convergence and stability by virtue of the law of large numbers. Offsetting extreme values leave the whole relatively unaffected, lending confidence to the use of historical data. Lastly, avoidance of circularity of logic requires that the reference group extend beyond the utility industry. Reliance on utilities whose earnings are regulated to set a fair return is a circular process, and standards other than the decisions of other regulators must be consulted.

(5) Downside Risk. Objection to the standard deviation is sometimes voiced on the grounds that investors are much more concerned with losing money than with total variability of return. If risk is defined as the probability of loss, it appears more logical to measure risk as the probability of achieving a return which is below the expected return. Figure 4-1 shows three frequency distribution of returns, one symmetrical, one skewed left, and one skewed right. If the probability distribution is symmetrical, specialized measures of downside risk are unnecessary, since a normal symmetrical distribution has no skewness[3]; the areas on either side of the mean expected return are mirror images of one another. Empirical studies of historical return distributions indicate that they are not significantly skewed, and as a practical expedient, measures of downside risk such as the

"semivariance" are highly correlated with traditional measures of risk such as the standard deviation.

Brigham & Crum (1977) suggest that the distribution of security returns for regulated utilities is more likely to resemble the negatively skewed distribution displayed in the middle of Figure 4-1. The process of regulation, by restricting the upward potential for returns and responding sluggishly on the downward side, may impart some asymmetry to the distribution of returns, and is more likely to result in utilities earning less, rather than more, than their cost of capital. Hence, the standard deviation is likely to provide a downward-biased estimate of the risk of public utilities relative to that of unregulated firms.

(6) Coefficient of Variation. The coefficient of variation, defined as the standard deviation divided by the mean, measures the amount of risk per unit of return. The coefficient of variation can be a useful measure of relative risk when two series of numbers are expressed in the same units but are of different magnitudes. For example, a standard deviation of earnings per share of $0.50 relative to a mean of $2.00 versus a standard deviation of stock price of $0.50 relative to a stock price of $20.00 implies a far more variable time series. Yet, both standard deviations are the same at $0.50; but the coefficient of variation is 0.25 for the earnings per share series, and 0.025 for the stock price series. In computing the coefficient of variation, care should be taken to measure relative peak to trough variability so as not to distort the relative risk of the variable in question. Further, the coefficient of variation can assume infinitely large values when dividing the standard deviation by the mean, if the mean is very small or approaches zero.

Figure 4-1

SKEWNESS IN PROBABILITY DISTRIBUTIONS OF
RETURNS

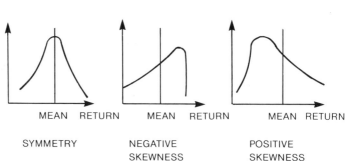

Moreover, if the mean is negative, the coefficient of variation implies negative risk, an implausible result.

When dealing with percentages as in the case of security returns, the use of the coefficient of variation is redundant, since a percentage is already a scaled measure, by definition.

(7) Multiple Risk Measures. Another commonly voiced objection to the standard deviation as a measure of risk is that it is insufficient. When dealing with the complex and multi-faceted notion of risk, one should not depend on the results of a single estimate of risk. Additional measures of risk, based on different concepts, are required to lend further reliability and credence to the results obtained from the standard deviation.

In practice, additional risk concepts should be employed for confirmation, such as beta coefficients and quality ratings[4]. In a large diversified portfolio, the volatility of the portfolio's return is much more closely related to the beta coefficients of the constituent stocks than to their standard deviations. Most institutional stock such as the stock of most utilities is held in such large diversified portfolios. A significant fraction of individuals' holdings is also invested in diversified portfolios. For undiversified portfolios, however, and even for reasonably diversified portfolios, there is evidence suggesting that investors' risk assessments depend also on the standard deviation of return. Friend & Westerfield (1980) and Morin (1981) summarize a myriad of evidence and supply evidence of their own that both beta and standard deviation are positively related to returns. Hence both the standard deviation and beta should be considered.

4.2 BETA AS A RISK MEASURE

Before discussing the practical usefulness of beta, it should be pointed out that the use of beta as an estimate of the relative risk of securities is not equivalent to acceptance of the Capital Asset Pricing Model (CAPM). The CAPM is a formal theory of how beta risk affects security prices, and is treated extensively in Chapter 10. Here, beta is used purely as one of several reasonable measures of risk to identify companies of comparable risk, and its use is not predicated on any formal security pricing theory.

Beta measures a security's volatility relative to that of the market, and is generally computed from a linear regression analysis based on past realized returns over some past time period, as shown on Figure 4-2. The dependent variable is the security's realized return over a certain time interval, and the independent variable is the corresponding return on some suitable market index, such as the Standard & Poor's 500 Industrial Index.

The beta coefficient is obtained from the estimated slope of the regression line, which has the form:

$$R_t = a + \beta R_{Mt} + \epsilon_t \tag{4-1}$$

Utilities generally have historical betas ranging from 0.50 to 0.80.

Practical and Conceptual Difficulties

(1) Computational Problems. Absolute estimates of beta may vary over a wide range when different computational methods are used. The time period used, its duration, the choice of market index, and whether annual, monthly, or weekly return figures are used influence the final result.

When the objective of estimating beta is to ascertain the relative values of beta for different firms rather than estimating the absolute value of beta for CAPM usage, it is reasonable to suppose that the relative ranking of the betas are less sensitive to the time period, length of return interval, and duration of time period, than are the absolute values of beta. For example, the ranking of all stocks based on Value Line betas, which is calculated using

Figure 4-2

GRAPH OF THE STANDARD REGRESSION MODEL
USED TO ESTIMATE BETA

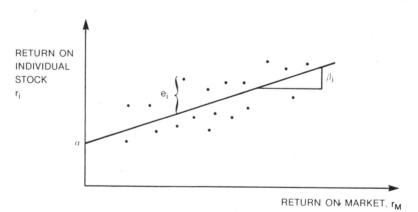

$r_i = a_i + B_i r_M + e_i$
r_i = RETURN ON STOCK i
a, B = LINEAR REGRESSION COEFFICIENTS
r_M = RETURN ON THE MARKET
e_i = ERROR

weekly returns, may not differ substantially from the ranking obtained using the Merrill Lynch beta, which is calculated using monthly returns.

A similar situation arises with the choice of the market index from which betas are estimated. In theory, unless the market index used is the true market index, fully diversified to include all securities in their proportion outstanding, the beta estimate obtained is potentially distorted[5]. Failure to include bonds, Treasury bills, real estate, etc., could lead to a biased beta estimate. But again, if beta is used as a relative risk ranking device, choice of the market index may not alter the relative rankings of security risk significantly.

To enhance statistical significance, beta should be calculated with return data going as far back as possible. But the company's risk may have changed if the historical period is too long. Weighting the data for this tendency is one possible remedy, but this presupposes some knowledge on how risk changes. A frequent compromise is to use a five-year period with either weekly or monthly returns. Value Line betas are computed based on weekly returns over a five-year period using the New York Stock Exchange Index; Merrill Lynch betas are computed with monthly returns over a five-year period using the Standard & Poor's 500 Industrials Index. In an empirical study of utility betas, Melicher (1979) found that while the beta estimating process differs between Merrill Lynch and Value Line, the beta estimates are reasonably comparable in absolute magnitude.

(2) Beta Stability. Several empirical studies of beta coefficients, notably by Blume (1975) and Levy (1971), have revealed the marked instability of betas over time. Both authors noted a pronounced tendency of betas to regress towards unity, that is for high betas to decline over time and for low betas to increase. Accordingly, many commercially available beta services such as Value Line and Merrill Lynch adjust for this regression tendency, so that the historical beta figures will more closely reflect the true beta[6].

Even with this adjustment, betas may still exhibit substantial instability. If betas are going to be applied to determine the cost of capital through the CAPM, stability of beta is crucial. If betas are not stable, any assessment of cost of capital based on historical beta estimates may not hold true for the future period during which the new allowed rates of return will be in effect. But if beta is going to be used to provide an estimate of the relative risk of various securities, the relative relationships between the betas are likely to be less sensitive to instability than are the absolute values of beta. There is some scant evidence by Melicher (1979) that beta estimates for utilities were stable, at least in the 1976-1979 period, more so than the betas of industrial companies.

(3) Historical versus True Beta. The true beta of a security can never be observed. Historically-estimated betas serve only as proxies for the true

beta. Current changes in the fundamentals of a company's operations and risk posture may not be fully reflected in the historically-estimated beta.

By construction, backward-looking betas are sluggish in detecting fundamental changes in a company's risk. For example, if a utility increased its debt to equity ratio, one would expect an increase in beta. However, if 60 months of return data are used to estimate beta, only one of the 60 data points reflects the new information, one month after the utility increased its leverage. Thus, the change in leverage only has a minor effect on the historical beta. Even one year later, only 12 of the 60 return points reflect the event.

Another example is shown graphically in Figure 4-3 where the true underlying beta of a utility is gradually increasing because of recently added risk factors, such as vast increases in plant construction costs, and increasing level of competition. Yet, the historical beta measured over a five-year estimation period lies midway between the true beginning-of-period beta and the current end-of-period beta, seriously underestimating the current beta.

This type of bias certainly applied to public utilities in the 1970-1983 period. The fundamental risks of utilities fluctuated markedly during that period. Environmental problems, demand uncertainties, inflation-related problems, deterioration in the quality of earnings, price decontrol, antitrust suits, nuclear uncertainties, contributed in raising the risk level of utilities in

Figure 4-3

BIAS IN ESTIMATING BETA FROM HISTORICAL DATA

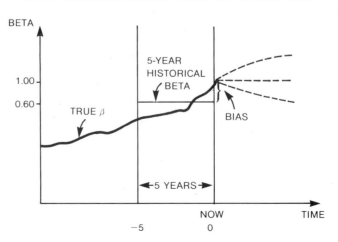

that era[7]. The structural shift in the risk of utilities was not fully reflected in the measured beta and standard deviation of utility stocks since such estimates were calculated using five years of past data using pre- and post-structural shift observations. So, any measured risk difference between utility stocks and stocks in general was misleading, and likely to be lower than that implied by a simple comparison of beta and standard deviation alone. A similar situation prevailed in the 1982-1983 for telecommunication utilities which were experiencing structural and fundamental shifts in risk, not fully reflected in historically measured betas.

For utilities with listed call options, Section 4.6 proposes a new tool designed to track short-run risk changes and detect possible biases in historical beta.

Brigham & Crum (1977) analysed the effects of risk non-stationarity in measured betas, hence on cost of capital, and concluded that a random shock that changes the true beta cannot be immediately measured by an estimated beta. For example, rising investor risk perceptions cause a decline in stock prices, which in turn produces low betas. The Brigham-Crum article generated voluminous discussion and controversy, reported in a special issue of Financial Management (Autumn 1978) devoted to the use of beta in utility regulation. The various comments offered by several noted financial scholars in that issue generally supported the view that betas could be biased, and that projecting beta from historical data could be dangerous. While beta is a sensible and objective risk measure, firmly anchored in modern portfolio theory, it should be used cautiously.

(4) Relevance of Beta. The basic issue of the relevance of beta as the only measure of risk remains. Both beta risk and standard deviation risk appear relevant to investors, based on the evidence cited in Section 4.1.

(5) Absence of Market Data. If the utility's stock is not publicly traded as in the case of wholly-owned subsidiaries of holding companies, or if making risk comparisons where no market data is available or if comparing the relative risks of the regulated with the unregulated subsidiaries of a parent company, the usual beta cannot be computed. Several alternate measures of beta risk based on company fundamentals and accounting data can be used in such situations. The next section elaborates on the use of company fundamental data for risk estimation.

4.3   RISK AND COMPANY FUNDAMENTALS

Earnings Beta

One attempt to circumvent the absence of market data problem is to compute an "earnings beta". Since beta is a measure of the co-movement between the returns of an individual company and those of the overall market, and since such co-movement is to a large extent determined by the co-movement of a company's earnings and the overall economy-wide corporate earnings, an "earnings beta" can be computed. A time series of a company's, subsidiary's, or division's quarterly earnings can be regressed on the corresponding index of aggregate quarterly corporate earnings published by the Commerce Department over the last ten years, and the slope coefficient from such a relationship is the "earnings beta". Since stock prices respond to earnings, the earnings beta and the usual stock beta should be highly correlated. The earnings beta is basically a measure of earnings cyclicality, that is, the extent to which fluctuations in a company's earnings mirror the fluctuations in aggregate earnings of all firms.

Gordon & Halpern (1974), for example, estimate the beta of a company division by assuming that the unobservable beta of the division is highly correlated with the slope coefficient from a regression of changes in divisional earnings on changes in total U.S. corporate profits. Growth in earnings per share and growth in after-tax cash flow per share are likely to be related to market return as well, and could be used instead of divisional earnings.

Pure-play Beta

Another approach to develop a beta for a non-publicly traded firm is the "pure-play" beta. This method attempts to identify firms with publicly traded securities whose operations are as similar as possible to the division or subsidiary in question. Once a sample of pure-play firms is identified, the average beta of the sample is used as a surrogate for the non-traded company's beta. One underlying assumption is that the beta and capital structure of the pure-play are similar to those of the division[8]. Fuller & Kerr (1981) provide empirical support for using the pure-play technique. The issue of determining the cost of capital for non-publicly traded subsidiaries is discussed further in Chapter 8. The search for pure-plays in the case of utility operations is relatively simple in most cases.

Accounting Beta

Given that accounting data capture the same events and information that influence market prices, and given that accounting data constitute an important source of information to investors in setting security prices, it stands to reason that accounting variables and market risk are related.

Beaver, Kettles, and Scholes (1970) were among the first to examine the relationship between accounting measures of risk and beta. They examined the statistical relationship between beta and seven "financial statement" variables: dividend payout, asset growth, leverage, liquidity, asset size, earnings variability, and earnings beta. Their results were consistent with what one would expect from financial theory. Firms with high dividend payout, low growth rates, low leverage, and which are large, highly liquid, and with stable earnings stream have lower risks[9].

The effects of company fundamentals on betas are usually estimated by relating beta to several fundamental variables via multiple regression techniques. An equation of the following form is typically estimated:

$$\beta = a_o + a_1X_1 + a_2X_2 + a_3X_3 + \ldots + a_nX_n + e \qquad (4\text{-}2)$$

where each X variable is one of the variables assumed to influence beta, and 'e' is the residual error term. The estimated historical relationship between accounting variables and beta can then be used to forecast the beta of a company. Following the Beaver, Kettle & Scholes study, several studies attempted to identify the accounting variables which are most highly correlated with beta. These studies, summarized in Myers (1977), generally find that four accounting variables contribute most significantly to betas:

i. Earnings Cyclicality: beta depends on the co-movement between swings in the firm's earnings and swings in earnings in the economy generally.

ii. Earnings Variability: beta is strongly related to the volatility of earnings.

iii. Financial Leverage: beta is highly related to financial risk.

iv. Growth: beta is positively related to growth, given the traditional association between rapid growth and high business risk.

The advantage of the accounting beta is that it responds quickly to a change in a company's fundamentals, unlike the historical beta. However, the weakness of the methodology is that the accounting betas are computed under the assumption that all companies respond in a similar manner to a change in fundamentals, that is, the regression coefficients in Equation 4-2 are equally applicable to all companies.

The accounting beta procedure was employed by Litzenberger (1979) in an actual rate case. This example is replicated below in order to convey the main idea of the approach which is to relate beta to an appropriate set of fundamental accounting variables. Several variants of methodology are possible.

ILLUSTRATION

In a 1979 testimony, Litzenberger developed a predicted value for AT&T's beta based upon a detailed analysis of a predictive model that takes into acount a number of market and accounting variables. The specifics of Litzenberger's approach are as follows:

First, the 5-year betas of each sample firm over the 1975-1979 "future period" are calculated. Second, the relation ship between these betas and a set of accounting variables calculated using data from the 1970-1974 period is estimated by multiple regression techniques, as in Equation 4-2. Third, the estimated relationship and the corresponding accounting variables for AT&T calculated using data for the 1975-1979 period are used to predict AT&T's beta for the future 1980-1984 period.

The accounting variables selected by Litzenberger as impacting the firm's future beta are: earnings beta (X1), growth in total assets (X2), book value to market price (X3), debt ratio (X4), historical beta (X5), historical standard deviation (X6), variation in cash flow (X7), current dividend yield (X8), and a dummy variable (X9) for dividend cuts in the previous 5 years.

The estimated relationship between future betas in the 1975-1979 period and the accounting variables over the 1970-1974 period was:

$$\text{Future Beta} = 0.326 - 0.015 \; X1 + .357 \; X2 + .125 \; X3$$
$$- 0.329 \; X4 + .334 \; X5 + 3.69 \; X6 + .04 \; X7$$
$$+ .201 \; X8$$

Inserting the following current values of the accounting variables for AT&T in the above equation:

X1 = 0.5798	X2 = 0.08771	X3 = 1.217
X4 = 0.3657	X5 = 0.4632	X6 = 0.02509
X7 = 0.1805	X8 = 0.09394	X9 = 0.00

The predicted 1980-1984 future beta for AT&T is 0.64.

Accounting-based approaches are useful tools to estimate the risks of a company for which no market data exist. For example, accounting-based techniques can be applied to estimate the relative risks of Bell operating companies since for several years following divestiture traditional techniques will be difficult to apply, given the paucity of market data.

An excellent example of using accounting data to infer the beta of companies without traded stock is contained in Pogue (1979). To infer the beta of unlisted oil pipeline companies, Pogue estimates the standard deviation in book rates of return for oil pipelines and for 18 reference industries for which market data is available. A beta prediction equation is developed from the 18 benchmark industry betas by relating the standard deviations of book returns for the 18 industries to their respective betas, using simple linear regression. By inserting the standard deviations for oil pipelines into the fitted beta estimation equation, he obtains beta estimates of oil pipelines. Pogue was careful in accounting for different debt ratios among the reference companies by working with unlevered betas[10]. Using the derived betas, Pogue estimates the cost of equity capital for the oil pipelines with the Capital Asset Pricing Model.

Fundamental Beta

The fundamental beta combines the techniques of historical betas and accounting betas into one system. Barr Rosenberg[11], who pioneered its development, found that fundamental beta is more accurate in predicting future beta than either historically derived estimates or accounting-based estimates alone.

Fundamental betas are developed through "relative response coefficients", defined as the ratio of the expected response of a security to the expected response of the market if both the security and the market are impacted by the same event, say inflation or energy. Those securities which react to an economic event in the same manner as the market will have high response coefficients, and vice-versa. The security's fundamental beta is determined by both the relative response of security returns to economic events and by the relative contributions of various types of economic events to market variance; the fundamental beta of a security is the weighted average of its relative response coefficients, each weighted by the proportion of total variance in market returns due to that specific event. To compute fundamental beta, it is necessary to consider the sources of economic events, to project the reaction of the security to such moves, and to assign probabilities to the likelihood of each possible type of economic event.

To forecast fundamental betas, Rosenberg uses a multiple regression equation similar to Equation 4-2, but with considerably more variables. A vast array of variables on market variability, earnings variability, financial risk, size, growth and a multitude of company and industry characteristics is used to capture differences between the betas of various companies and industries. Fundamental betas are commercially available from the firm of Barr Rosenberg & Associates.

4.4   OTHER RISK MEASURES

In the absence of market data, or as an adjunct to the beta and standard deviation measures of risk, several quantitative accounting-based proxies for risk and qualitative risk indicators are available.

Quantitative Accounting Risk Measures

As a proxy for beta and standard deviation, the volatility of the firm's earnings stream or the volatility of its book return on common equity can be computed using several common statistical measures.

The average deviation around growth trend of earnings per share, or the standard deviation of changes in earnings per share over time are plausible measures of risk. The "smoothness" of earnings, dividends, or sales, can be measured as well, using the mean absolute deviation of the actual values from their time trend; a perfectly smooth series will have a smoothness measure of zero.

The volatility of the book rate of return on common equity is also an indicator of risk. The standard deviation, the mean absolute year-to-year percentage change, or the mean deviation around time trend can all be computed from a time series of annual figures of book return on common equity to serve as risk proxies. The reader is referred to Pogue (1979) for a practical application of accounting risk proxies in an actual rate case.

While it is sensible to infer that firms with volatile earnings will have volatile stock prices, this argument is relevant only to the extent that total risk is relevant to investors, rather than beta risk. In practice, beta and standard deviation are highly correlated for public utilities, and high total risk generally implies high market risk.

Chandrasekaran & Dukes (1981) found that the most important variables used by investment bankers to evaluate the risk of public utilities were the times interest earned (Earnings before Tax and Interest/Interest) and overall cash-flow coverage ratios. Regulatory lag and high interest rates were considered significant for the risk in utility firms. In a study of the importance of variables related to risk, Dukes & Chandy (1983) found that the majority of both utility firms and commissions considered the interest coverage variable the most important. High levels of importance were also ascribed to internal cash generated as a per cent of construction expenditures, market-to-book ratio, and internal generation of funds. A large proportion of AFUDC in relation to earnings available to common shareholders was also considered a crucial risk variable by utility firms and commissions.

Qualitative Accounting Risk Measures

Quality ratings published by several investment analysis services such as Fitch, Moody's, Standard & Poor's, Duff & Phelps, Canadian Bond Rating Service provide subjective assessments of risk which influence the formation of investors' assessment of future risk.

For common stocks, useful risk analysis tools include the Standard & Poor Quality Rating, which is based principally on growth and stability of earnings and dividends over a ten-year period, and the Value Line Safety Rating[12]. The latter is based 80% on the stability of the stock price adjusted for trend, measured by the standard deviation of weekly percent changes in the stock's market prices over a five-year period, and 20% on subjective factors. The subjective factors include company size, financial leverage, earnings quality, balance sheet condition, and market penetration.

Other useful risk indicators published by Value Line include the Price Stability Index, Financial Strength Rating, and Earnings Predictability Index.

Bond ratings by Moody's, Standard & Poor's, and Duff & Phelps are useful risk analysis tools. Bondholders are concerned with the risk of default on debt obligations and stockholders are concerned with the possibility of corporate bankruptcy. Investors rely greatly on agency bond ratings as a source of information on default risk because agency bond ratings reflect the risk of default and are closely tied to risk premiums.

Concrete evidence supporting the relationship between bond ratings and the quality of a security is abundant. The empirical evidence gathered by Hickman (1958) supports the notion of a tradeoff between bond ratings or risk premiums, which in turn reflect default risk, and expected return. In studies by Schwendiman & Pinches (1975) and Melicher & Rush (1974), beta values were consistently associated with deteriorating bond ratings.

The criteria for determining bond ratings are discussed in most investments textbooks. Standard & Poor's (1982) *Credit Overview: Corporate and International Ratings* outlines the procedures for determining bond ratings for various industry groups, including utilities. Briefly, bond ratings vary directly with profitability, size, and earnings coverage, while they move inversely with financial leverage and earnings stability. Interest coverage is one of the principal tests used by rating agencies to establish bond ratings. Coverage represents the protection of assets or the number of times earnings are greater than fixed contractual charges or interest costs. Maintaining an earnings level sufficient to provide a minimum post-tax interest coverage of a certain amount (3.25 for AAA bonds for example) is considered as necessary on a consistent basis to retain a given current bond rating. The relationship between the allowed return on common equity and the resulting interest coverage ratio is discussed in Chapter 13.

The ratings assigned to bond issues are important in terms of the marketability and effective cost to the ratepayer. The top four letter ratings, AAA down to BBB, are considered to be investment-grade securities, meaning that financial institutions are potential purchasers of such bonds without violating the laws of prudent investment. Not only is an investment-grade bond rating crucial for a utility to maintain continued access to capital, but the rating determines the cost and terms of the issue. Corporate bonds are discounted at progressively higher discount rates as their ratings deteriorate.

Two inadequacies of bond ratings are noteworthy. First, they are sluggish in changing to new conditions, due perhaps to inertia and slow reaction time by the ratings agencies. Typically, other barometers of risk will have changed well before the bond rating is altered by the agency. Evidence gathered by Wakeman (1978) and Weinstein (1978) shows that changes in bond ratings are not treated as new information by investors. Changes in bond ratings usually occur several months after investors have already reacted to the fundamental change in the bond's quality. Nevertheless, bond ratings are useful and valuable in that they provide unbiased estimates of bond risk. Second, one has to go beyond the mere examination of ratings in evaluating the risk of a company. A given bond rating class is broad, and an investor is still left with an enormous range of issues from which to select. Four investment-grade ratings categories is not a very discriminating classification system when 90% of all rated bonds are included in that system.

Bond ratings and stock ratings can be used as risk screening devices to identify companies of comparable risk. If a utility's bonds are rated BBB, for example, a reasonable risk filter would eliminate all companies with a rating other than BBB.

Market Reaction Measure of Risk

An alternative to the use of market and accounting data to measure risk is to examine how investors react to risk. The behavior of a utility's price/earnings ratio relative to that of the market as as whole, or a comparison of relative market-to-book ratios can reveal investors' reaction to risk, assuming that all other things are the same. An example of this approach is the study by Brigham (1977). He demonstrates that the fundamental risks faced by utilities increased markedly during the 1960-1980 period, as evidenced by the relative decrease of market-to-book values of utilities with respect to industrials. He also notes that utility price-earnings ratios trended downward during that period compared with those of industrials, and reinforces his conclusion by a thorough examination of the behavior of a wide assortment of variables relating to the quality of earnings, inflation, construction program, etc.

Quality of Earnings

A major factor influencing quality of earnings, particularly in the electric utility industry, is the accounting for construction work in progress (CWIP). When the latter is included in the rate base, the current construction financing costs are realized in cash. When CWIP is not included in the rate base, an allowance for funds used during construction (AFUDC) is estimated and added to income. This lets public utilities capitalize the costs of debt and equity funds used in building new facilities.

Utility profits are composed of both AFUDC and operating income from sales of services. Since AFUDC does not generate cash, an increasing proportion of reported utility profits is unavailable for capital expenditures and dividend payments. When AFUDC is capitalized, increased uncertainty is injected into the reported income stream since it may never be realized in cash. The cost of capital is affected through this increase in risk.

Empirical research by Fitzpatrick & Stitzel (1978), Lerner and Breen (1981), Brigham (1979), and Westmoreland (1979) has shown that firms which capitalize AFUDC are riskier because of increased fluctuations in operating incomes and cash flows over the construction cycle, augmenting business risk. The financial risk premium is increased as well, because of negative effects on cash coverage ratios, bond indenture clauses, and more frequent financing. Regulatory risk is also enhanced because the cash realization of AFUDC depends on prompt and reasonable rate relief over the life of the construction assets. Therefore, the higher the percentage of AFUDC in reported income, the greater the risks borne by shareholders, resulting in reduction in market-to-book ratios.

Whether the tax savings attributable to accelerated depreciation and the investment tax credit are "normalized" or are used to reduce taxes for regulatory purposes ("flow through") can also exert a perceptible effect on risk and cost of capital. Relative to companies which normalize tax savings, flow through companies generate less cash flow per dollar of earnings and interest coverage ratios per dollar of interest expense are lower, thereby increasing risk and capital costs. This is shown in detail in Hyman (1983).

The results of empirical studies by Berndt (1979) and Morris (1980) indicate that companies operating under flow through experience an increase in cost of debt of the order of 25 to 35 basis points relative to firms operating under tax normalization. The question of whether utilities should be required to flow through the tax benefits of accelerated depreciation and investment tax credits remains controversial, although the 1981 tax laws have made the debate largely academic because such tax benefits cannot be obtained if they are flowed through.

Regulatory Climate Ranking

Regulatory risk can be assessed by means of ratings assigned to regulatory bodies by investment firms. More than 20 investment and research firms, including Argus Research, Value Line, Merrill Lynch, Salomon Brothers, Goldman Sachs, and Duff & Phelps, rate individual state public utility commissions based on the stringency with which they regulate rates. States where the regulatory climate is rated as "very favorable" are typically characterized by a relatively high allowed rate of return on equity, minimal regulatory lag, forward test year, inclusion of CWIP in rate base, normalization of tax benefits, and automatic fuel adjusted clauses. States where the regulatory climate is rated as "unfavorable" are typically characterized by low allowed returns, substantial regulatory lag with no interim rate relief, flow through treatment of tax benefits, historical test year, and AFUDC treatment of CWIP. As documented by Navarro (1983), the allowed rate of return on equity and the inclusion of CWIP in the rate base are particularly significant to investors in measuring the regulatory climate for public utilities.

Several recent studies have shown that an unfavorable regulatory climate is associated with a higher cost of capital. Studies by Trout (1979), Archer (1981), Fitzpatrick & Stitzel (1978), Dubin & Navarro (1983), Hadaway et al. (1982), Navarro (1983), and Davidson & Chandy (1983) have established that utility capital costs are strongly related to regulatory climate ratings. High ratings result in low capital costs and low ratings in high capital costs. In a cost-benefit analysis of utility bond ratings, Hadaway concludes that electric utilities with high bond quality ratings on average provide lower cost services than financially weaker lower rated companies.

4.5 RISK FILTER: AN ILLUSTRATION

An example of a risk filter employing several of the risk measures discussed in this chapter is shown in Table 4-1. The object of the risk filter was to identify companies comparable in risk to American Telephone & Telegraph Co. in a 1983 rate case before divestiture[13]. The group of companies was developed by screening the Value Line Data Base according to strict quality, or risk, criteria: The companies had to be industrials listed on the New York Stock Exchange to ensure comparable liquidity, excluded all utilities to circumvent the problem of circular logic, and included only companies with beta coefficients less than 1, standard deviations less than 4%, equity capital in excess of $100 million, a Standard & Poor stock rating of A+, a Standard & Poor bond rating of AAA, a Value Line Safety rank of 1, and for which corporate financial data were available in the Value Line Data Base. Eighteen high-quality industrial companies survived all screens, and are shown in Table 4-1.

TABLE 4-1 RISK FILTER ILLUSTRATION: AT&T

MEASURES OF
RISK FOR 18 HIGH-QUALIFTY INDUSTRIALS

COMPANY	BETA	STD. DEV.	S&P STOCK RATING	S&P BOND RATING	MOODY'S BOND RATING	FINANCIAL STRENGTH
(1)	(2)	(3)	(4)	(5)	(6)	(7)
American Home Prods	0.85	2.926%	A +	–	–	A + +
Beatrice Foods Co.	0.85	3.013	A +	AAA	Aaa	A +
Bristol-Myers Co.	1.00	3.378	A +	AAA	Aaa	A + +
Carnation Co.	0.75	3.183	A +	AAA	Aaa	A + +
Coca-Cola Co.	0.85	3.305	A +	AAA	Aaa	A +
Donnelley (R R) & Sons	0.85	3.271	A +	–	–	A + +
Eastman Kodak Co.	0.95	3.305	A +	–	–	A + +
Exxon Corp.	0.90	2.793	A +	AAA	Aaa	A + +
Federated Dept. Stores	0.90	3.697	A +	AAA	Aaa	A + +
General Electric Co.	0.95	2.840	A +	AAA	Aaa	A + +
Genuine Parts Co.	0.85	3.804	A +	–	–	A + +
IBM	0.95	2.990	A +	AAA	Aaa	A + +
Kellogg Co.	0.70	3.193	A +	AAA	Aaa	A + +
Merck & Co. Inc.	0.85	3.114	A +	AAA	Aaa	A + +
Minn. Mng. & Mfg. Co.	0.95	3.107	A +	AAA	Aaa	A + +
Procter & Gamble	0.75	2.423	A +	AAA	Aaa	A + +
Timken Co.	0.80	3.323	A +	–	–	A + +
Weis Markets, Inc.	0.60	2.347	A +	–	–	A +
AVERAGE	0.85	3.11%	A +	AAA	Aaa	
AT&T	0.65	2.00%	A +	AAA	Aaa	

Source: *Value Line Data Base*, November 1982
Wall Street Journal, January 11, 1983

4.6   A NEW RISK ESTIMATION TOOL: CALL OPTION PRICING

Evidence of investor risk perceptions of utility common stocks over time can be extracted from market data on utility call options listed on the Chicago Board Option Exchange (CBOE). Options on the common stock of several utilities are traded daily in large volumes on the CBOE. Listed option quotations are available daily from the Wall Street Journal.

A call option is simply a right to buy a share of common stock at a predetermined price ("exercise price"), over a stated period of time ("maturity"). The holder of an option can exercise the right to purchase the stock at the stated price anytime before or at maturity, or let the option expire unexercised.

A well-established body of financial theory has emerged in recent years on the valuation and pricing of call options[14]. Essentially, three factors determine the price that an investor will pay for a call option. First, the maturity or time to expire of the option; the longer the maturity, the more valuable the option, since the probability is greater that the actual common stock price will exceed the exercise price, and make exercise attractive. Second, the exercise price; the lower the exercise price, the more valuable the option. Third, the volatility of the underlying stock; the more volatile the underlying stock, the more valuable the option, since the probability that the stock price will exceed the exercise price is greater, the more variable is the stock price's behavior.

The valuation process of options by investors was formalized by Professors Black and Scholes[15]. The seminal Black-Scholes option valuation model is reproduced in Appendix 4A, along with a numerical example for AT&T. The Black-Scholes option pricing formula formally incorporates the three determinants of an option's value discussed above.

The market's consensus opinion of the future volatility of a public utility's common stock is contained implicitly in the market price of the option. By taking the price of the option, and working backwards through the Black-Scholes pricing formula, the volatility that is implicit within that option price can be obtained. Referring to the AT&T example of Appendix 4A, upon observing that the value of an option with $S = \$60$, $T = .241$, and $r = 6\%$ was $10.60, one would discover that the implicit price volatility of that option is 0.40, since if that volatility were used in the pricing formula, the price of the option observed in the market would be replicated.

Figure 4-4 is taken from an actual cost of capital testimony presented in a 1983 rate hearing by the author[16], and shows the standard deviation of return implied by AT&T call option prices over various time periods. These calculations of implied risk were performed by means of the Fischer Black Option Analysis Program, available commercially through Chase Economet-

Figure 4-4

IMPLIED STANDARD DEVIATIONS FOR AT&T, 1977-1982

AT&T
IMPLIED STOCK VOLATILITY

TIME PERIOD	RISK
12/31/76 - 12/31/77	.08
12/30/77 - 12/31/78	.10
12/29/78 - 12/31/79	.10
12/31/79 - 12/31/80	.17
12/31/80 - 12/31/81	.17
12/31/81 - 12/15/82	.19

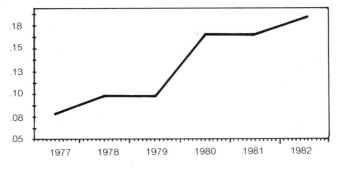

SOURCE: MORIN (1983C)

rics/Interactive Data Corporation. The obvious trend implied by AT&T's call option data during the 1977-1983 period is the steady upward trend in the risk perceived by investors, which the traditional historical beta risk measure is unable to discern clearly. The great advantage of the option-based technique is that risk perceptions can be tracked on a daily basis, and that changes in risk can be readily detected. The drawback of the technique is that it can only be applied to utilities with traded options. The apparent complexity of the technique is likely to be a deterrent as well.

Notes
[1] Blume & Friend (1978) found that the standard deviation of returns is widely used by investors.

[2] These problems are not as serious for the standard deviation as for most of the other risk measures, such as beta.

[3] For a detailed analysis of the effect of skewness on security returns, see Francis (1975), Friend, Westerfield and Granito (1980), Kraus & Litzenberger (1976), and Morin (1976).

[4] Section 4.5 provides an example of a risk filter used in an actual rate hearing which relies on several measures of risk.

[5] Kolbe & Read (1983) have shown that the omission of other assets seriously distorts the actual beta values of utilities. Conventionally calculated betas are too low for public utilities, and should be estimated with a market index that includes the returns on fixed-income securities, since the return pattern of utility stocks is similar to that on bonds.

[6] High estimated betas will tend to have positive error and low estimated betas will tend to have negative error. There are two methods to compress the betas toward one. The first is to measure the extent to which estimated betas tend to regress towards the mean over time. This adjustment employs the formula: Adjusted beta = 1.0 + K (B - 1.0), where K is an estimate from past data of the extent to which estimated betas regress towards the mean. The second method is an application of Bayesian statistics and is a weighted average of the prior estimate, 1.0, and the sample estimate of beta, where the weights are the error variances on these two estimates. See Elton & Gruber (1981), Chapter 5, for more details.

[7] For an analysis of the factors which contributed to increasing the relative risks of utilities in the 1960-1979 period, see Brigham (1979).

[8] Chapter 15 will describe a technique and provide examples for purging the estimated beta of its financial risk component. The resulting unlevered beta can then be relevered by applying the desired capital structure.

[9] Dividend payout and beta should be negatively correlated to the extent that investors perceive that dividend payments are less risky than capital gains, and/or to the extent that high payout is indicative of management's confidence concerning the level of future earnings. Hence, a utility with a high payout is less risky. Growth is usually perceived by investors as being positively associated with beta; high growth companies are perceived to be more risky than low growth firms. Since leverage increases the volatility of earnings, it increases risk and beta. Firms with high liquidity are thought to be less risky than firms with low liquidity. Large firms are less risky than small firms because of superior diversification and/or superior access to capital markets. Firms with volatile earnings streams, and with earnings streams highly correlated with the market have higher betas.

[10] See footnote #8.

[11] For an analytical description of fundamental betas, see Rosenberg & McKibben (1973), and Rosenberg & Guy (1976). Elton & Gruber (1981), Chapter 5, and Hagin (1979), Chapter 33, provide non-technical summaries of fundamental betas.

[12] Wagner & Lau (1971) found a significant relationship between beta and Standard & Poor's Stock Quality Rating. Stocks with high quality ratings had low betas, and vice versa. The ratings and the average beta for each quality group were as follows: A+ 0.74, A 0.80, A- 0.89, B+ 0.87, B 1.24, B- and C 1.23.

[13] See Morin (1983C).

[14] For an overview of option concepts and valuation, see Brealey & Myers (1984), Chapter 20.

[15] See Brealey & Myers (1984), Chapter 20.

[16] See Morin (1983C).

APPENDIX 4-A
Call Option Valuation

BLACK – SCHOLES FORMULA

$$C = S\ N(d_1) - Ee^{-rt}\ N(d_2)$$

Where,   C = price of a call option

S = price of the stock

T = time to expiration

E = exercise price

r = interest rate

σ = volatility of the stock

$$d_1 = \frac{\ln(S/E) + (r + \tfrac{1}{2}\sigma^2 T)}{\sigma\sqrt{T}}$$

$$d_2 = d_1 - \sigma\sqrt{T}$$

NUMERICAL EXAMPLE

Use of the formula requires the input of 5 variables: stock price, exercise price, time to maturity, interest rate, volatility of the stock. To calculate the value of a Utility X October 60 option with 88 days to expiration, and with particular observable values of the 5 variables as follows:

$$S = 68$$
$$E = 60$$
$$T = 88/365 = 0.241\ \text{years}$$
$$r = 6\%$$
$$\sigma = .4$$

Substituting the values of the variables in the formula, we have the option price as:

$$C = 68 \; N(d_1) - 60e^{-0.06 \; (.241)} \; N(D_2)$$

Where,
$$d_1 = \frac{\ln^{68}\!/_{60} + (0.6 + \tfrac{1}{2}.16).241}{.4 \times .491} = .808$$

$$d_2 = .808 - .196 = .612$$

and using the normal distribution tables:

$$N(d_1) = N(.808) = .79$$
$$N(d_2) = N(.612) = .73$$

we obtain the call option price:

$$C = 68 \times .79 - 60e^{-0.01446} \; (.729) = \underline{\underline{\$10.60}}$$

Part Two

The Cost of Equity Capital

CHAPTER 5

DISCOUNTED CASH FLOW CONCEPTS

Consistent with the basic premises of rate of return regulation enunciated in Chapter 1, a public utility's allowed rate of return on equity must be sufficient to enable it to attract capital, and must be commensurate with the return on investments in other firms with similar risks; otherwise, the ability to attract funds is impaired. The return required by equity owners for a given risk class is implicitly embedded in the share price of that firm. In order to estimate the required return on equity, or cost of equity, the determinants of stock price must be understood, which requires knowledge of the investor's valuation process.

Discounted Cash Flow (DCF) Models occupy the next four chapters. This chapter outlines the basic notions of security valuation which underlie Discounted Cash Flow (DCF) models of cost of equity capital. The first section reviews the classical theory of security valuation. A generalized stock valuation model is derived in the second section. The third section describes the standard DCF model prevalent in most regulatory hearings. The determinants of the dividend growth rate which appears in most DCF models are analyzed in the fourth section. The Earnings/Price approach to cost of equity determination, which is a special case of the standard DCF model, is reviewed in the last section. The necessary assumptions behind all the models are discussed extensively throughout the chapter.

In the next chapter, several refinements and more advanced versions of the standard DCF approach are described. The actual implementation of the DCF models and the difficulties encountered in actual regulatory proceedings are discussed in the third and fourth chapters of the DCF sequence.

5.1 THE BASICS OF VALUATION

The Concept of Value

Classical valuation theory focuses on the true, or intrinsic, value of a security. This theory holds that the value of a financial asset is determined by its earning power, its ability to generate future cash flows. The fundamental value of the asset is the discounted sum of all future income flows that will be received by the owner of the asset. The seminal notion that the value of an asset stems from the discounted present value of its future cash flow stream was first advanced by Fisher (1907) around 1900, and later expanded by J.B. Williams in his classic 1938 book, *The Theory of Investment Value*. Molododvsky (1974) disseminated the use of the technique among financial analysts. In essence, the application of classical valuation theory by analysts involves estimating and adding up the present values of the future cash flows expected by the security holder.

Present Value. The concept of present value is designed to estimate how much an investment is worth today, given its expected future cash flows. Consider an investment which is expected to pay $100 one year from now. Its value today depends on the return one expects to make on other investments of comparable risk. If competing investments of similar risk are offering a return of 10%, an investment of $90.91 today, that is $100/1.1, is also expected to produce $100 one year from now. So, the original investment has a present value of $90.91. The process of computing present values of future sums is known as discounting, or capitalizing. To determine the present value of a future sum, the future amount is multiplied by a discount factor available from standardized financial tables for various combinations of discount rate and number of time periods[1]. The discount factor reflects the investor's opportunity, or foregone, rate of return on investments in a given risk class. The present value of any future stream of cash flows can be determined by this approach.

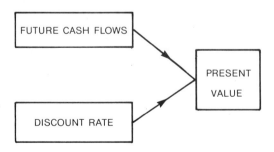

The formula for the present value of an amount, F, due in n years, given i as the time value of money, is given by:

$$PV = \frac{\acute{F}}{(1 + i)^n} = F(1 + i)^{-n} \qquad\qquad (5\text{-}1)$$

For example, how much is a bond worth which will pay $150 per year for three years, and an additional amount of $1000 three years from now, given that the opportunity cost of money for investments of comparable risk is 15%? Using the assumed discount rate of 15% and the corresponding discount factors available from a set of present value tables, or applying Equation 5-1 directly, the present value of $150 one year from now is $130.43, the present value of $150 two years from now is $113.42. The present value of the final $1150 to be received three years from now is $756.14. Adding each separate present values, the present value of the bond investment is $1000.

$$PV = \$150/(1 + .15) + \$150/(1 + .15)^2 + (\$150 + \$1000)/(1 + .15)^3$$
$$= \$130.43 + \$113.42 + \$756.14$$
$$= \underline{\$1,000}$$

This procedure is equally applicable to the case of common stocks. The aggregate present value of the discounted cash flows from holding the stock will equal the present value of the stock. Two characteristics distinguish the case of common stocks from bonds. First, the future cash flows from the stock are uncertain and probably uneven over time, unlike the cash flows from bonds which are contractually set and known with relative certainty. Second, since the risk of holding stock exceeds that of holding bonds, the expected future cash flows from the stock must be discounted at a higher opportunity rate of interest, reflecting the additional risk.

Common Stock Valuation

The cash flows expected by investors holding common stock are dividends and changes in stock price.

One-year Holding Period

Consider an investor with a one-year holding period. For example, if a dividend of $5 and a resale price of $26 are expected at the end of the first year, and the stock is currently trading at $25, then the net cash flow expected by the investor is:

$$\text{cash flow} = \text{expected dividend} + \text{change in stock price}$$
$$= \$5 + (\$26 - \$25)$$
$$= \$6$$

By dividing the cash flow expected from the investment by the current stock price, the cash flow can be expressed as a rate of return per dollar of investment:

$$\text{return} = \text{cash flow} / \text{investment}$$
$$= \$6 / \$25$$
$$= 24\%$$

The investor's return can be broken down into its two component parts, dividend yield and capital appreciation:

$$\text{return} = \frac{\text{first-year dividend}}{\text{current stock price}} + \frac{\text{change in stock price}}{\text{current stock price}}$$
$$= \$5 / \$25 + (\$26 - \$25) / \$25$$
$$= 20\% + 4\% = 24\%$$

Generalizing the above example using algebraic notation, where D_1 is next year's expected dividend, P_1 is the price expected to prevail at the end of the year, and P_0 the current stock price, the one-year return expected by the shareholder, denoted by the symbol K_e, can be expressed as:

$$K_e = D_1 / P_0 + (P_1 - P_0) / P_0 \qquad (5\text{-}2)$$

Equation 5-2 demonstrates how the return required by the shareholder, or cost of equity, is set by the market through the market price. That return is the sum of the expected dividend yield, D_1 / P_0, and the expected capital gains or losses, $(P_1 - P_0) / P_0$. The stock price at any point in time is set such that shareholders obtain a return of K % on their investment, reflecting their opportunity cost. If the current price of the stock is above P_0, the shareholder will not buy the stock since the dividends and end-of-period stock price are insufficient to cover opportunity cost. Conversely, if the current price is less than P_0, the investor will buy the stock since the return offered exceeds the opportunity cost.

By rearranging Equation 5-2 and solving for the stock price, an expression is obtained, which is consistent with the basic tenet of classical valuation theory, namely, that the value of the stock is the present value of the cash flows expected from the investment discounted at the investor's required rate of return.

$$P_o = \frac{D_1}{1 + K} + \frac{P_1}{1 + K}$$

In the numerical example:

$$\$25 = \$5/1.24 + \$26/1.24$$

Two-year Holding Period

If in the above numerical example, the investor possesses a two-year holding period, the stock price can be expressed as the sum of cash flows for both future periods, discounted at the average required rate of return for the two periods. If for example a dividend of \$5.25 and a resale price of \$27.30 are expected at the end of the second year, we have:

$$25 = \frac{5}{1 + K} + \frac{5.25}{(1 + K)^2} + \frac{27.30}{(1 + K)^2}$$

Solving for K, the investor's required return up to year 2 on the stock is 24%.

Thus, the DCF valuation framework is easily extensible over as many periods as desired, provided that reasonable estimates of future cash flows are available.

Realized Returns

The cost of common equity capital is sometimes estimated by calculating realized returns on equity over arbitrarily chosen historical time periods. The historical rate of return for a given period is the actual dividend yield plus the actual capital gain or loss. The basic measure of realized return is the same as Equation 5-2, except that actual realized data are used.

For example, to find the realized return to holders of a common stock over two periods, the first period return, K_1 is:

$$K_1 = \frac{D_1 + (P_1 - P_o)}{P_o}$$

and the second period return, K_2, is:

$$K_2 = \frac{D_2 + (P_2 - P_1)}{P_1}$$

The average return over the two periods can be computed by either the arithmetic average of the two period returns, or by their geometric average[2].

The arithmetic average is simply $(K_1 + K_2)/2$. The geometric average of the two period returns is computed by:

$$K_e = \sqrt[2]{(1 + K_1)\ (1 + K_2)} - 1$$

Since the first period return is 24% and the second period is 21%, the average arithmetic average is $(24\% + 21\%) / 2 = 22.5\%$. The geometric average for the period is:

$$K_e = \sqrt[2]{(1 + .24)(1 + .21)} - 1$$

$$= .2245 \text{ or } 22.45\%$$

The realized return approach is frequently encountered in measuring cost of equity. Typically, the monthly realized returns are computed as above over a 10-year period and the arithmetic or geometric mean of the monthly returns is computed to arrive at the average realized return. The latter is then used as an estimate of cost of capital.

Cost of capital is a forward-looking long-run expectational concept while realized return reflects only one of many outcomes initially envisaged by the investor in a probability distribution of several outcomes. It is important to keep in mind when using realized return as a proxy for expected return that the former measures what actually happened, and not what investors expect to happen.

Averaging realized returns provides only a broad indication of the relevant range over which expectations lie. These averages provide useful information only to the extent that they cover a long period of time and many securities, and that no major change has occurred in the economy.[3] It would be hazardous to rely on five years of historical returns for a particular public utility as a guide to investors' expectations for the future. A simple example will illustrate this.

In the one-year holding period example of the previous section, suppose that the actual resale price turns out to be $20 instead of the expected $25. Then, the after-the-fact realized return is:

$$K_1 = \frac{D_1 + (P_1 - P_o)}{P_o} = \frac{D_1}{P_o} + \frac{P_1 - P_o}{P_o}$$

$$= \$5 \ / \ \$25 \ + \ (\$24 \ - \ \$25) \ / \ \$25$$

$$= 20\% \ - \ 4\% \ = \ \underline{16\%}$$

versus the expected 24%. Reliance on realized return provides a distorted measure of investors' expected return.

Or suppose investors become disenchanted with utility stocks because of inclement regulation, and now require a 30% return. With the increase in required return, the stock price will fall to $23.85 in order for investors who purchase the stock now to get a 30% return:

$$P_0 = \frac{D_1}{1 + K} + \frac{P_1}{1 + K}$$
$$= \$5 \ / \ 1.30 \ + \ \$26 \ / \ 1.30$$
$$= \$3.85 \ + \ \$20 \ = \ \underline{\$23.85}$$

5.2 THE GENERAL DCF MODEL

Extending the concepts of the previous section from a one-year and two-year holding period to a multi-year holding period, consider an investor with an horizon of 'n' periods. The investor buys stock at the beginning of year 1, expects to receive dividends of D_1 at the end of year 1, D_2 at the end of year 2, D_3 at the end of year 3, etc., and expects to sell the stock at a price of P_n at the end of year 'n'. If the investor's required return corresponding to the riskiness of those expected cash flows is K, the present value of the first year's expected dividend D_1 is:

$$\frac{D_1}{1 + K}$$

The present value of the second year's dividend D_2 is:

$$\frac{D_2}{(1 + K)^2}$$

and similarly for the other cash flows. The present value, and hence the price, of all the future expected cash flows from owning the stock is:

$$P_0 = \frac{D_1}{1 + K} + \frac{D_2}{(1 + K)^2} + \frac{D_3}{(1 + K)^3} + \ .... \ +$$

$$\frac{D_n}{(1 + K)^n} + \frac{P_n}{(1 + K)^n}$$

(5-3)

In abbreviated form, the equation can be compressed as:

$$P_o = \sum_{t=1}^{n} \frac{D_t}{(1 + K)^t} + \frac{P_n}{(1 + K)^n} \qquad .(5\text{-}4)$$

Given the current price, the expected dividends up to period n and the price in period n, an estimate of the cost of equity, K, can be obtained.

Alternately, the value of common stock can be expressed as the present value of an infinite stream of dividends extending to infinity. This can be justified either by assuming that the investor has an infinite investment horizon, or by assuming that the expected resale price at the end of a limited horizon, P_n, is itself a present value of the expected dividends following year n to the new purchaser:

$$\textbf{Present Value} = \frac{D_1}{1 + K} + \frac{D_2}{(1 + K)^2} + \frac{D_3}{(1 + K)^3} \ldots. \textbf{ and so on indefinitely}$$

In short-hand form:

$$P_o = \sum_{t=1}^{\infty} \frac{D_t}{(1 + K)^t} \qquad (5\text{-}5)$$

Equation 5-5 is the seminal DCF dividend valuation model of common stocks, the mother lode equation for all the various DCF approaches discussed in this book.

General DCF Assumptions

The four crucial assumptions of the general DCF model are:

(1) that investors in fact evaluate common stocks in the classical valuation framework, and trade securities rationally at prices reflecting their perceptions of value. Given the universality and pervasiveness of the classical valuation framework in investment education and in the professional investment community, this assumption is plausible.

(2) that investors discount the expected cash flows at the same rate K in every future period. In other words, a flat yield curve is assumed. If K varies over time, there is no single required return rate, and practical estimates of the required return must be considered as weighted averages of $K_1, K_2, K_3 \ldots .K_n$. Since each of the one-period return requirements can be thought of as an interest rate plus risk premium, the required return to a multiple time horizon can be viewed as an average interest rate plus an average risk premium. More complex discounting models which incorporate these "yield curve effects" are available, but are of limited practical usefulness.[4]

(3) that the K obtained from the fundamental DCF equation corre-

sponds to that specific stream of future cash flows alone, and no other. There may be alternate company policies which would generate the same future cash flows, but these policies may alter the risk of the cash flow stream, and hence modify the investor's required return, K.

(4) that dividends, rather than earnings, constitute the source of value. The rationale for computing the value of common stock from dividends is that the only cash values ever received by investors are dividends. Earnings are important only insofar as they provide dividends.

Focusing on the present value of expected earnings can be misleading. It is earnings net of any investment required to produce the earnings that are of interest, and not earnings alone. For example, a company expects earnings per share of $1.00 per year; but to sustain the stream of future earnings, the company needs to invest in real assets at the rate of $1.00 per year. Since an amount equal to each year's earnings must be channeled into new asset investment, no sustainable dividend payout, hence value, is possible. In general, even for a non-dividend paying company, earnings will eventually outrun the firm's need for additional asset investment, creating the capacity to pay dividends.

The finance literature has produced three general approaches to determine value, each involving discounting three different streams of money: (1) the present value of expected dividends, (2) the present value of expected earnings net of required investment, and (3) the present value of the cash flows produced by assets. All three approaches are equivalent, provided they are properly formulated.[5]

In summary, classical valuation theory states that the present value of a share of common stock can be derived from the discount rate and the expected dividend stream:

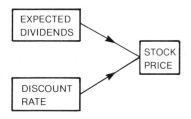

The process can be reversed to arrive at the implicit discount rate from the present value (current price) and the dividend stream. Given estimates of the current price and future dividends, the stock's implicit discount rate can be calculated. The discount rate is that rate of return (cost of equity) that equates the current price with the forecast dividend stream:

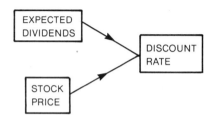

5.3 THE STANDARD DCF MODEL

The general common stock valuation model embodied in Equation 5-5 is not very operational, since it requires an estimation of an infinite stream of dividends. But by assigning a particular configuration to the dividend stream, a more operational formula can be derived. Assuming that dividends grow at a constant rate forever, that is,

$$D_t = D_o \ (1 + g)^t \qquad (5\text{-}6)$$

where g = expected dividend per share growth

and substituting these values of future dividends per share into Equation 5-5, the familiar reduced form of the general dividend valuation model is obtained[6]:

$$P_o = \frac{D_1}{K - g} \qquad (5\text{-}7)$$

In words, this fundamental equation states that the market price of a share of common stock is the value of next year's expected dividend discounted at the market's required return net of the effect of growth. Solving the equation for K, the cost of equity capital, the standard DCF formulation widely used in regulatory proceedings is obtained:

$$K = D_1 / P_0 + g \qquad (5\text{-}8)$$

This formula states that under certain simplifying assumptions discussed below and which investors frequently make, the equity investor's expected return, K, can be envisaged as the sum of an expected dividend yield, D_1/P_0, plus the expected growth rate of future dividends, g. Investors set the equity price so as to obtain an appropriate return consistent with the risk of the investment and with the return foregone in investments of comparable risk.

The basic idea of the standard DCF approach to estimating the cost of equity capital is to infer K from the observed share price and from an estimate of investors' expected future dividends. The principal appeal of the approach is its simplicity and its correspondence with the intuitive notion of dividends plus capital appreciation as a measure of investors' total expected return. The assumptions underlying the model are well-known and are generally applicable to utilities. They are discussed in detail below. Essentially, a constant average growth trend for both dividends and earnings, a stable dividend payout and capital structure policy, and a discount rate in excess of the expected growth rate are assumed. A simple example will illustrate the standard DCF model.

EXAMPLE

We have the following market data for Utility X:

> current dividend per share = $1.62
> current stock price = $13.00
> expected dividend growth = 4%

From Equation 5-8, the standard DCF model produces a cost of equity of:

$$
\begin{aligned}
K &= D_1 / P_0 + g \\
&= D_0(1 + g) / P_0 + g \\
&= \$1.62\ (1.04) / \$13 + .04 \\
&= 13\% + 4\% = \underline{17\%}
\end{aligned}
$$

Note that next year's expected dividend is the current spot dividend increased by the expected growth rate in dividends. In general, implementation of the approach requires finding D_0 and P_0 from readily available sources of market data; the growth rate, g, can be estimated using several techniques. One way is to extrapolate the historical compound growth of dividends over some past period. Chapters 7 and 8 will discuss the applicational aspects of the DCF formulation in detail.

Standard DCF Model Assumptions

The assumptions underlying the standard DCF model have been the source of unjustified controversy, confusion and misunderstanding in rate hearings. This section will hopefully clarify these assumptions.

Theories are simplifications of reality and the models articulated from theories are necessarily abstractions from the existing world so as to facilitate understanding and explanation of the real world. The DCF model is no exception to the rule. A model should not be judged by the severity and surrealism of its assumptions but rather by its intended use, ability to predict, explain and help the decision-maker attain his goal. The assumptions of the standard DCF model are as follows.

Assumption #1. The four assumptions discussed earlier in conjunction with the general classical theory of security valuation still remain in force.

Assumption #2. The discount rate K must exceed the growth rate, g. In Equation 5-7, it is clear that as g approaches K, the denominator gets progressively smaller, and the price of the stock infinitely large. If g exceeds K, the price becomes negative, an inplausible situation. In the derivation of the standard DCF equation (5-7) from the general stock valuation equation (5-5), it was necessary to assume g less than K in order for the series of terms to converge toward a finite number[7]. With this assumption, the present value of steadily growing dividends becomes smaller as the discounting effect of K in the denominator more than offsets the effect of such growth in the numerator.

This assumption is realistic for most public utilities. Investors require a return commensurate with the amount of risk assumed, and this return likely exceeds the expected growth rate in dividends for most public utilities. Although it is possible that a firm sustain very high growth rates for a few years, no firm could double or triple its earnings and dividends indefinitely.

Assumption #3. The dividend growth rate is constant in every year to infinity. This assumption is not as problematic as it appears. It is not necessary that g be constant year after year to make the model valid. The growth rate may vary randomly around some average expected value. Random variations around trend are perfectly acceptable, as long as the mean expected growth is constant. The growth rate must be "expectationnally constant" to use formal statistical jargon. This assumption greatly simplifies the model without detracting from its usefulness.

If investors expect different growth patterns to prevail in the future other than constant infinite growth, more complex DCF models are available. For example, investors may expect dividends to grow at a relatively quick pace for the first five years and to resume a slower normal steady-state course thereafter. The general valuation framework of Equation 5-5 can handle such situations. The "non-constant growth" model presented in the next chapter is an example of such a model.

It should be pointed out that the standard DCF model does not require infinite holding periods to remain valid. It simply assumes that the stock will be yielding the same rate of return at the time of sale as it is currently yielding.

EXAMPLE

To illustrate this point, consider a three-year holding period in the previous numerical example. If both price and dividends grow at the 4% expected rate, dividends for each of the next three years are $1.68, $1.75, $1.82 respectively, and the price at the end of the third year is $13(1 + .04)^3 = $14.62. If the investor sells the stock at the end of the third year, the return expected by the investor is still 17%, because the present value of the dividend stream and the stock price at resale is exactly equal to the current purchase price:

$$P_o = \frac{1.68}{1.17} + \frac{1.75}{1.17^2} + \frac{1.82}{1.17^3} + \frac{14.62}{1.17^3}$$

$$= \$13$$

This will be true for any length of holding period. The main result of the DCF model does not depend on the value of 'n'.

Another way of stating this assumption is that the DCF model assumes that market price grows at the same rate as dividends. Although 'g' has been specified in the model to be the expected rate of growth in dividends, it is also implicitly the expected rate of increase in stock price (expected capital gain) as well as the expected growth rate in earnings per share. This can be seen from Equation 5-7 which in period 1 would give:

$$P_1 = D_2/K - g$$

but
so that

$$D_2 = D_1(1 + g), \text{ and } P_o = D_1/K - g$$
$$P_1 = D_1(1 + g)/K - g = P_o(1 + g)$$

Hence, 'g' is the expected growth in stock price. Similarly, if a fixed fraction of earnings are distributed in dividends, then:

$$D_1 = aE_1$$
$$D_2 = aE_2$$

where a is the constant payout ratio and E the earnings per share. Since

$D_2 = D_1(1 + g)$, we also have $E_2 = E_1(1 + g)$ and, hence, 'g' is the expected growth in earnings per share.

Still another way of stating the assumption that the validity of the standard DCF model does not depend on the value of the investor's holding period is to say that investors expect the ratio of market price to dividends (or earnings) in year 'n', P_n/D_n, to be the same as the current price/dividend ratio, P_o/D_o. This must be true if the infinite growth assumption is made. Investors will only expect $(P/E)_n$ to differ from $(P/E)_o$ if they believe that the growth following year 'n' will differ from the growth expected prior to 'n', since the price in year 'n' is the present value of all subsequent dividends from n + 1 to infinity.

The constancy of the price/earnings (P/E) assumption is not prohibitive to DCF usage. If there is reason to believe that stock price will grow at a different rate than dividends, because for example the stock price is expected to converge to book value, a slightly more complex model is warranted. Such a model is presented in the following chapter.

Assumption #4. Investors require the same K every year. The assumption of a flat yield curve was alluded to earlier, but requires elaboration. A firm's cost of capital, K, varies directly with the risk of the firm. By assuming the constancy of K, the model abstracts from the effects of a change in risk on the value of the firm. If K is to remain constant, the firm's capital structure policy and dividend payout policy must be assumed to remain stable so as to neutralize any effect of capital structure changes or dividend policy changes on K.

The assumption of a constant dividend payout policy not only simplifies the mathematics but also insulates the model from any effects of dividend policy on risk, if any, and hence on K. Besides, this assumption was indirectly stated earlier; a constant dividend policy implies that dividends and earnings grow at the same rate. The assumption of constant dividend payout is realistic. Most firms, including utilities, tend to maintain a fixed payout rate when it is averaged over several years.

The simplification of a constant capital structure is acceptable, given the near constant debt-equity ratios exhibited over time by most utilities. It is sometimes argued that debt-equity considerations cannot be ignored in the presence of corporate income taxes, in view of the tax savings attendant to debt financing. This argument loses its impact, given that regulators set an after-tax return, that is, once the rate is set, taxes are then added as an expense in establishing revenue requirements[8].

Assumption #5. The standard DCF model assumes no external financing. All financing is assumed to be conducted by the retention of earnings. No new equity issues are used or, if they are, they are neutral in effect with respect to existing shareholders. The latter neutrality occurs if the market-to-book ratio is one. Without this assumption, the per share dividends could be watered down by a new stock issue, violating the constant growth assumption. A more comprehensive model allowing for external stock financing is presented in the following chapter.

5.4 THE DETERMINANTS OF DIVIDEND GROWTH

It is instructive to describe the factors which cause growth in dividends to occur and to disaggregate the 'g' term in the standard DCF model into its contributory elements.

The "retention ratio" is defined as the percentage of earnings retained by the firm for reinvestment. The fraction of earnings not ploughed back into the firm's asset base is paid out as dividends, and is referred to as the "dividend payout ratio". Under the DCF assumption of no external financing, if a firm is expected to retain a fraction 'b' of its earnings and expected to earn a book return of 'r' on common equity investments, then its earnings, dividends, book value, and market price will all grow at the rate 'br'. In short, a firm's sustainable dividend growth rate is its expected return on book equity times its retention ratio if all incremental equity investments are financed by the ploughback of earnings.

The relationship between a utility's book return on equity, retention ratio, payout ratio, book value, and dividend growth rate can best be understood by reference to the following numerical illustration.

TABLE 5-1 THE DETERMINANTS OF DIVIDEND GROWTH

YEAR	EQUITY BASE	EARNINGS	DIVIDENDS	RETAINED EARNINGS	STOCK PRICE
1	$100.00	$10.00	$5.00	$5.00	$100.00
2	105.00	10.50	5.25	5.25	105.00
3	110.25	11.02	5.51	5.51	110.25
4	115.76	11.58	5.79	5.79	115.76
–	–	–	–	–	–
–	–	–	–	–	–
–	–	–	–	–	–
etc.	etc.	etc.	etc.	etc.	–
	$g = 5\%$	$g = 5\%$	$g = 5\%$	$g = 5\%$	$g = 5\%$

Table 5-1 shows a firm earning a 10% book return on an initial equity capital base of $100. Its dividend policy consists of paying out 50% of its earnings in dividends, and conversely to retain 50% of earnings for reinvestment. Earnings on an initial capital base of \$100 are thus \$10, from which \$5 are paid in dividends, and \$5 are retained and added back to the initial equity base of \$100. An equity base of \$105 is carried forward to the second year. Repeating the cycle in the second year, earnings are \$10.50, or 10% on equity, \$5.25 are paid out in dividends, and 50% or \$5.25 are reinvested, bringing the equity base to \$110.25 in the third year. The process continues in an identical manner in each subsequent year. The stock price is shown in the last column at an arbitrarily assumed price/earnings multiple of 10 times earnings, in keeping with the DCF assumption of a constant price/earnings ratio. Note that if the book return on equity, r, and the retention ratio, b, remain constant, the dividends per share grow by r times b, or .10 x .50 = 5% per year. The book value of equity, earnings, stock price also grow at the same rate of 5%.

In summary:

$$K = D_1/P_o + g$$

but

$$g = br \tag{5-9}$$

so,

$$K = D_1/P_o + br \tag{5-10}$$

5.5   THE EARNINGS-PRICE RATIO

Another method to estimate the cost of equity is the Earnings-Price ratio. The rationale for the relationship of earnings to current stock price as a measure of equity cost is as follows[9]. The legal claim of common shares relates to the residual income earned after all operating and all other financial charges against revenue have been met. By definition, the current return to shareholders is the after-tax earnings remaining after subtraction of dividends owing to preferred stock. Irrespective of whether earnings are retained or paid out as dividends, they are the property of common equity holders. Dividends and earnings retained from current net income are simply the division of a stream of earnings into parts. The shareholder's claim is against both parts. Implicitly, the common shares also enjoy the claim to the future dividends generated by incremental assets financed by earnings retained. In short, the stream of net earnings in total is the return to common stock. Thus, the market price of common stock is the valuation of the stream of anticipated earnings, and the relationship of earnings to price per share is the current rate of return on market value. If anticipated earnings per share are E_1 and current price per share is P_o, this measure of equity rate of return K is:

$$K = E_1/P_o \qquad (5\text{-}11)$$

An alternate interpretation of this relationship as a measure of equity cost is to view this return of earnings to shareholders as a cost to the company of equity funds. Under this interpretation, the same rate of return must be earned on equity-financed assets to equal the cost rate. Otherwise, earnings produced will fall short of the requirement implied in the current earnings/price relationship.

The Earnings/Price Ratio was discussed extensively in the corporate finance literature in the 1960's, and enjoyed some notoriety in regulatory hearings in that period. Today, the method has almost vanished in use because it can produce unreliable results if not properly applied. In fact there are only two limiting cases in which the Earnings/Price yield constitutes an accurate measure of the cost of equity and reduces to the standard constant-growth DCF model. The specific circumstances under which the E/P ratio collapses to the standard DCF model are two-fold: (1) the case where all earnings are paid out in dividends, and (2) the case of an "ordinary" firm.

(1) All Earnings are Paid in Dividends

Consider the seminal DCF equation:

$$K = D_1/P_o + g$$

If all earnings are paid out as dividends, then D_1 equals earnings per share, E_1, and growth is zero. The above equation is rewritten as:

$$K = E_1/P_o + 0$$

and the cost of equity is simply the earnings/price ratio. This case lacks realism since most companies, including regulated utilities do in fact retain earnings.

(2) The "Ordinary Firm"

An ordinary firm is defined as one without profitable opportunities; the firm earns a return on its new equity investments that is just equal to the cost of equity, that is, to investors' required return. In this case, $r = K$. If assets financed by the equity base at book value are allowed to earn the earnings rate of return on equity's market value, the standard DCF model resolves into the Earnings/Price model. This is shown as follows. Starting with the standard DCF equation with the growth term $g = br$:

$$K = D_1/P_o + br \qquad (5\text{-}10)$$

If $r = K$, the latter can be substituted for r. Also, if the fraction of earnings retained is b, the fraction of earnings paid as dividends is $(1-b)$. Hence, anticipated dividends are equal to the fraction of earnings distributed as $D_1 = (1\text{-}b)E_1$. Substituting K for r and $(1-b)E_1$ in place of D_1 in Equation 5-10 and simplifying:

$$K = \frac{(1-b)\ E_1}{P_o} + bK$$

$$K(1-b) = \frac{(1-b)\ E_1}{P_o} \qquad (5\text{-}12)$$

Dividing both sides of the equation by $(1-b)$ reduces the equality to:

$$K = E_1/P_o \qquad (5\text{-}13)$$

which is the Earnings/Price ratio model. Thus the Earnings/Price ratio is an estimate of the cost of equity when there are no investments which yield returns different in magnitude than the cost of equity; in a regulated utility, this will occur when the allowed return equals the overall cost of capital or market price equals book value per share.

Solving the latter equation for the stock price P_o:

$$P_o = E_1/K \qquad (5\text{-}14)$$

Hence, stock price exceeds the earnings yield E_1/K only when $r > K$, that is, when the firm earns on its incremental equity investments a return in excess of the discount rate employed by investors to value its shares. In the case of profitable investment, the Earnings/Price ratio underestimates the cost of equity capital. To demonstrate this, suppose in fact the rate of return to equity holders due to investment were to exceed the required return by '$a\%$', that is, $r = K + a$. Substituting for $r = K + a$ in Equation 5-10, and following the same algebraic substitution as above, the equation would reduce to:

$$E_1/P_o = K - (b/1\text{-}b)a \qquad (5\text{-}15)$$

confirming that the earnings/price ratio understates the cost of equity when there are profitable investments. Intuitively, if a firm invests in projects whose returns are just equal to shareholders' opportunity costs, no impact on stock price will occur, although the firm's future earnings expand. But if very attractive investments are undertaken, the stock price will increase, but the earnings figure E_1 does not reflect the very large increase in earnings expected. So, the earnings/price ratio underestimates the cost of equity K.

EXAMPLE

(1) As a matter of policy, a corporation distributes all of its net income per share. Anticipated earnings for the coming year are $10 per share, and current market price, P_o is $50 per share.

$$K = E_1/P_o = \$10/\$50 = 20\%$$

(2) The same corporation chooses to divide its net income fifty-fifty between dividends and retained earnings. Therefore,

$$b = .5 \text{ and } 1 - b = .5$$

The capital expenditures policy of the company succeeds in choosing assets so that earnings on the rate base in turn produce a return on the book value of equity equal to market value cost of equity of 20%. Earnings per share are $10 and market price is $50.

$$K = r = 20\%$$

$$K = D_1/P_o + br$$
$$K = (1-b)E_1/P_o + br$$
$$= .5 \times \$10/\$50 + (.5 \times .20)$$
$$= .10 + .10 = .20 \text{ or } 20\%$$

It is interesting to speculate that if regulation worked perfectly with no regulatory lag and with the allowed rate of return continuously set equal to the cost of equity at all points in time, the earnings/price ratio would constitute a simple yet ideal method to compute cost of equity. The Earnings/Price ratio is rarely used in rate cases. If it is, extreme care and caution must be exercised that the assumptions underlying its use are not violated. One practical difficulty is to obtain an estimate of anticipated earnings, E_1, especially if earnings are subject to substantial seasonal fluctuation. Extrapolating historical earnings would pose additional problems if unrepresentative growth rates have distorted past earnings. Finally, the numerator of the earnings/price ratio is subject to the vagaries of accounting treatment and differences between companies respecting the impact of inflation.

Notes

[1] The use of specialized financial calculators greatly facilitates the process of discounting.

[2] The arithmetic average of 'n' successive one-period rates of return, $\overline{R}$, is defined as:

$$\frac{1}{n} \sum R_t$$

The arithmetic mean can be very misleading however. For example, an asset is purchased for $100; its price falls to $50 after one year, then rises back to $100 after two years. The arithmetic average return is $(-50\% + 100\%) / 2 = 50\%$. An asset bought for $100 and sold for $100 two years later clearly did not earned 50%, it earned zero percent. The arithmetic average is clearly not equal to the true average return over multiple periods. The true return over 'n' periods is the geometric return, defined by:

$$\sqrt[n]{(1 + R_1) \ (1 + R_2) \ ..... \ (1 + R_n)} - 1$$

The arithmetic average of successive one-period returns is only an approximation of the true multiperiod return. As the volatility of the one-period returns grows smaller, the approximation improves. See Francis (1976), Appendix J. Maximizing the geometric mean return of a portfolio also has some appealing theoretical and practical properties. See Elton & Gruber (1981), Chapter 9.

[3] Ibbotson-Sinquefield (1982) compile historical returns on stocks, bonds, and Treasury Bills from 1926 to the present for various holding periods. Both arithmetic and geometric mean returns are reported.

[4] Discounting at a constant risk-adjusted rate of return implicitly assumes that risk increases at a constant rate as the futurity of the cash flows increases. See Brealey & Myers (1984), Chapter 9.

[5] The equivalence between the three approaches is demonstrated in several financial texts. See for example Francis (1976), Chapter 9.

[6] To derive the standard DCF model, start with the general DCF valuation model of Equation 5 – 5:

$$P = \sum_{t=1}^{\infty} \frac{D_t}{(1 + K)^t}$$

If future dividends are growing at a constant rate of 'g', then:

$$P = \frac{D_1}{(1 + K)} + \frac{D_1(1 + g)}{(1 + K)^2} + \frac{D_1(1 + g)^2}{(1 + K)^3} + \ldots \frac{D_1(1 + g)^{n-1}}{(1 + K)^n}$$

where 'n' is the number of years. Hence, stock price P is the sum of an infinite geometric progression whose first term (f) is $\frac{D_1}{1 + K}$ and whose constant ratio (R) is $\frac{1 + g}{1 + K}$. The standard formula for the sum of a geometric series is: $f/1 - R$. Applying this formula:

$$P = \frac{D_1}{1 + K} \bigg/ \left(1 - \frac{1 + g}{1 + K}\right) = \left(\frac{D_1}{1 + K}\right) \bigg/ \frac{K - g}{1 + K} = \frac{D_1}{K - g}$$

Solving for the required rate of return (cost of equity):

$$K = \frac{D_1}{P} + g$$

[7] See the derivation of the standard DCF model in footnote #6. For the geometric to converge, it is necessary that the constant ratio R be less than one, that is, $1 + g < 1 + K$.

[8] The effects of capital structure on the cost of equity are discussed at length in Chapters 14 and 15.

[9] This section draws heavily on Andrews in Morin & Andrews (1983A).

CHAPTER 6

DCF MODEL EXTENSIONS

This chapter describes alternate formulations and refinements of the basic DCF approach. Essentially, the models presented in this chapter result from relaxing some of the more restrictive assumptions of the standard DCF model and from introducing some real world institutional elements in the standard DCF model. In the first section, the assumption of constant growth is dropped, and a more general DCF model is derived capable of handling various assumed growth profiles. The second section relaxes the assumption of no external stock financing, and restates the standard DCF model under more general conditions. Adjustment of the DCF model for flotation costs is analysed in the third section.

6.1 THE NON-CONSTANT GROWTH DCF MODEL

In Chapter 5, a generalized security valuation model was presented. The central idea was that the price of a share of common stock is the present value of the stream of expected dividends discounted at the cost of equity capital. The general DCF model equation was given by:

$$P_o = \sum_{t=1}^{\infty} \frac{D_t}{(1 + K)^t} \qquad (6\text{-}1)$$

where P_o = current price per share
D_t = dividend payment in period t
K = cost of equity capital

This general valuation model can be adapted to suit a variety of growth situations. The simplest assumption is that dollar dividends are constant; this reduces to the Earnings/Price model, discussed in the previous chapter. The most popular assumption is that future dividends and earnings are expected to grow indefinitely at a constant rate due to future investments financed through the retention of earnings; this assumption gives rise to the standard DCF model, also discussed in the previous chapter.

Dividends need not be, and probably are not, constant from period to period. Moreover, there are circumstances where the standard DCF model cannot be used to assess investor return requirements. For example, if a utility's common stock is selling at a significant discount or premium from book value, and there is reason to believe that investors expect a recovery of stock price to book value, the standard DCF model is invalid. This is because the expected growth in stock price has to be different from that of dividends, earnings, and book value if the market price is to converge toward book value.

The DCF model will now be restated under more plausible and realistic estimates of future dividend growth rates. In essence, the following question will be answered: Given the actual stock price, and given a forecast of growth in dividends for the next 'n' years and a subsequent constant normal growth rate thereafter, what is the implied rate of return required by investors? Expanding the above general stock price equation for a limited horizon of 'n' years on the part of investors, we obtain:

$$P_o = \frac{D_1}{1 + K} + \frac{D_2}{(1 + K)^2} + \; .... \; \frac{D_n}{(1 + K)^n} + \frac{P_n}{(1 + K)^n} \qquad (6\text{-}2)$$

where $D_1 D_2 \, ... D_n$ = expected dividends in each year
$\qquad$ P_n = expected stock price in year n
$\qquad$ P_o = current stock price
$\qquad$ K = required return on equity

In words, Equation 6-2 states that current stock price P_o is the present value of the dividends to be received in each of the next 'n' years and of the stock price prevailing at the end of the nth year. Returns to common equity holders consist of dividends to a finite time horizon and the sale price, or liquidation value, of the equity at that time. The cost of common equity in market terms is the rate of discount required to equate the flow of future dividends plus market price at the horizon to current price.

If the growth rate beyond year 'n' is to be constant, the expected value of P_n is then:

$$P_n \; = \; \frac{D_n + 1}{K - g} \; = \; \frac{D_n(1 + g)}{K - g} \qquad (6\text{-}3)$$

that is, the standard constant growth DCF model prevails beyond year 'n'. Substituting Equation 6-3 into Equation 6-2:

$$P_o = \frac{D_1}{1 + K} + \frac{D_2}{(1 + K)^2} + \cdots \frac{D_n}{(1 + K)^n} + \frac{D_n(1 + g)}{K - g} \frac{1}{(1 + K)^n} \tag{6-4}$$

Knowing the current stock price, P_o, and given estimates of D_1 through D_n and of the constant growth beyond year 'n', g, one can solve Equation 6-4 for the implicit return on equity required by investors.

It should be stressed that the Non-Constant Growth model embodied in Equation 6-4 is quite consistent with current valuation practices of institutional investors and is a common estimation technique used by financial analysts[1]. The model is known under various aliases, including Limited Horizon Model and Finite Horizon Model, and is used by many financial institutions to improve security valuation. Security analysts routinely estimate the model's required inputs, basing their forecasts on historical and on current and foreseeable future conditions for the economy and the company. Forecasts of earnings, dividends, earnings growth rates and payout ratios are used to derive anticipated future dividends, and the rate that equates the discounted stream of these anticipated future dividends to the current price is the required return on equity.

EXAMPLE

Assume a two-year time horizon. Current market price is $50 per share, dividends are predicted to be $5 in the first year and $5.40 per share in the second year. Dividend growth at the rate of 8% per year will prevail in third year and perpetually thereafter.

$$P_o = \$50$$
$$D_1 = \$5$$
$$D_2 = \$5.40$$
$$g = 8\%$$

From Equation 6-3, the market price prevailing at the end of year 2 will equal:

$$P_2 = \frac{D_2 (1 + g)}{K - g} = \frac{\$5.40 (1.08)}{K - 0.08} \tag{6-5}$$

Therefore, from Equation 6-4:

$$P_o = \frac{D_1}{1 + K} + \frac{D_2}{(1 + K)^2} + \frac{P_2}{(1 + K)^2}$$

$$\$50 = \frac{\$5.00}{1 + K} + \frac{\$5.40}{(1 + K)^2} + \frac{\$5.40 \ (1.08)}{K - 0.08} \ \frac{1}{(1 + K)^2}$$

Solving this equation for K by successive iteration, the cost of equity is obtained:

$$K = 21.8\%$$

Dividends estimates can be found by direct means or taken from an independent source, such as Value Line. To illustrate the latter methodology[2], the following example derives an explicit estimate of Utility X's cost of equity, based on data from Value Line, one of many firm in the securities industry which provides estimates for the values of the variables in Equation 6-4.

EXAMPLE

The current issue of Value Line Investment Survey projects Utility X's earnings and dividends for 1984 and averages for 1986 – 1988. Interpolating for 1985, 1986, and 1987, and using the 1986 – 1988 forecast as the 1987 estimate, the following earnings and dividends per share estimates are obtained, along with the implied retention ratio, b.

	1983	1984	1985	1986	1987	1988
	ACTUAL	PROJECTED				
Earnings per Share	$2.38	2.45	2.63	2.82	3.00	3.18
Dividends per Share	1.66	1.74	1.83	1.92	2.00	2.08
Retention Ratio	30%	29%	30%	32%	33%	35%

The resulting compound growth rate in earnings for 1984 – 1988 is 6.74%, while the growth in dividends is 4.56% for the same period. Following this 5 – year period, dividends will resume a constant normal growth rate, which can be obtained by multiplying the 1988 implied retention ratio of 35% by the 1986 – 1988 return on equity of 15% forecast by Value Line. The estimated constant growth rate is:

$$g = br = .35 \times .15 = 5.25\%$$

Substituting these estimates into Equation 6-4 with n = 5 years, and using the current stock price of $15 5/8, we obtain:

$$\$15.625 = \frac{1.74}{1+K} + \frac{1.83}{(1+K)^2} + \frac{1.92}{(1+K)^3} + \frac{2.00}{(1+K)^4} + \frac{2.08}{(1+K)^5} + \frac{2.08\,(1.0525)}{K-0.0525}\,\frac{1}{(1+K)^5}$$

Solving this equation for K, the implied expected rate of return on common equity is 16.2%.

Another application of the Finite Horizon DCF model is when stock price and dividends cannot grow at the same rate by virtue of realistic circumstances in the capital markets[3]. A projected change in the price/earnings ratio or a shift in dividend growth for periods beyond the investment horizon will produce a capital gain or loss to the investor which is a legitimate part of investor return requirements. Carleton (1980) argues that when estimating the cost of equity for utilities whose market price differs from book value, the standard DCF model must be corrected because the growth in stock price has to differ from the growth in dividends if the stock price is to converge to book value. The standard DCF model suppresses such capital gains or losses by assuming an infinite investment horizon.

When a utility's stock price is below book value or when regulatory lag is present, it is reasonable to assume that investors expect future increases in the utility's market-to-book ratio through upward adjustments in the allowed rate of return. This is because proper regulation requires a market-to-book ratio of at least one. The expected increase in market-to-book ratio would result in the rate of price appreciation that exceeds the growth in earnings, contrary to the standard DCF model's assumptions that the firm's earnings per share grow at a constant rate foreover and/or that the firm's price/earnings ratio is constant. Application of the standard DCF model would result in a downward-biased estimate of the cost of equity to a public utility whose current market-to-book ratio is less than one and which is expected to converge towards one by investors.

In the context of Equation 6-2, a forecast by investors that the stock price will ultimately reach book value after a regulatory lag period of 'n' years means that $P_n = B_n$, where B_n is the book value per share in year 'n'[4].

If the eventual recovery of stock price to book value is assumed to occur in 'n' years, and that two growth rates can be estimated, one for dividends per share, g, and one for book value per share, g_B, to year 'n', Equation 6-2 becomes:

$$P_o = \frac{D_o(1+g)}{1+K} + \frac{D_o(1+g)^2}{(1+K)^2} + \cdots + \frac{D_o(1+g)^n}{(1+K)^n} + \frac{B_o(1+g_B)^n}{(1+K)^n}$$

where B_o is the current book value per share. K is then the return expected over the following 'n' years during which the periodic cash flows are the growing dividends, and for which the final cash flow is the market price at that date, assumed equal to book value at that date, $B_o(1 + g_B)^n$.

EXAMPLE

If the current dividend is $6 per share, dividend growth is 2%, book value growth is 5%, current stock price is $80, and current book value per share is $100, for a recovery period of 2 years ($n = 2$), we obtain[5] from Equation 6-2:

$$\$80 = \frac{6 \times 1.02}{1 + K} + \frac{6 \times 1.02^2}{(1 + K)^2} + \frac{100 \ (1.05)^2}{(1 + K)^2}$$

from which $K = 24.6\%$.

For a recovery period of 4 years ($n = 4$) we obtain:

$$\$80 = \frac{6 \times 1.02}{1 + K} + \frac{6 \times 1.02^2}{(1 + K)^2} + \ldots \frac{6 \times 1.02^4}{(1 + K)^4} + \frac{100 \ (1.05)^4}{(1 + K)^4}$$

from which $K = 17.8\%$.

6.2 THE DCF MODEL WITH EXTERNAL STOCK FINANCING

In developing the standard DCF model, only one source of equity financing was recognized, namely the retention of earnings. But growth in earnings and dividends can also be achieved by the sale of new common equity. The standard DCF model can be expanded to explicitly allow for the case of continuous new equity financing[6].

In Gordon's expanded DCF model, which is derived in Appendix 6-A, utilities are seen as engaging in two kinds of operations: 1) investment decisions on which they earn the rate of return 'r', and 2) stock financing operations on which they earn at the rate 'vs'. If a utility is expected to stock finance at the rate 's', the standard cost of equity model:

$$K = D_1/P + g$$

is altered as follows. Since growth in book value per share results from both types of operations, now $g = br + sv$ and not simply br, where

s = funds raised from the sale of stock as a fraction of existing common equity

v = fraction of the funds raised from sale of stock that accrues to shareholders at the start of the period

The only change required in the standard DCF model to recognize the expectation of continuous stock financing at the rate 's' is the change in the expected rate of growth from 'br' to 'br + sv', as demonstrated by Gordon (1974). The expanded DCF model of the cost of equity takes the form:

$$K = D_1/P + br + sv \qquad (6\text{-}6)$$

In this expanded DCF model, v is the fraction of earnings and dividends generated by the new funds accruing to existing shareholders. To understand the meaning of 'v', consider a new stock issue sold at a price equal to book value, $P = B$. The equity of the new shareholders is equal to the funds they invest, and the existing shareholders' equity is not changed. But if the stock is sold at a price greater than book value, $P > B$, a portion of the funds accrues to the existing shareholders. And if the stock is sold at a price less than book value, $P < B$, existing shareholders experience a dilution of their equity position. Specifically, Gordon[7] has shown that

$$v = 1 - B/P \qquad (6\text{-}7)$$

is the portion of the new funds raised that increases/decreases the book value of the existing shareholders' equity depending on whether $P > B$ or $P < B$.

The expanded DCF model in Equation 6-6 reduces to the standard DCF version if either the company does not regularly sell new stock, $s = 0$, or if new stock is sold at a price equal to book value, $v = 0$. In the latter case, new stock financing has no impact on stock price. $B/P = 1$ in Equation 6-7, and v is thus 0. An alternate way of expressing this condition is that if the expected book return on equity is set equal to the cost of equity, then $P/B = 1$, and v is 0. A simple manipulation of Equation 6-7 is most revealing in that regard. Starting from the extended growth expression of Equation 6-7, it can be shown[8] that:

$$v = (r - K)/(1 - b)r \qquad (6\text{-}8)$$

Substituting Equation 6-8 into the extended growth expression $g = br + sv$, we obtain:

$$g = br + s (r - K)/(1 - b)r \qquad (6\text{-}9)$$

If the utility does not engage into external stock financing, s = 0, and growth is simply the product of the retention ratio and book profitability. Positive common stock financing increases this growth only if return on investment exceeds the cost of equity, that is, only if the proceeds of the stock issue are invested to earn more than the cost of capital[9].

EXAMPLE

To estimate the cost of equity of Utility X, where:

- expected dividend yield D_1/P_0 = .12
- expected return on book equity r = .13
- expected retention ratio b = .40
- expected growth in the number of shares s = .05
  (historical 10 - year average)
- expected profitability of stock investment v = - .011
  (market-to-book ratio of 0.90)

The expanded growth expression is given by:

$$
\begin{aligned}
g &= br + sv \\
&= .40 \times .13 + .05 \times (-.011) \\
&= .0520 - .0056 \\
&= .0464 \text{ or } 4.64\%
\end{aligned}
$$

Combined with the expected dividend yield of 12%, the cost of equity is estimated as 12% + 4.64% = 16.64%.

An analogous extended DCF model was derived by Miller and Modigliani (1961), who used a slightly different valuation approach to arrive to an expression which is equivalent to Gordon's model in Equation 6-6. Miller & Modigliani obtained:

$$K = D_1/P + r (b_r + b_s(1 - B/P)) \qquad (6\text{-}10)$$

where b_r = fraction of earnings retained
b_s = new equity raised by stock sale
as a fraction of earnings

Using the appropriate notational translations, several authors, including Davis & Sparrow (1972) and Arzac & Marcus (1981), have shown the equivalence of the Gordon and Miller & Modigliani versions.

One difficulty in applying the extended DCF model in regulatory proceedings is that the quantities 's' and 'v' are not easily measurable nor intuitively understandable. By effecting the following simple notational translation[10]:

$$G = br + s \qquad (6\text{-}11)$$

The following equation for the allowed rate of return on equity is obtained (see derivation in Appendix 6-B):

$$r = G + (M/B)(K - G) \qquad (6\text{-}12)$$

where now G is the growth rate in total, not per share, book equity, and M/B is the market-to-book ratio. Equation 6-12 effectively tranforms the investor's required rate of return, K, into the utility's required return on book equity[11]. This notational translation results in a more empirically tractable equation, since the quantity G is likely to be be more understandable and measurable than the quantities 's' and 'v'. As discussed further in Chapter 12, the application of this equation depends upon the M/B value that is used. If a target M/B ratio of 1 is selected, then r = K in Equation 6-12, as in the standard DCF model. New stock issues at a price equal to book value do not exert any dilutive or expansive impact on existing shareholders, so that g = br. Setting the allowed return on equity equal to the standard DCF cost of equity is appropriate under these circumstances.

6.3 FLOTATION COSTS AND THE UNDERPRICING ALLOWANCE

This section demonstrates that an adjustment to the market-based cost of capital is necessary for flotation costs associated with new issues, and discusses the mechanics of applying this adjustment. A typical utility is continuously issuing stock through its dividend reinvestment plan and employee stock option plan, or sells new shares to the public on a regular basis in order to maintain its construction program and meet its mandated service requirements. The costs of issuing securities are just as real as operating and maintenance expenses or costs incurred to build utility plants, and fair regulatory treatment must permit the recovery of these costs.

The criterion laid down in the landmark *Hope* and *Bluefield* cases requires that a utility's financial integrity, credit, and ability to attract capital be maintained. This criterion mandates that the utility be able to obtain new equity capital at a price which does not dilute the book value per share of existing shareholders. If investors were to expect continuing confiscation of their equity investment with each new stock issue, the utility's cost of capital would reach unacceptably high levels. In the absence of flotation costs, the financial integrity of the utility is maintained when the allowed return is set equal to investors' required return on equity, because only then will the utility's stock price be driven to book value per share, that is, the market-to-book ratio will be one[12].

When a utility issues new stock however, three factors result in the utility receiving as net proceeds from the issue an amount less than the preannouncement stock price: (1) the costs associated with floating the new issue, such as the fee to the underwriter and other related administrative financing expenses such as printing, legal, and accounting expenses, (2) the downward market pressure connected with the increased supply of stock, because large blocks of new stock may cause significant pressure on market prices, even in stable markets, and (3) the potential market price decline related to external market variables; this is often referred to as the allowance for "market break". To prevent the dilution of existing shareholders' investment resulting from these three factors, an amount must be added to the rate of return on common equity to obtain the final cost of equity financing[13]. This incremental return is referred to as the "underpricing allowance", and is the sum of flotation costs, market pressure, and market break.

To demonstrate the need for adjusting the market-determined return on equity for underpricing costs, consider the following simple example. Shareholders invest $100 of capital on which they expect to earn a return of say 10%, or $10, but the company nets $95 because of issuance costs. It is obvious that the company will have to earn more than 10% on its net book investment (rate base) of $95 to provide investors with a $10 return on the money actually invested. To provide earnings of $10 on a $95 capital base requires an allowed return of $10/$95 = 10.53%.

Size of the Underpricing Allowance

The underpricing allowance is estimated at approximately 5% to 10%, depending on the size and risk of the issue. A more precise figure can be obtained by surveying empirical studies on utility security offerings. According to recent studies by Logue & Jarrow (1978) and Bower & Yawitz (1980), underwriting costs and expenses average 4% of gross proceeds for utility stock offerings. As far as the market pressure effect is concerned, these same studies suggest an allowance of about 1%. Logue & Jarrow found that the absolute magnitude of the relative price decline due to market pressure was less than 1.5%. Bower and Yawitz examined 278 public utility stock issues and found an average market pressure of 0.72%. According to these empirical studies then, total flotation costs including market pressure amount to about 5%.

The problem in measuring market pressure effects is to disentangle the downward effect on stock price resulting from the increased supply of stock from the effect of general movement in the stock market. One simple and effective method of isolating the market pressure effects from the market's aggregate effect proposed by Patterson (1973) is to compute the following statistic for a series of past stock offerings, and use the average as a measure of the market pressure effect:

$$\text{market pressure} = 1 - \frac{P_{LOW} + R}{P_{ANN}\left(\dfrac{I_{LOW}}{I_{ANN}}\right)} \tag{6-13}$$

where P_{LOW} = low market price during the issue period
$\quad\quad P_{ANN}$ = market price two days prior to announcement of the issue
$\quad\quad I_{LOW}$ = level of the market index on the date of P_{LOW}
$\quad\quad I_{ANN}$ = level of the market index two days prior to announcement date
$\quad\quad R$ = value of one right on date if a rights issue

EXAMPLE

Two days prior to the announcement of a common stock issue, Utility X's stock price is $60, while the Dow Jones Industrial Index is at 1200. During the issue period, Utility X's stock price reaches a low of $56 while the Dow Jones is at 1220 on the corresponding date. The market pressure effect can be computed as:

$$\begin{aligned}
\text{market pressure} &= 1 - \$56/\$60\ (1220/1200) \\
&= 1 - .949 \\
&= .051 \text{ or } 5.1\%
\end{aligned}$$

The allowance for market break is even more complex to gauge accurately. Some cushion should be provided against market declines from external causes. Regulated utilities are mandated to provide quality service and to expand when warranted by demand. Unlike unregulated companies who have the luxury to postpone the issuance of new securities when market conditions are unfavorable, utilities do not have the same flexibility, and they must obtain capital when needed regardless of market conditions. A precise quantification of this effect is difficult. One way to assess the magnitude of market break is to compare current utility Price/Earnings ratios with their historical levels, and the higher the current P/E ratios, the greater is the possible decline.

In summary, based on empirical studies, total flotation costs including market pressure amount to approximately 5% of gross proceeds. This is consistent with the fact that several utilities raise a substantial portion of their external equity every year through an automatic dividend reinvestment plan and offer a 5% discount, suggesting that the savings from abstaining from a public issue of common stock are at least 5%. The underpricing allowance of 5% is likely to be conservative, since no explicit allowance for market break is incorporated; if negative events should occur during the time period from announcement of a public issue to actual pricing, the price could fall below book value unless a sufficient margin is maintained. Moreover, the 1% allowance for market pressure is probably conservative for large stock issues.

Regulatory Treatment

In theory, underpricing costs could be expensed and recovered through rates as they are incurred. This procedure is not considered appropriate, however, because the equity capital raised in a given stock issue remains on the utility's common equity account and continues to provide benefits to ratepayers indefinitely. It would be unfair to burden the current generation of ratepayers with the full costs of raising capital when the benefits of that capital extend indefinitely. Although flotation costs are not expensed, they must nevertheless be recovered.

An analogy with bond issues is useful here in order to understand the treatment of issue costs in the case of common stock issues[14]. In the case of bonds, flotation costs are recovered over the life of the bond in two steps: (1) flotation costs are amortized over the life of the bond and the annual amortization charge is incorporated into revenue requirements, in much the same way that funds invested in utility plant is recovered through depreciation charges. (2) The unamortized portion of flotation costs is included in rate base, and a return is earned on the unamortized costs, in the same way that a return is earned on the undepreciated portion of a utility's plant. The recovery continues year after year regardless of whether the utility raises new debt capital until the recovery process is terminated, in the same way that the recovery of utility plant investments continues whether the utility constructs new facilities or not.

Unlike the case of bonds, common stock has no finite life so that flotation costs cannot be amortized and must therefore be recovered via an upward adjustment to the allowed return on equity.

Flotation Cost Adjustment

From the standard DCF model, the investor's required return on equity capital is expressed as:

$$K = D_1/P_0 + g \tag{6-14}$$

If P_0 is regarded as the proceeds per share actually received by the company from which dividends and earnings will be generated, that is, P_0 equals B_0, the book value per share, then the company's required return is:

$$r = D_1/B_0 + g \tag{6-15}$$

Denoting the percentage flotation costs 'f', proceeds per share B_0 are related to market price P_0 as follows:

$$P - fP = B_0$$

$$P (1 - f) = B_0 \tag{6-16}$$

Substituting Equation 6-16 into 6-15, we obtain:

$$r = D_1/P (1 - f) + g \tag{6-17}$$

which is the utility's required return adjusted for underpricing[15]. Equation 6-17 is often referred to as the "conventional approach" to flotation cost adjustment. Its use in regulatory proceedings by cost of capital witnesses is widespread. The formula is derived in several college level corporate finance textbooks, such as Brigham (1982A).

The flotation cost adjustment can also be approached in the context of the more general extended DCF model discussed in the previous section. Recall the extended DCF expression for cost of equity capital under the assumption of continuous external stock financing:

$$K = D_1/P + br + sv \tag{6-18}$$

The expression for v was $v = 1 - B/P$. To incorporate underpricing, v needs to be redefined as:

$$v = 1 - B/P (1 - f) \tag{6-19}$$

where $P(1 - f)$ are the net proceeds from a stock issue. This recognizes that when a utility engages in external financing, it is the net proceeds per share which have an impact on existing shareholders rather than the full market price. To avoid any dilution in the existing shareholders' claim, v must be set equal to zero. Setting Equation 6-19 equal to zero, we obtain

$B = P(1 - f)$. By substituting Equation 6-19 into Equation 6-18, and by recognizing also that setting $v = 0$ implies $g = br$, Equation 6-18 is restated as follows to incorporate the effect of underpricing:

$$r = D_1/P\ (1-f) + g \qquad (6\text{-}20)$$

The latter expression is identical to that obtained from the standard DCF model adjusted for underpricing in Equation 6-17.

The more practical version of the extended DCF model cast in terms of G, the growth rate in total book equity, also collapses to an identical expression. From Equation 6-12:

$$r = G + (M/B)\ (K - G) \qquad (6\text{-}21)$$

To avoid dilution, $v = 0$, which in turn implies $G = g = br$. Equation 6-21 reduces to Equation 6-20 under the condition that $M/B = 1/(1 - f)$:

$$\begin{aligned} r &= g + (1/(1 - f))\ (K - g) \\ &= g + (1/(1 - f))\ D_1/P \\ &= D_1/P\ (1 - f) + g \end{aligned}$$

Flotation Cost Controversies

Several important controversies have surfaced regarding the underpricing allowance. The first is the contention that an underpricing allowance is inappropriate if the utility is a subsidiary whose equity capital is obtained from its parent. This objection is unfounded since the parent-subsidiary relationship does not eliminate the costs of a new issue, but merely transfers them to the parent. It would be unfair and discriminatory to subject parent shareholders to dilution while individual shareholders are absolved from such dilution. Fair treatment must consider that if the utility-subsidiary had gone to the capital market-place directly flotation costs would have been incurred.

A second controversy is whether the underpricing allowance should still be applied when the utility is not comtemplating an imminent common stock issue. A related controversy is whether or not the retained earnings component of equity requires a flotation cost adjustment.

Arzac & Marcus (1981) developed an alternative approach to accounting for flotation costs in regulatory hearings. To avoid dilution of the initial shareholders' equity, the allowed rate of return should equal:

$$r = \frac{K}{1 - \dfrac{fh}{1 - f}} \qquad (6\text{-}22)$$

where h = external equity financing rate, as a percentage of earnings, and the other symbols are as before.

Patterson (1983) formally compares the properties of the Arzac-Marcus adjustment with those of the conventional adjustment, and shows that the former is equivalent to expensing issue costs in each period when a stock issue occurs. In other words, if Equation 6-22 is consistently applied, the utility is reimbursed its flotation costs in each year as they are incurred.

Patterson also shows that the present value of flotation cost adjustments received by the utility is the same for both the conventional and the Arzac-Marcus adjustments[16]. The only difference between the two methods, if properly applied, is in the intergenerational allocation of flotation costs. The conventional approach amortizes then over an infinite period, while the Arzac-Marcus approach expenses them. The choice of method is a matter of public policy. It is important that whatever method is selected be applied consistently over the life of the utility.

It should be pointed out that the Arzac-Marcus method is based on the assumption that the flotation costs of past stock issues have been fully recovered, and hence, the recovery of future flotation costs is the primary basis for adjustment. The method is inappropriate if that assumption is not met.

On grounds of fairness alone, the conventional approach would seem preferable. Since the equity capital has long-term implications for both the company and ratepayers, imputing the flotation costs to ratepayers who happen to be extant at the time of each specific stock issue appears unreasonable. The conventional approach in effect normalizes the potential dilution issue over a period of years. To charge ratepayers for the full magnitude of stock issue costs at the time of each stock issue would impose an unfair burden on ratepayers at that time.

It is important to note that, under the conventional approach, flotation costs are only recovered if the rate of return is applied to total equity, including retained earnings, in all future years, even if no future financing is contemplated. The next two examples will demonstrate this. The first example is adapted from Brigham (1979A) and shows that even if no further common stock offerings are contemplated, an underpricing adjustment is still permanently required to adjust for past offerings. The second example, adapted from Richter (1982), shows that the allowance applies to retained earnings as well as to the original capital.

EXAMPLE

A new utility is formed, and it must raise $1,000 of capital to purchase assets to serve the public. Stock can be sold to investors at a price of $11 per share, but at a 10% flotation cost, so that the company nets $10 per share. To raise the $1,000, the company must sell $1,000/$10 = 100 common shares. For expository clarity, let's assume that all earnings are paid out as dividends. Assume moreover that investors require a return of 10%.

Since the company has a capital base of $1,000 but investors have actually invested $1,100 of their capital ($11 x 1,000) the company's annual profits must be 0.10 x $1,100 = $110. To obtain such profits, the rate of return on rate base of $1,000 must be 11% computed as follows:

$$r = \$110 \; / \; \$1,000 \; = \; 11\%$$

The impact on book value and the M/B ratio is noteworthy. Book value per share is $1,000/100 = $10 which represents the net proceeds per share after flotation costs. Under fair regulatory treatment, earnings per share will equal book value per share times the fair allowed return, which equals $10 x 0.11 = $1.10. Since the market required return is 10%, the stock price will be $1.10/0.10 = $11. The M/B ratio is thus $11/$10 = 1.10.

If no underpricing allowance is made, then the utility is allowed to earn only 10% on its $10 book value. Earnings per share are only $1.00, and the stock price would decline to $1.00/0.10 = $10. The M/B ratio is thus equal to one, but an unfair loss of $1.00 per share is inflicted upon shareholders.

The underpricing is permanent rather than transitory. If the 11% return is allowed only during the year when the stock is issued, with the allowed return reduced to 10% the subsequent year, then the stock price would fall during the second year to $10. Since the capital raised by the stock issue is permanent capital, the corresponding adjustment must be in force permanently.

EXAMPLE

Shareholders invest $1,100 of equity capital, and the net proceeds of the issue to the company are $1000. The investor's required return is 10%, broken down as follows: 5% from dividend yield and 5% from growth.

$$K \; = \; D_1/P \; + \; g \; = \; 5\% \; + \; 5\% \; = \; 10\%$$

In order to support the 5% dividend requirement, the company must pay $55 in dividends, and the utility's rate base investment must grow by $50 through the retention of earnings to fulfill the expected 5% growth. So, in total, the utility must earn $105, $55 for dividends and $50 for retained earnings. It follows that the utility must earn a return of 10.5% on its book equity, that is $105/$1000. At the end of the first year, book equity will total $1050 ($1000 + $50).

The same scenario repeats in the second year. The investors expect a 5% increase in dividends, and so the company needs to pay $57.75 in dividends. Its book value must increase by 5% through retained earnings, that is, $52.50. The company must therefore earn a total of $110.25, $57.75 for dividends and $52.50 for growth, on its book equity of $1050. The required return on book equity is again 10.5% ($110.25/$1050), even though no additional stock was sold. The higher return requirement induced by the underpricing allowance applies to both retained earnings and the original equity capital. The results for a five-year period are presented in tabular form below.

YEAR	BOOK EQUITY (BOY)	STOCK PRICE* (BOY)	EARNINGS	DIVIDENDS	RETAINED EARNINGS
1	$1000.00	$11.00	$105.00	$55.00	$50.00
2	1050.00	11.55	110.25	57.75	52.50
3	1102.50	12.13	115.76	60.64	55.12
4	1157.62	12.74	121.55	63.67	57.88
5	1215.50	13.38	127.63	66.85	60.77

*$P = D_1/(K - g)$

All quantities are growing at a 5% rate. The book returns and the M/B ratios are constant every year at 10.5% and 1.10 respectively. The dividend yield is 5% and the growth is 5% for a total return of 10% to investors. In order to provide the investor with a 10% return, the company must earn 10.5% not only on the original equity capital but also on all subsequent retained earnings.

Richter (1982) also demonstrates that the underpricing allowance applicable to all the company's book equity is a weighted average of the current allowances required for each past financing, and suggests some practical means of circumventing the problem of vintaging each equity source. Richter essentially suggests sourcing book equity by broad categories of equity, such as dividend reivestment plan equity, stock option equity, and public issue equity, and calculating a weighted average underpricing factor.

Notes

[1] The majority of college level investments and corporate finance textbooks describe the Finite Horizon DCF model. See for example Reilly (1979), Sharpe (1981), and Brigham (1982A).

[2] For an example of this approach in regulatory proceedings, see: Federal Energy Regulatory Commission, The Georgia Power Company. Prepared Testimony, R.A. Morin, FERC Docket 81-730, 1981.

[3] This discussion draws on Carleton, W. T., "Alternative Formulations and Extensions of the Basic DCF Equation in the Context of a Regulated Public Utility." Reproduced in North Carolina Utilities Commission, Prepared Testimony, Docket # P-55, Sub 784, 1980.

[4] For an actual example of this approach in regulatory testimony, see Carleton (1980).

[5] Examples drawn from Carleton (1980).

[6] For a complete discussion of the extended DCF model, see Gordon (1974).

[7] Gordon (1974) provides a more rigorous development of the term 'v'.

[8] This can be shown as follows. By definition, $v = 1 - B/P$. But from the standard DCF valuation equation $P = E(1-b)/K-g$ and since $E = rB$, then $P = rB(1-b)/K-g$ and $P/B = r(1-b)/K-g$. Inverting the latter expression and substituting in the definition of v, Equation 6-8 follows.

[9] The dependence of g on K prompted Myers (1971) to employ simulation techniques for the determination of K.

[10] See Richter (1982) for a formal demonstration of this approach.

[11] Litzenberger (1979) and Dwyer (1979) employed similar transformation equations to derive the appropriate return on book equity.

[12] Chapter 13 contains a formal exposition of the relationship between the allowed rate of return, the cost of equity capital, and the market-to-book ratio.

[13] An alternate way of stating this requirement is that the utility's stock must be maintained at some minimum market-to-book ratio in such a way that the proceeds from new stock issues will not decline below book value per share.

[14] See Brigham (1982)

[15] Another way to look at it is that in order to prevent dilution of book value per share, the market-to-book ratio must be at least $1/(1-f)$. The Target Market-to-Book method discussed in Chapter 13 can be used to translate the DCF cost of equity figure into an appropriate allowed return on book equity. As shown in Chapter 13, the allowed return consistent with a target M/B ratio which allows for the recapture of flotation costs is:

$$r = P/B (K-g) + g$$

[16] Howe (1983) also compares the two flotation cost adjustment methods, and provides guidance for implementation. He shows that the conventional method

actually slightly underestimates the adjustment, and that the Arzac-Marcus slightly overestimates the magnitude of the adjustment.

APPENDIX 6-A

Derivation of Extended DCF Model

Gordon's DCF model with continuous new equity financing is derived as follows. Starting with the general stock valuation formula:

$$P = \sum_{t=1}^{n} \frac{D_t}{(1 + K)^t} \qquad \text{(A)}$$

But dividends, D_t, equal earnings, E_t, times the payout ratio, $(1 - b)$, where b is the fraction of earnings retained:

$$D_t = E_t(1 - b) \qquad \text{(B)}$$

Substituting (B) into (A)

$$P = \sum_{t=1}^{n} \frac{E_t(1 - b)}{(1 + K)^t} \qquad \text{(C)}$$

An expression for future earnings, E_t, and future dividends, D_t, with continuous equity financing is now developed. If a firm's initial book equity is B_0, next year's book equity B_1 will be B_0 plus additional equity generated by the retention of earnings, plus new equity raised from sale of new stock. If earnings per share of E_1 are generated in the first year on N_1 shares outstanding, the additional equity from retention is given by $b E_1 N_1$. The additional equity from new issues is $s B_0$, where s = funds raised from sale of stock as a fraction of existing book equity. So, we have

$$B_1 = B_0 + b E_1 N_1 + sB_0 \qquad \text{(D)}$$

Since the return on equity, r, equals $\dfrac{N_1 E_1}{B_0}$ by definition, $N_1 E_1 = rB_0$. Substituting in (D):

$$B_1 = B_0 + br B_0 + s B_0 \qquad \text{(E)}$$

$$B_1 = B_0 (1 + br + s)$$

Generalizing, the book equity in any given year 't' is therefore:

$$B_t = B_0 (1 + br + s)^{t-1} \tag{F}$$

In other words, total equity in any period is increased by the retention of earnings, br, and the sale of additional shares, s.

Not all the equity accrues to existing shares. In any year 't', the total equity includes the equity of the initial shareholders at $t = 0$, and the equity arising from new stock during the period. Letting B_t^* be that portion of the total equity that belongs to the shares outstanding at $t = 0$, and letting 'v' be the fraction of the new funds provided during the period that accrues to the original shareholders at the start, then:

$$B_t^* = B_0 (1 + br + sv)^{t-1} \tag{G}$$

A fuller explanation of the meaning of 'v' is contained in the main body of the text and in Gordon (1974).

Multiplying both sides of (G) by r, and dividing both sides by the original number of shares outstanding, N, an expression for earnings per share in any given year t is obtained:

$$\frac{rB_t^*}{N} = \frac{rB_0}{N} (1 + br + sv)^{t-1}$$

$$E_t^* = E_0 (1 + br + sv)^{t-1} \tag{H}$$

Multiplying both sides of H by $(1 + b)$, the payout ratio, an expression for per share dividends in any given year t is obtained

$$(1 - b)E_t^* = (1 - b)E_0 (1 + br + sv)^{t-1} \tag{I}$$

$$D_t^* = D_0 (1 + br + sv)^{t-1}$$

Substituting (I) in (A):

$$P = \sum_{t=1}^{n} \frac{D_0 (1 + br + sv)^{t-1}}{(1 + K)^t} \tag{J}$$

(J) is a geometric progression whose sum converges to (see footnote 6, Chapter 5):

$$P = \frac{D_1}{K - br - sv} \qquad \text{(K)}$$

Solving for K:

$$K = \frac{D_1}{P} + br + sv \qquad \text{(L)}$$

APPENDIX 6-B

The Cost of Equity and the Allowed Return on Book Equity

This appendix derives an equation which transforms the investor's required return on equity into the firm's allowed return on book equity.

From Equation (K) in Appendix 6-A:

$$P = \frac{D_1}{K - br - sv}$$

but $D_1 = E_1(1-b)$ and $E_1 = rB_0$; substituting and dividing both sides by B:

$$P/B = \frac{(1-b)r}{K - br - sv}$$

$$P/B(K - br) - P/B(sv) = (1-b)r$$

$$\text{but } v = (1 - B/P)$$

substituting and rearranging:

$$P/B(K - br) - P/B\ s + s = (1-b)r$$

$$P/B(K - br - s) + s = (1-b)r$$

$$\text{but } G = br + s \text{ by definition}$$

so: $$P/B(K - G) + s = (1-b)r = r - br$$

solving for r:

$$r = br + P/B(K - G) + s$$

$$\boxed{r = G + P/B(K - G)}$$

CHAPTER 7

DCF APPLICATION

The purpose of DCF is to estimate the opportunity cost of shareholders, or cost of equity capital. From the standard DCF model, the cost of equity is the sum of the expected dividend yield, D_1/P_o, and the expected growth, g. It would be a relatively simple matter to calculate the cost of equity capital if investor expectations were readily observable. Projections of dividends and growth would be looked up, the stock price observed, and K calculated, based on this one-firm sample. Reality is not so convenient however, and the purpose of this chapter is to analyze the practical problems associated with the estimation of the inputs to the DCF model. The conceptual material of the two previous chapters will be put into practical perspective. The chapter reviews the practical implementation of the DCF technology, the difficulties encountered, potential tools and solutions along with their practical usefulness.

The first section briefly describes readily available computerized sources of investment information useful in the implementation of DCF. In the second section, the issues of spot dividend yield versus expected dividend yield, and the appropriate stock price to employ are discussed. In the third section, methods of estimating expected growth are outlined, including historical growth, analysts forecasts, and sustainable growth. The next chapter stresses the need to broaden the sample to include other investment alternatives, and discusses the design of comparable risk groups of companies through the use of risk filters. Other complications which arise in determining the cost of equity, such as the absence of market data, the case of subsidiary utilities, and violation of DCF assumptions are also discussed in the next chapter.

7.1 DATA SOURCES

Several techniques described in this and subsequent chapters rely on the availability of historical and forecast information. The most widely used and comprehensive data bases in the determination of the cost of capital are reviewed in this section[1].

A wealth of investment information is available in the publications of investment advisory services. The major services are:

Moody's Investor Services Inc.
Standard & Poor's Corporation
The Value Line Investment Survey

A comprehensive and abundant flow of bulletins and reports emerges daily, weekly, and monthly from these services, compiled in reference volumes each year for various fields, including public utilities. Compendiums of information on individual companies are also available from Moody's and Standard and Poor's[2].

Of particular interest are the computerized data bases and computer-generated reports and tabulations offered by the major services to investors. A major data compilation, first developed by Standard & Poor's, is Compustat. This data base is available via magnetic tape directly from a subsidiary of Standard & Poor's, Investors Management Sciences Inc., or remotely through a number of time-sharing systems, such as Interactive Data Corp. (IDC). The latter has taken over a number of electronic services from Standard & Poor's and provides access to additional financial data banks. IDC maintains or makes available a number of large-scale financial data bases and a variety of software programs to access and process the data, including[3]:

The Security Master Data Base
The Prices Data Base
The Split and Dividend Data Base
The Compustat Data Bases
The Value Line Data Bases
The I/B/E/S Summary Data Base

The Compustat tapes contain 20 years of annual data, updated regularly, for approximately 2,200 listed industrial companies, 900 over-the-counter companies, 155 utilities, and others. Quarterly data for the industrial companies are available for the past 10 years and for utilities over the past 12 years. Composite company group data can be extracted from the Compustat tapes based on various selected financial criteria and ratios of which there is an almost infinite number.

The Value Line Investment Survey covers 1640 stocks in 75 industries, and essentially provides a reference and current valuation service. Each stock in the list is reviewed in detail quarterly. Each week the new edition of the Value Line Survey covers four to six industries on a rotating basis. Each industry report contains reports on individual stocks. About 125 stocks are covered weekly in the order of their industries. After all 1640 stocks have been covered in 13 weeks, the cycle is repeated. A plethora of investment information is made available for each company, including growth rates, risk measurements, quality rating, historical performance data, and financial ratios.

The Value Line Data Base contains historic annual and quarterly financial records for 1,500 companies beginning in 1954 for annual data and 1963 for quarterly figures. Comprehensive financial statements, precalculated ratios, return rates, per share data, measures of risk and earnings predictability, dividends and earnings forecasts, and countless other investment data are easily accessed.

The advent of personal computers and communications software has greatly facilitated ready access to financial data bases. For example, the Dow Jones News/Retrieval and The Source offer on-line access to comprehensive financial information on a paid subscription basis through a personal microcomputer.

7.2 DIVIDEND YIELD ESTIMATION

According to the standard DCF formulation, the cost of equity is estimated by the formula:

$$K = D_1/P_o + g \qquad (7\text{-}1)$$

The measurement of K can be broken down into two components: measurement of the expected dividend yield, D_1/P_o, and the measurement of growth, g. The next two sections will consider each in turn. This section focuses on the dividend yield component.

Two issues are involved in the determination of the dividend yield. First, the appropriate stock price to employ, and second, the relative merits of using a spot dividend yield versus an expected dividend yield.

Stock Price

The stock price to employ in the standard DCF formula is the current price of the security at the time of estimating the cost of capital, rather than some historical high-low or weighted average stock price over an arbitrary time period. The reason is that the analyst is attempting to determine a utility's cost of equity in the future, and since current stock prices provide a better indication of expected future prices than any other price according to the basic tenets of the Efficient Market Hypothesis[4], the most relevant stock price is the most recent one. Use of any other price violates the Efficient Market Hypothesis.

Market Efficiency

The purpose of the equity market is to allow risk bearing in the economy in an efficient manner. An efficient market is one where at any point in time security prices fully reflect all the relevant information available at that time. An efficient market implies that prices adjust instantaneously to the arrival of new information, and that therefore prices reflect the intrinsic fundamental economic value of a security. The market is efficient with respect to a given set of information if there is no way for investors to use that information set to select stocks and reap abnormal risk-adjusted returns.

Investors set stock prices by estimating a stream of expected dividends and an end-of-period price and by discounting those future cash flows at a required rate of return commensurate with the risk of the security. The market is efficient if, on average, required market rates of return equate to expected market rates of return. Investors could not continue to receive rates of return in excess of the minimum necessary to pay for the risk of the company for very long, unless the market was hopelessly inefficient. Investors would bid up prices of the undervalued stock, and thereby restore the stock's expected return to its risk-adjusted level. Similarly, if the stock's expected returns were less than required, investors would dump the stock, thereby lowering its price, restoring the expected return to its appropriate risk-adjusted level.

A massive body of empirical evidence indicates that U.S. capital markets are remarkably efficient with respect to a broad set of information, including historical and publicly available information[5].

The efficiency of the stock market has several implications. First, it indicates that observed prices at any time represent the true fundamental equilibrium value of a security, and that a cost of capital estimate should be based on current prices rather than on an average of past prices. Conceptually, there is no validity to smoothing stock price series. The measurement of K rests on the assumption that a utility's stock is accurately priced relative to other equivalent-risk investments; the Efficient Market Hypothesis validates that assumption. Second, the assumption of perfect markets which is embodied into DCF valuation models is validated by the existence of efficient markets. And third, market efficiency confirms that the estimated K reflects returns in investments of similar risks, since observed stock prices reflect information about possible alternative investments with different risks and returns.

A frequent objection to the use of spot prices is that they may reflect abnormal conditions, making it more useful to use average prices over a period of time for purposes of estimating the cost of capital. Notwithstanding the fact that this assertion is a direct contravention of the Efficient Market Hypothesis, this may be partly correct under special circumstances. Visual inspection of a chart of daily closing prices over the last few weeks should reveal whether the current stock price is representative or is an outlier. If the current stock price is not an outlier, the use of the current stock price is corroborated. If the current stock price is indeed an outlier, there is some justification for averaging over several trading days to smooth out market aberrations, as would be the case after a stock goes ex-dividend for example. But the longer the past period over which stock prices are averaged, the more severe the violation of market efficiency. A stock price dating back to the previous month, or even to the previous year as some analysts would have it, would not be representative of current market conditions and could not be used to derive a company's current cost of capital.

An analogy with with interest rates will clarify this point. If for example interest rates have climbed from 10% to 12% over the past six months, it would be incorrect to state that the current interest rate is in the range of 10% to 12% just because this is the interest rate range for the past six months. Analogously, it is incorrect to state that the cost of equity, which has also risen along with interest rates, is in some given six-month range. Just as the current interest rate is 12%, the cost of equity is currently that which is obtained from the standard DCF using current spot prices.

In the special case of certain utility stocks traded over the counter, an estimate of current price may be obtained by averaging the most recent bid and ask prices. If the stock is thinly traded, there is some justification for averaging over several trading days, at the expense of market efficiency.

There is yet another justification for using current stock prices. In measuring K as the sum of dividend yield and growth, the period used in measuring the dividend yield component must be consistent with the estimate of g which is paired with it. Since the current stock price P_0 is caused by the g foreseen by investors at the present time and not at any other time, it is clear that the use of spot prices is preferable.

Dividend Yield

DCF theory states very clearly that the expected rate of return on a stock is equal to the expected dividend for the next period divided by the current stock price, plus the expected growth rate. In implementing the standard DCF model, it is the dividend that an investor who purchases the stock today expects a company to pay during the next twelve months that should be used, and not the dividend that was paid last year. The investor's valuation process is forward-looking and based on expected future cash flows. The standard DCF formula requires the use of the expected dividend in the next period. The dividend next period is just equal to the dividend this period times the growth rate, that is,

$$D_1 = D_o(1 + g) \qquad (7\text{-}2)$$

If the analyst uses the current dividend yield, D_o/P_o, instead of D_1/P_o, he is incorrect. The magnitude of the error can be substantial. For example, with $P_o = \$20$, $D_o = \$2$ and $g = 5\%$, the current dividend yield is 10%; the theoretically correct dividend yield is $\$2(1 + .05)/\$20 = 10.5\%$, or 50 basis points higher.

Comprehensive dividend yield information for utility stocks is available from Value Line, Argus Utility Scope Monthly Handbook, and the Wall Street Journal on a daily basis.

One of the assumption of the standard DCF model is that dividend payments are made annually whereas in fact most utilities pay dividends on a quarterly basis. Clearly, quarterly dividends are preferred by investors to a lump sum end of the year payment equal to the sum of the quarterly payments because there is time value of money. The quarterly dividends, when reinvested until the end of the year, are worth more to the investor.

The exact nature of the adjustment to the dividend yield becomes more complex if the quarterly timing of dividends and the interval between dividend payments are recognized. If dividends are paid once a year and increased each year in response to the growth in earnings, as is assumed in the standard DCF model, then the appropriate adjustment is to multiply the spot dividend yield, D_o/P_o, by $(1 + g)$; the spot dividend yield is obtained by dividing the dividends paid over the year ending on the purchase date by the stock price on that date.

But in the more realistic case of quarterly dividends, if the dividend is increased each year, the adjustment factor is in excess of $(1 + g)$. This is shown formally in Appendix 7-A, which contrasts the standard DCF model with the quarterly timing version of the model explicitly recognizing the value of receiving money earlier than later. The quarterly DCF model incorporates all the same assumptions as the standard model, including constant growth, except that the dividends are paid quarterly rather than annually. It is shown that the standard DCF model understates a company's cost of equity capital by failing to account for the time value of money when quarterly dividends are involved[6]. The magnitude of the error using the annual model rather than the quarterly model is of the order of 50 basis points (0.5%) for any reasonable values of the parameters of the model. Even if the adjustment factor is applied to the spot dividend yield, defined as

4 times the current quarterly installment, the adjustment factor remains above $(1 + g)$, although somewhat reduced.

Finally, if the conventional method of flotation cost adjustment is used by the regulator, the expected dividend yield must be adjusted for underpricing allowance by dividing it by $(1 - f)$, where f is the underpricing allowance factor:

$$K = D_1/P_0(1 - f) + g \qquad (7\text{-}3)$$

7.3   GROWTH ESTIMATES: HISTORICAL GROWTH

The principal difficulty in calculating the required return by the DCF approach is in ascertaining the growth rate which investors are currently expecting. While there is no infallible method in assessing what the growth rate is precisely, an explicit assumption about its magnitude cannot be avoided. Estimate of the growth component is the most difficult and controversial step in implementing DCF since it is a quantity which lies buried in the minds of investors. All one can hope for is to analyze and measure available data which are logically linked to 'g', or that influence 'g', and then decide judgmentally the usefulness of the proxy data. Three general approaches to estimate expected growth can be used:

– historical growth rates
– sustainable growth rates
– analysts' forecasts

This section describes the historical growth approach while the next two sections address the other two approaches.

A convenient starting point is to focus on the utility in question, and to assume that its future growth is relatively stable and predictable; it is therefore reasonable to use past growth trends as one of many proxies for investor expectations. Historical rates of growth in earnings, dividends, market prices, and book values during some past period are among the most widely used proxies for expected growth. The fundamental assumption is made that investors arrive at their expected 'g' by simply extrapolating past history. In other words, historical growth rates affect investor anticipations of long-run dividend growth rate.

In computing historical growth rates, three decisions must be made: 1) which historical data series is most relevant for estimating expected 'g', 2) over what past period, and 3) which computational method is most appropriate.

Historical Series

DCF proponents have variously based their historical computations on earnings per share, dividends per share, and book value per share. Of the three possible growth rate measures, growth in dividends per share is likely to be preferable. After all, DCF theory states clearly that is is expected future cash flows in the form of dividends which constitute investment value.

Since the ability to pay dividends stems from a company's ability to generate earnings, growth in earnings per share can be expected to influence the market's dividend growth expectations. Dividend growth can only be sustained if there is growth in earnings. Using earnings growth as a surrogate for expected dividend growth can be difficult, however, since historical earnings per share are frequently more volatile than dividends per share.

Past growth rates of price and earnings per share tend to be very volatile and lead to unreasonable results, such as consistently negative growth rates. For example, in the 1970's and beginning of the 1980's especially, utility earnings growth rates were so unstable and volatile that they could not reasonably be expected to continue. Several empirical studies have shown that earnings growth rates are not persistent[7].

Dividend growth rates are considerably more stable (see Table 7-1 example). They are not as nearly affected by year-to-year inconsistencies in accounting procedures, and they are not as likely to be distorted by an unusually poor or bad year. Most companies, and utilities in particular, are reluctant to alter their dividend policy in response to transitory earnings variations.

The major disadvantage of using dividends rather than earnings is the discretionary aspect of dividends. Frequently, dividend increases are made in discrete, sometimes large steps, at management's discretion, and historical dividend growth may not be an adequate surrogate of the average expected growth over some future time period. Historical growth rates derived over specific periods can be biased by short-run changes in the dividend payout of a firm or through abnormal earnings that are unsustainable. A change in dividend policy would create growth in dividends that is more fictitious than real. Of course, if no change in long-run payout policy is anticipated, the expected average growth in dividends will equal the expected average growth in earnings.

Historical growth in book value per share may be a useful proxy for future dividend growth under certain limited circumstances. Book value per share tends to be less volatile than earnings per share and dividends per share. While book value is largely irrelevant for unregulated companies, it is a principal determinant of earnings for utilities in original cost jurisdictions because allowed earnings are determined by regulatory commissions on the basis of the level of book assets. Earnings per share is the product of book value per share and rate of return on book equity so that historical growth in book value per share may provide an indication of the growth in earnings that would have occurred if past rates of return had remained constant.

Past growth in book value per share is an adequate proxy for future growth only if two crucial assumptions are met, however: First, that investors expect no change in earnings per share arising from changes in future book rate of return on equity. Second, that market-to-book ratios have remained stable. The latter assumption is vital, because book value may increase or decrease based on issuances of common stock at a premium or discount from existing book value. Growth from this source alone is largely unsustainable. An analysis of the historical relationship between per share earnings, book value, dividends, and the stability of earned returns on book equity and market-to-book ratios should provide valuable insights in assessing the merits of looking at history as a valid proxy for the future[8].

Other historical series sometimes used by analysts as proxies for future dividend growth are revenues, assets, and net plant. Too many explicit assumptions are required to link the growth of these series with dividend growth. Reliance on such proxies is dangerous and unlikely to provide insights into future dividend growth. Some analysts average together the growth rate in customers, revenues, earnings, dividends, and book value. This procedure is highly questionable; the quantities of interest are dividends and earnings. One might be interested in how growth in customers, sales, or book value influence growth in earnings and dividends through regression analysis, but otherwise the procedure is unjustified.

Time Period

Once an appropriate historical series has been selected, the period over which the growth is to be measured must be determined. The period must be long enough to avoid undue distortions by short-term influences and by abnormal years, and short enough to encompass current and foreseeable conditions relevant for investors' assessment of the future. Dividend growth over the past year is hardly representative of a trend. Similarly, it is meaningless to measure growth during a long extended period when dividend payout ratio was 60% and earned returns on book equity were 10% if investors, based on existing trends, expect the future payout to be 40% and future returns to be 13%.

Historical growth rates are customarily computed over the last five and ten years. An average of the five-year and ten-year growth rates is a reasonable compromise between the conflicting requirements of representativity and statistical adequacy.

A useful test of the reliability of historical growth as a surrogate for future growth is to measure its sensitivity to the period selected. If historical dividend growth is between say 5% and 6% regardless of the length of the period over which it is measured, one can conclude that the relationship between the historical growth rate and investors's expected growth rate is reliable. If the computed growth rate is highly sensitive to the length of the period, then it does not provide useful information.

Growth Rate Computation

The method of calculating growth is most meaningful in the context of compound interest. If dividends grow from $2 to $3 over a ten-year period, for example, the total growth is 50%, or a simple average per annum rate of 5%. But 5% is not a meaningful expression of the growth rate because it ignores compounding, that is, the accrual of interest on interest as well as on the original value. Assuming annual compounding, $2 grows to $3 in ten years at a rate of 4.1%. The latter can be obtained either from standard compound interest tables or from a specialized financial calculator.

Use of the compounding method of calculating growth is vulnerable to a potential distortion. If either the initial or terminal values are unrepresentative, unusually high or low, the resulting growth rate will not truly reflect the developments during the period. For example, if the terminal year happens to be one of severely depressed earnings due to inflation or acute regulatory lag, and the initial year one of boom, the indicated growth rate will be unrealistically low. The reverse may also be true. This potential distortion can be avoided in one of two ways. Either select initial and terminal end points that have similar economic characteristics, or do not use single years' data, but rather the averages of the first few and last few years' data as end points. The latter method is preferable because it involves less subjective judgment. The historical five-year and ten-year compound growth rates available in the Value Line Data Base for earnings, dividends, book value, revenues, and cash flows are computed in this manner. Base periods used by Value Line are three-year averages in order to temper cyclicality and to mitigate any potential distortion due to sensitivity to end points in the calculation.

A more sophisticated method of calculating a growth rate is to fit a "least-squares line" to the logarithms of all the data in the series. This method is known under various names, such as log-linear trend line, log linear regression, or least-squares exponential regression analysis. Essentially, an equation of the form:

$$y = Ae^{bx} \tag{7-4}$$

is estimated, where A is the intercept, b is the continuous growth rate, y is the historical data, and x is the time period. Taking the logarithms of both sides of the above equation:

$$\log y = A + bx \qquad (7\text{-}5)$$

hence the name log-linear trend line. To implement the method, a straight line is fitted to the logarithm of the series of interest by regression techniques, and the slope estimate of the regression, b, provides a measure of the growth rate.

The log-linear method is theoretically more precise than the compound growth rate method in that it includes each observation of the period rather than merely the end points. In normal circumstances however, the added precision is not worth the substantial extra calculation effort. In certain extreme cases, the usefulness of the growth proxy may be improved if one or more abnormal years are omitted or adjusted.

The numerical example shown in Table 7-1, portrays a history of The Southern Company's earnings and dividends per share. Compound growth rates, smoothed compound growth rates, and exponential growth rates for earnings and dividends are computed for the last ten and five years. Compound growth is computed by solving the orthodox compound value formula for g:

$$F = P (1 + g)^n \qquad (7\text{-}6)$$

where F = terminal value, P = initial value, and n = number of periods. For example, to get the 10-year dividend growth rate, the following formula is solved for g by either consulting standard compound interest tables or by using a financial calculator:

$$1.66 = 1.34 (1 + g)^{10}$$

Base periods used in the computation of the smoothed compound growth rates are three-year averages in order to temper cyclicality and reduce sensitivity to end points. For example, base periods for the 5-year and 10-year growth rate calculations through the end of 1982 are 1980-1982 versus 1976-1978 and 1971-1973 respectively. The exponential growth rates are obtained by estimating the value of the exponent in Equation 7-4 through least-squares regression techniques.

TABLE 7-1 GROWTH COMPUTATIONS FOR THE SOUTHERN COMPANY

YEAR	EARNINGS PER SHARE	DIVIDENDS PER SHARE
1971	$1.77	$1.26
1972	1.88	1.30
1973	2.07	1.34
1974	1.41	1.39
1975	2.26	1.40
1976	1.62	1.41
1977	1.95	1.48
1978	1.45	1.54
1979	1.51	1.54
1980	2.23	1.56
1981	1.81	1.62
1982	2.38	1.66

Source: The Southern Company's Annual Reports

	EARNINGS GROWTH	DIVIDENDS GROWTH
– 5-year compound growth (1978-1982)	10.42%	1.51%
– 10-year compound growth (1973-1982)	1.41%	2.16%
– 5-year compound growth (1978-1982), three-year base periods	5.08%	1.70%
– 10-year compound growth (1973-1982), three-year base periods	1.14%	2.10%
– 5-year exponential growth (1978-1982)	11.70%	2.01%
– 10-year exponential growth (1973-1982)	1.47%	2.31%

Hazards of Historical Growth Rates

Past growth rates in earnings or dividends may be misleading, since past growth rates may reflect changes in the underlying relevant variables that cannot reasonably be expected to continue in the future, or may fail to capture known future changes.

The future need not be like the past. For example, assets may grow at a different rate, or utilities may be more or less profitable. Since investors take such factors into account in assessing future earnings and dividends, historical growth rates could provide a misleading proxy for future growth.

The standard DCF model assumes that a company will have a stable dividend payout policy and a stable earned return on book equity, and thus that earnings, dividends, and book value per share will in the future grow at the same rate. The DCF model also assumes that the financing mix, that is, the proportions used of retained earnings, debt, and new stock issues, remains constant. If they change, the growth rates will change and the past growth rates will not reflect future growth rates. While it is appropriate to make such assumptions for forecasting purposes, these assumptions are frequently violated when examining historical data. Payout ratios or earned returns on equity may have been historically unstable, and hence earnings, dividends, and book value did not grow at the same growth rate.

This was certainly the case for most utilities in the 1970's and beginning of the 1980's when double-digit inflation increased plant, capital, and operating costs while regulatory lag held down price increases. The depressing effect of inflation on utility earnings, dividend, and book value growth was compounded by the necessity to sell stock at prices below book value, which diluted book value and retarded growth further. These low historical growth rates were not representative of future growth rates and could not be extrapolated into the future. The utility industry experienced a turnaround starting in the middle of 1982. Inflation abated, utilities were authorized and were earning higher rates of return than in earlier years; market-to-book ratios increased, so that stock sales no longer diluted book value to the same extent it did earlier. As a result, security analysts and investors were forecasting higher growth rates in the future compared to the past.

Brigham (1983) provides an interesting demonstration of how historical book value growth rate is a downward-biased estimator of future growth if the book return on equity has been rising. Table 7-2 and Figure 7-1 illustrate that historic book value growth rates understate the future DCF dividend growth rate if the return on equity is rising. Brigham's demonstration works in reverse as well, that is, if earned returns were falling, historical growth would overestimate future growth.

Another example, articulated by Gordon (1977) in a New York Telephone rate case, displayed in Table 7-3, shows what happens to historical earnings growth when return on equity is increased. With a 4% earnings growth before period 4, and a 6% growth rate after period 4, the arithmetic mean rate of growth over the five years is 18%. This is due to an increase in book equity return from 10% to 15% and the 56% earnings growth in period 4. Extrapolation of the 18% growth rate over this 5-year period would appear to be quite unreasonable.

Another potential problem with the use of historical growth rates is that there is no convenient method to adjust the results if the company's risk changes. For example, the stock price of an electric utility which diversifies

Figure 7-1

THE HAZARDS OF HISTORICAL GROWTH RATES

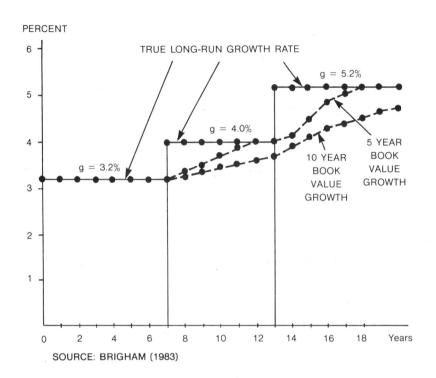

SOURCE: BRIGHAM (1983)

into oil exploration or solar conservation reflects both the risk of electric generation and of peripheral energy activities. Historical growth rates may be quite different from those expected in the future.

The major point of all this is that it is perilous to apply historical growth when a utility is in a transition between growth paths. When payout ratios, equity return, and market-to-book ratios are changing, reliance on historical growth is hazardous. Such transitions can occur under variable inflation environments, or under fundamental environmental shifts such as deregulation.

Given the choice of variables, length of historical period, and the choice of statistical methodologies, the number of permutations and combinations of historical growth rates is such that other methods and proxies for expected growth must be explored. Historical growth rates constitute a useful starting point and provide useful information as long as

TABLE 7-2 ILLUSTRATION OF GROWTH RATE ESTIMATES

Year (1)	ROE (2)	Book Value Per Share, BVPS (Beginning of Year) (3)	Earnings Per Share, EPS (BVPS × ROE) (4)	Payout Rate, (POR) (5)	Dividends Per share, DPS (EPS X POR) (6)	Predicted Growth Rate, Based On			Expected Data $g = b(ROE) =$ $(1-POR)(ROE)$ (10)	Actual Growth Rates in EPS, DPS (11)
						Past Data (5-Year Averages)				
						BVPS (7)	EPS (8)	DPS (9)		
1	8%	$10.0000	$0.8000	0.60	$0.4800	–	–	–	3.20%	3.20%
2	8	10.3200	0.8256	0.60	0.4954	–	–	–	3.20	3.20
3	8	10.6502	0.8520	0.60	0.5112	–	–	–	3.20	3.20
4	8	10.9910	0.8793	0.60	0.5276	–	–	–	3.20	3.20
5	8	11.3427	0.9074	0.60	0.5445	3.15%	3.15%	3.15%	3.20	3.20
6	8	11.7056	0.9365	0.60	0.5619	3.15	3.15	3.15	3.20	3.20
7	10	12.0802	1.2080	0.60	0.7248	3.15	7.61	7.61	4.00	28.99
8	10	12.5636	1.2564	0.60	0.7538	3.30	10.00	10.00	4.00	4.00
9	10	13.0662	1.3066	0.60	0.7840	3.54	10.23	10.23	4.00	4.00
10	10	13.5888	1.3589	0.60	0.8153	3.77	8.23	8.23	4.00	4.00
11	10	14.1324	1.4132	0.60	0.8479	3.92	3.92	3.92	4.00	4.00
12	10	14.6977	1.4698	0.60	8.8819	3.92	3.92	3.92	4.00	4.00
13	13	15.2856	1.9871	0.60	1.1923	3.92	9.17	9.17	5.20	35.20
14	13	16.0804	2.0905	0.60	1.2543	4.15	12.02	12.02	5.20	5.20
15	13	16.9166	2.1992	0.60	1.3195	4.50	12.37	12.37	5.20	5.20
16	13	17.7963	2.3135	0.60	1.3881	4.84	10.09	10.09	5.20	5.20
17	13	18.7217	2.4338	0.60	1.4603	5.07	5.07	5.07	5.20	5.20
18	13	19.6952	2.5604	0.60	1.5362	5.07	5.07	5.07	5.20	5.20

SOURCE: BRIGHAM (1983)

TABLE 7-3 THE IMPACT OF A CHANGE IN RATE OF RETURN ON EARNINGS GROWTH

YEAR	BOOK VALUE (1)	EARNINGS PER SHARE (2)	DIVIDENDS PER SHARE (3)	RETAINED EARNINGS (4)	GROWTH RATE OF EARNINGS (5)
1	$10.00	$1.00	$0.60	$0.40	
2	$10.40	$1.04	$0.62	$0.42	0.04
3	$10.82	$1.08	$0.65	$0.43	0.04
4	$11.25	$1.69	$1.01	$0.67	0.56
5	$11.92	$1.79	$1.07	$0.72	0.06
6	$12.64	$1.90	$1.14	$0.76	0.06

Column (1): Value for previous year plus retained earnings in previous year
Column (2): 10% of book value in first three years, and 15% of book value in last three years
Column (3): 60% of earnings
Column (4): 40% of earnings

Source: Gordon, M.J., N.Y. State Public Service Commission, Case 267755

the necessary conditions and assumptions outlined in this section are not dramatically violated. Although historical information provides a primary foundation for expectations, investors use additional information to supplement past growth rates. Extrapolating past history alone without consideration of historical trends and anticipated economic events would assume either that past rates will persist over time or that investors' expectations are based entirely on history. Analysts' forecasts provide a supplementary source of information on growth expectations.

7.4 GROWTH ESTIMATES: ANALYSTS' FORECASTS

Since investor growth expectations are the quantities desired in the DCF model, the use of forecast growth published by investment services merits serious consideration. The growth rates assumed by investors can be determined by a study of the analyses of future earnings and projected long-run growth rates made by the investment community. The anticipated long-run growth rates actually used by institutional investors to determine the desirability of investing in different securities influence investors' growth anticipations.

Growth rate forecasts of several analysts are available from published sources. For example, The I/B/E/S Summary Statistic Data Base systematically tabulates analysts' earnings forecasts on a regular basis. The Rodney L. White Center for Financial Research at the Wharton School of Finance regularly surveys long-run growth projections of some 50 institutional investors.

Typically, growth forecasts are in the form of earnings per share and dividends per share over periods ranging from one to 5 years, and are supported by extensive financial analysis. Table 7-4, drawn from a 1982 Southern Bell rate case, tabulates analysts' projections made in the March-June 1983 period for AT&T. The average growth rate estimate for dividends and earnings measures the consensus expectation of the investment community. The truncated mean of the forecasts, defined as the average of all the forecasts after removing the high and the low estimate, is also a useful measure of consensus.

Major brokerage firms which publish growth forecasts are listed on the table. This list is not exhaustive of course, but is nevertheless representative. Other sources of published growth forecasts include Ford Investment Service, Argus Research, Salomon Brothers, and Drexel Burnham.

A test of whether such growth projections are typical of the market as a whole is their uniformity. For example, in Table 7-4, 10 out of 15 analysts forecasts growth in the 7% – 9% range; hence, the probability is high that their analysis reflects a degree of consensus in the market as a whole.

Because of the dominance of institutional investors and their influence on individual investors, analysts' forecasts of long-run growth rates provide a sound basis for estimating required returns[9]. Financial analysts also exert a strong influence on the expectations of many investors who do not possess the resources to make their own forecasts, that is, they are a cause of 'g'. The accuracy of these forecasts in the sense of whether they turn out to be correct is not at issue here, as long as they reflect widely held expectations. As long as the forecasts are typical and/or influential in that they are consistent with current stock price levels, they are relevant. The use of analysts' forecasts in the DCF model is sometimes denounced on the grounds that it is difficult to forecast earnings and dividends for only one year, let alone for longer time periods. This objection is unfounded however because it is present investor expectations that are being priced; it is the consensus forecast which is embedded in price and therefore in required return, not the future as it will turn out to be.

Several empirical studies have shown that analysts' forecasts represent the best possible source of DCF growth rates, and are more accurate than forecasts based on historical growth rates. These studies show that investors rely on analysts' forecasts to a greater extent than on historic data only. A study by Brown & Rozeff (1978) shows that analysts, as proxied by Value Line analysts, make better forecasts than could be obtained using only

TABLE 7-4 STOCK ANALYSTS' FORECASTS OF AT&T's GROWTH RATE POST JANUARY 1982 DIVESTITURE ANNOUNCEMENT

FIRM	EPS	DPS	COMMENT
L.F. Rothschild, Unterberg Towbin, *AT&T*, 1/25/82	10-12%	–	Next several years
E.F. Hutton, *Earnings & Valuation Digest*, 7/82	7.0	7.0	Next 5 years
Bache, *Quantitative Investment Strategies*, 8/82	8.0	6.2	Through 1986
First Boston Research, *Review and Comment*, 8/82	8.0	6.0	Next 5 years
Smith Barney, *Statistical Summary*, 9/82	5.7	8.7	Through 1987, EPS is normalized
Argus Research, *A Progress Report*, 9/24/82	8.0	–	Through 1987
Merrill Lynch, *Monthly Research Review*, 10/82	9.0	8.0	Next 5 years
Janney Montgomery Scott, *Research Department Coverage*, 10/5/82	7.0	–	Next 5 years
Donaldson, Lufkin, & Jenrette, *AT&T*, 10/6/82	7.25-7.80	–	Through 1984
Dean Witter, *Technology Group*, 10/11/82	8.0-9.0	–	Normalized, next 5 years
Paine Webber, *Telecommunications Monthly*, 10/15/82	5.4	5.6	Through 1987
Salomon Brothers, *Monthly Stock Review*, 10/15/82	6.5	6.5	Next 5 years
Value Line, *Investment Survey*, 10/29/82	0.5	1.5	1979-1981 to 1985-1987
Kidder Peabody, *Monthly Valuation Information*, 11/82	7.8	6.1	Next 5 years
Wells Fargo, *Security Market Plane* 11/82	8.3	–	Next 5 years
Average Growth Rate Estimates	7.21%	6.18%	
Truncated Mean	7.44%	6.49%	

SOURCE: MORIN (1983C)

historical data, because analysts have available not only past data but also a knowledge of such crucial factors as rate case decisions, construction programs, new products, cost data, and so on. Brown & Rozeff test the accuracy of analysts' forecasts versus forecasts based on past data only, and conclude that their evidence of analyst superiority means that analysts' forecasts should be used in studies of cost of capital. Their evidence supports the hypothesis that Value Line analysts consistently make better predictions than time series models.

Empirical studies have been conducted showing that investors who rely primarily on data obtained from several large reputable investment research houses and security dealers obtain better results than those who do not[10]. Thus, both empirical research and common sense indicate that investors rely primarily on analysts' growth rate forecasts rather than on historical growth rates alone.

Ideally, one could decide which analysts make the most reliable forecasts and then confine the analysis to those forecasts. This would be impractical since reliable data on past forecasts are generally not available. Moreover, analysts with poor track records are replaced by more competent analysts, so that a poor forecasting record by a particular firm is not necessarily indicative of poor future forecasts. In any event, analysts working for large brokerage firms typically have a following, and investors who heed to a particular analyst's recommendations do exert an influence on the market. So, an average of all the available forecasts from large reputable investment houses is likely to produce the best DCF growth rate.

One problem with the use of published analysts' forecasts is that some forecasts cover only the next one or two years. If these are abnormal years, they may not be indicative of longer run average growth expectations. Another problem is that forecasts may not be available in sufficient quantities or may not be available at all for certain utilities, in which case alternate methods of growth estimation must be employed.

Some analysts are uncomfortable with the assumption that the DCF growth rates are perpetual growth rates, and argue that above average growth can be expected to prevail for a fixed number of years and then the growth rate will setlle down to a steady-state long-run level, consistent with that of the economy. Extended DCF models are available to accomodate such assumptions, and were discussed in Chapter 6.

7.5 GROWTH ESTIMATES: SUSTAINABLE GROWTH METHOD

Another method, alternately referred to as the "ploughback", "sustainable growth", and "retention ratio" method, used by investment analysts to predict future growth in earnings and dividends is to multiply the fraction of earnings expected to be retained by the company, b, by the expected return on book equity, r. That is,

$$g = b \times r$$

The conceptual premise of the method, enunciated in Chapter 5, Section 4, is that future growth in dividends for existing equity can only occur if a portion of the overall return to investors is reinvested into the firm instead of being distributed as dividends.

For example, if a company earns 16% on equity, and pays all the earnings out in dividends, the retention factor, b, is zero and earnings per share will not grow. Conversely, if the company retains all its earnings and pays no dividends, it would grow at an annual rate of 16%. Or again, if the company earns 16% on equity and pays out 70% of the earnings in dividends, the retention factor is 30%, and earnings growth will be 30% x 70% = 4.8% per year.

In implementing the method, the retention rate, b, should be the rate that the market expects to prevail in the future. If no explicit forecast is available, it is reasonable to assume that the utility's future retention ratio will, on average, remain unchanged from its present level. Or, it can be estimated by taking a weighted average of past retention ratios as a proxy for the future on the grounds that utilities' target retention ratios are usually, although not always, stable[11].

Both historical and forecast values of 'r' are used to estimate g, although forecast values are far superior since adjustment for current and foreseen changes are incorporated. The use of historical realized book returns on equity rather than the expected return equity is highly question- able since reliance on achieved results involves circular reasoning. Realized returns are the results of the regulatory process itself, and are also subject to tests of fairness and reasonableness. As a gauge of the expected return on book equity, either direct published analysts' forecasts of the long-run expected return on equity, or authorized rates of return in recent regulatory cases can be used as a guide. As a floor estimate, it seems reasonable for investors to expect allowed equity returns by state regulatory commissions to be in excess of the current cost of debt to the utility in question.

Another way of estimating the return on equity investors are expecting is proposed by Copeland (1979). Since earnings per share (E) can be stated as dividends per share (D) times the payout ratio (1 – b), the earnings per share capitalized by investors can be inferred by dividing the current dividend by an expected payout ratio. Since most utilities follow a fairly stable dividend policy, the possibility of error is less when estimating the payout than when estimating the expected return on equity or the expected growth rate. Using this approach, and denoting book value per share by B, the expected return on equity is:

$$r = E/B = (D/(1-b)) / B \qquad (7\text{-}7)$$

Estimates of the expected payout ratio can be inferred from historical 10-year average payout ratio data for utilities. Since individual averages frequently tend to regress toward the grand mean, the historical payout ratio needs to be adjusted for this tendency, using statistical techniques for predicting future values based on this tendency of individual values to regress toward the grand mean over time[11].

An application of the sustainable growth method is shown in the following example, adapted from testimony presented by the Georgia Power Company in a 1983 rate filing.

EXAMPLE

As a gauge of the expected return on equity, authorized rates of return in recent regulatory cases for Eastern U.S. electric utilities as reported by Value Line for 1982 and 1983 averaged 15.62%, with a standard deviation of 1%. In other words, the majority of those utilities were authorized to earn 15.6%, with the allowed return on equity ranging from 14.6% to 16.6%.

As a gauge of the expected retention ratio, the average 1982 payout ratio of 34 eastern electric utilities as compiled by Value Line was 73% which indicates an average retention ratio of 27%. This was consistent with the long-run target retention ratio indicated by the management of The Southern Company, parent of Georgia Power. It is therefore reasonable to postulate that investors expect a retention ratio ranging from 25% to 35% for the company with a likely value of 30%. In Table 7-5 below, expected retention ratios of 25% to 35% and assumed returns on equity from 14.6% to 16.6% are combined to produce growth rates ranging from 3.65% to 5.82% with a likely value of 4.69%.

TABLE 7-5 ILLUSTRATION OF THE SUSTAINABLE GROWTH METHOD

EXPECTED GROWTH RATE: $g = br$

Expected Retention Ratio	Expected Return on Book Equity (r)		
	14.6%	15.6%	16.6%
25%	3.65%	3.90%	4.16%
30%	4.38	4.69	4.99
35%	5.11	5.47	5.82

Source: Georgia Public Service Commission, Docket Testimony of Dr. R. A. Morin, 1983.

It should be pointed out that published forecasts of the expected return on equity by analysts such as Value Line are sometimes based on end-of-period book equity rather than on average book equity. The following formula[12] adjusts the reported end-of-year values so that they are based on average common equity:

$$r_a = r_t \left(\frac{2B_t}{B_t + B_{t-1}} \right) \qquad (7\text{-}8)$$

where r_a = return on average equity

r_t = return on year-end equity as reported

B_t = reported year-end book equity of the current year

B_{t-1} = reported year-end book equity of the previous year

The sustainable growth method can also be applied using Gordon's expanded growth formula, which allows for external financing. The expanded growth estimate (see Chapter 6.4) is:

$$g = br + sv$$

where b, r are defined as previously, 's' is the expected percent growth in number of shares to finance investment, and 'v' is the profitability of the equity investment. The variable 's' measures the long-run expected stock financing that the utility will undertake. If the utility's investments are growing at a stable rate and if the earnings retention rate is also stable, then 's' will grow at a stable rate. 's' can be estimated by taking a weighted average of past percentage increases in the number of shares. This measurement is difficult however owing to the sporadic and episodic nature of stock financing, and smoothing techniques must be employed. 'v' is the profitability of the equity investment and can be measured as the difference of market price and book value per share divided by the latter, as discussed in Chapter 6.

Generally, there are two problems in the practical application of the sustainable growth method, neither of which are prohibitively serious. The first is that it may be even more difficult to estimate what b and r investors have in mind than it is to estimate what g they envisage. Second, there is a potential element of circularity in estimating g by a forecast of b and r for the utility being regulated, since r is determined in large part by regulation. To estimate what r resides in the minds of investors is equivalent to estimating the market's assessment of the outcome of regulatory hearings. Expected r is exactly what regulatory commissions set in determining an allowed rate of return. If a commission were to set the rate of return too high because it relied on too high a g forecast as a result of an inflated r forecast, the prophecy of an exaggerated r would become self-fulfilling. This problem can be circumvented by applying the DCF method to a broad sample of comparable risk firms, instead of only to forecast values of the utility being regulated.

The circularity problem is not as severe as it appears because of the self-correcting nature of the DCF model. If a high equity return is granted, the stock price will increase in response to the unanticipated favorable return allowance, lowering the dividend yield component of market return in compensation for the high g induced by the high allowed return. At the next regulatory hearing, more conservative forecasts of r would prevail. The impact on the dual components of the DCF formula, yield and growth, are at least partially offsetting.

Notes

[1] An exhaustive catalogue of sources of investment information is contained in the following investments textbooks: Cohen, Zinbarg & Zeikel (1977), Sharpe (1981), and Francis (1976).

[2] Services offered by Standard & Poor's are described in a booklet entitled "Standard & Poor's Services and Publications Cover Every Financial Information Need", which may be obtained by writing to Standard & Poor's at 345 Hudson St., New York, N.Y. 10014. Moody's services are described in a publication entitled "How Moody's Can Help You", and may be obtained by writing to Moody's Investor Service Inc., 99 Church St., New York, N.Y. 10007.

[3] For a description of IDC/Chase Econometrics financial services, write to company at 486 Totten Rd, Waltham, Mass. 02154.

[4] The Efficient Market Hypothesis, pioneered by Fama (1970), is the cornerstone of modern investment theory, and is described in most college level investment textbooks. For an excellent treatment, see Reilly (1979), Sharpe (1981), and Brealey & Myers (1984).

[5] An excellent summary of the empirical evidence can be found in Reilly (1979).

[6] For a derivation, discussion, and implementation of the quarterly DCF model in regulatory hearings, see Friend (1983), and Litzenberger (1979).

[7] The lack of persistence of earnings growth rates is documented in studies by Little (1962), Murphy (1966), and Lintner & Glauber (1967). The time series properties of earnings data are analysed in Brown & Rozeff (1978).

[8] Changes in accounting practices can create problems of data comparability and consistency; the analysis should thus be confined to those years following the accounting changes. When using per share data series, care must be taken to take into account changes in capitalization, such as stock splits and stock dividends.

[9] The rest of this section is adapted from Brigham (1983).

[10] Examples of such studies include Stanley, Lewellen, and Schlarbaum (1981) and Touche Ross Co. (1982).

[11] Statistically superior predictions of future averages are made by weighting individual past averages with the grand mean, with the variance within the individual averages and the variance across individual averages serving as weights. See Efron & Morris (1975) for an excellent discussion of this method.

[12] The return on year-end common equity (r) is defined as $r = E/B_t$, where E are earnings per share, and B_t is the year-end book value per share. The return on average common equity (r_a) is defined as:

$$r_a = E/B_a$$

where B_a = average book value per share. The latter is by definition:

$$B_a = \frac{B_t + B_{t-1}}{2}$$

where B_t is the year-end book equity per share and B_{t-1} is the beginning-of-year book equity per share. Dividing 'r' by 'r_a', and substituting:

$$\frac{r}{r_a} = \frac{E/B_t}{E/B_a} = \frac{B_a}{B_t} = \frac{B_t + B_{t-1}}{2B_t}$$

Solving for 'r_a', a formula for translating the return on year-end equity into the return on average equity is obtained, using reported beginning-of-the year and end-of-year common equity figures:

$$r_a = r\left(\frac{2B_t}{B_t + B_{t-1}}\right)$$

APPENDIX 7-A

DCF MODEL
Quarterly Timing Adjustment

We start with the seminal notion that market price is the present value of expected future cash flows and assume for simplicity a one-year holding period. If D_{10}, D_{20}, D_{30}, D_{40} represent the dividends paid each quarter in the year preceding the purchase date, and P_0 is the stock price, P_1 the stock price one year from now, we can write:

$$P_0 = \frac{D_{10}(1+g)}{(1+K)^{1/4}} + \frac{D_{20}(1+g)}{(1+K)^{1/2}} + \frac{D_{30}(1+g)}{(1+K)^{3/4}} + \frac{D_{40}(1+g)}{(1+K)} + \frac{P_1}{1+K} \quad ①$$

where g = annual growth rate on earnings and dividends

Noting that $P_1 = P_0(1+g)$, we multiply the numerator and demoninator of each term by the following factors so as to facilitate algebraic manipulation.

$$P_0 = \frac{D_{10}(1+g)(1+K)^{3/4}}{(1+K)^{1/4}(1+K)^{3/4}} + \frac{D_{20}(1+g)(1+K)^{1/2}}{(1+K)^{1/2}(1+K)^{1/2}} +$$

$$\frac{D_{30}(1+g)(1+K)^{1/4}}{(1+K)^{1/4}(1+K)^{3/4}} + \frac{D_{40}(1+g)}{(1+K)} + \frac{P_0(1+g)}{1+K}$$

$$= \left[\frac{D_{10}(1+K)^{3/4}}{1+K} + \frac{D_{20}(1+K)^{1/2}}{1+K} + \frac{D_{30}(1+K)^{3/4}}{1+K} + \frac{D_{40}}{1+K} \right]$$

$$(1+g) + \frac{P_0(1+g)}{1+K}$$

Solving for K, by multiplying through by $(1+K)$ and dividing through by P_0, we get

$$K = \left[\frac{D_{10}(1+K)^{3/4} + D_{20}(1+K)^{1/2} + D_{30}(1+K)^{1/4} + D_{40}}{P_0} \right](1+g) + g \quad ②$$

The standard DCF model by analogy is

$$K = \frac{D_0 (1 + g)}{P_0} + g \qquad \text{③}$$

Clearly, the expression in large brackets in ② is greater than D_0 in ③ since $D_0 = D_{10} + D_{20} + D_{30} + D_{40}$ and K is a positive number. Consequently, if dividends are paid quarterly, the appropriate adjustment to the current dividend yield is higher than $(1 + g)$. If the adjustment is applied to the spot dividend yield, defined as $4 \, D_{40}$, the adjustment factor is still in excess of $(1 + g)$, although reduced. This can be seen by transforming as an approximation into:

$$K = \frac{D_{40}}{P_0} \left[\frac{(1 + K)^{3/4}}{(1 + g)^{3/4}} + \frac{(1 + K)^{1/2}}{(1 + g)^{1/2}} + \frac{(1 + K)^{1/4}}{(1 + g)^{1/4}} + 1 \right] (1 + g) + g$$

Since $K > g$, the bracketed expression above multiplied by D_{40} is higher than the spot dividend rate, $4 \, D_{40}$.

The difference in cost of capital estimate can be substantial. Subtracting (3) from (2), we obtain the difference between the annual and quarterly DCF estimates:

$$\frac{\left[\left(D_{10} (1 + K)^{3/4} + D_{20} (1 + K)^{1/2} + D_{30} (1 + K)^{1/4} + D_{40} \right) - D_0 \right] (1 + g)}{P_0}$$

To obtain an idea of the magnitude of the difference, take representative values for the parameters of the above equation applicable to The Southern Company. The quarterly dividends on the current year are 0.425, the range in growth rate g is 3% – 5%, the stock price $P_0 = \$16$. The magnitude of the difference in cost of capital estimates from the above equation is approximately 50 basis points:

	Quarterly DCF	Annual DCF	Difference
g = 3%	14.50%	13.94%	0.56%
g = 4%	15.65%	15.05%	0.60%
g = 5%	16.81%	16.16%	0.65%

CHAPTER 8

DCF COMPARABLE GROUPS

There are several reasons why the determination of cost of capital should not rest on a sample of one firm:

(1) Consistency with the notions of fair and reasonable return promulgated in the *Hope* and *Bluefield* cases. The basic premise in determining a fair return is that the allowed return on equity should be commensurate with returns on investments in other firms with comparable risk, hence the need to extend the sample to firms of comparable risk. Moreover, the equity costs of other firms represent economic opportunity costs which directly impact the cost of equity for the utility being studied.

(2) Added reliability. Confidence in the reliability of the estimate of equity cost can be enhanced by estimating the cost of equity capital for a variety of risk-equivalent companies. Such group comparisons not only act as a useful check on the magnitude of the cost of equity estimate obtained from a single company, but also mitigate any distortion introduced by measurement errors in the two components of K, namely dividend yield and growth. For example, in a large group of companies, positive and negative deviations from the expected growth will tend to cancel out owing to the law of large numbers, provided that the errors are independent[1]. The average growth rate of several comparable firms is less likely to diverge from expected growth than is the estimate of growth for a single firm. More generally, the assumptions of the DCF model are more likely to be fulfilled for a group of companies than for any single firm.

(3) Abnormal conditions. When there is reason to believe that the standard DCF model is inapplicable to a particular utility, or when a utility is experiencing extraordinary circumstances, such as General Public Utilities following the Three Mile Island accident, or Washington Power Public Service following the default on its bonds, the use of a benchmark group of companies is the only viable alternative to measure equity costs through the DCF method.

(4) Circularity problem. Stock price, hence cost of equity capital, depends on investors' growth expectations, which in turn depend partially on investors' perception of the regulatory process. The net result is that the cost of equity depends in part on anticipated regulatory action, since both

components of K, yield and growth, are influenced by the regulatory process. Carried to its extreme, this implies that regulation would in effect deliver whatever equity return investors expect.

This calls to mind Myer's (1972) reference to the gaming aspects of regulation. Suppose that stock price is initially below book value, and that regulators announce that they will subscribe to the standard DCF method of measurement. Stock price will then rise, since investors expect a higher allowed return to come out of the rate hearing. But if stock price rises, the regulators will underestimate the cost of equity if they assume that investors expect a continuation of historical growth. If investors in turn recognize the regulator's error in assessing their expectations, a complex circular game between investors and regulators ensues. Myer's solution to this predicament is to extend the sample to include several comparable risk firms.

It is thus imperative to examine market data not related to the firm's financial statistics as a check on the standard DCF model. The circularity problem, to the extent that it exists, can be mitigated by referencing data on non-regulated companies as well as on other utilities.

This chapter illustrates the design of comparable risk groups and offers solutions to special problems encountered in applying DCF by means of comprehensive case studies, drawing on the material of previous DCF chapters. The various measures of risk and the design of risk filters discussed in Chapters 3 and 4 are also illustrated.

8.1   DCF COMPARABLE GROUPS: CASE STUDIES

The Southern Company

The application of the DCF approach to other companies as a means of comparison first requires a specification of a risk-equivalent class of securities, since the basic notion underlying the cost of common equity capital is that securities are priced so that all securities of equivalent risk offer the same expected return at any point in time. For The Southern Company, the basic problem is thus to determine the expected rate of return for its particular risk class. Three groups of companies similar in risk to The Southern Company are studied.

The first group of companies is a selection of companies which are primarily in the same industry as The Southern Company, and is designated as "Eastern Electric Utilities – East" by Value Line. Besides The Southern Company, this group of 34 companies, listed in Table 8-1, includes eastern electric utilities whose common shares are publicly listed and are therefore subject to the opinions and actions of investors in a measurable way.

Although there may be substantial differences in characteristics between these companies which may result in varying risk assessments by investors, they are all subject to similar kinds of economic and regulatory risk influences, and the average risk of the group can be considered comparable to The Southern Company.

To determine the comparability of risk, two quantitative and objective measures of risk were utilized, the beta coefficient and standard deviation of returns. Columns two and three of Table 8-1 show the two risk measures estimated over a five-year period using weekly returns for each company as calculated by Value Line. The data show that The Southern Company's beta estimate of 0.65 is identical to the 0.65 average beta for the group. The betas for the companies in the group are remarkably homogeneous. Similarly for the standard deviation of return, The Southern Company's risk of 2.54% is close to the group's average risk of 2.79%.

Application of DCF is performed as follows. The fourth column of Table 8-1 shows the current dividend yield for each of the 34 electric utilities, including The Southern Company, as of the date of case preparation, using the ratio of the current indicated dividend rate to the closing market price as of that date. The next two columns show the rate of growth in dividends per share experienced by each company over the past 5 and 10 years. The average of the 5-year and 10-year growth rates is shown at the bottom of column six.

While the historical growth rate may not be representative of investors' expectations of future growth in the case of a single company, in the case of a large group of comparable companies, positive and negative deviations from the expected growth will tend to cancel out, provided there are no systematic industry-wide effects which affect all the companies in the group. The estimate for the group is thus more reliable than the estimate based on a single company.

The average dividend yield and the average historical growth rate for the group are summed to arrive at the investors' required return. The resulting estimate for the group is 15.68% based on an average for all companies. The latter must be adjusted upward since the spot dividend yield was used in computing the return rather than the conceptually correct expected dividend yield. As shown in the upper panel of Table 8-2, the adjustment is obtained by multiplying the average spot dividend yield for the group by $(1 + g)$. That is, $D_1/P_o = D_o(1 + g)/P_o$. The adjusted dividend yield is thus $11.08\%(1 + 4.6\%) = 11.58\%$ to produce an average return on equity of $11.58\% + 4.68\% = 16.18\%$.

TABLE 8-1 REQUIRED MARKET RETURN AND MEASURES OF RISK FOR 34 EASTERN ELECTRIC UTILITIES

COMPANY	BETA	STANDARD DEVIATION	CURRENT DIVIDEND YIELD	5-YEAR DIVIDEND GROWTH	10-YEAR DIVIDEND GROWTH	DIVIDEND GROWTH FORECAST	EXPECTED RETENTION RATIO	EXPECTED BOOK RETURN ON EQUITY	RETENTION RATIO GROWTH
(1)	(2)	(3)	(4)	(5)	(6)	(7)	(8)	(9)	(10)
1 ALLEGHENY PWR SYS INC	0.75	2.76	9.8	4.5	4	6.5	0.29	14.5	4.2
2 AMERICAN ELEC PWR INC	0.70	2.44	13.0	2.0	3.0	2.0	0.17	13.5	2.3
3 ATLANTIC CITY ELEC CO	0.60	2.74	10.0	6.0	4.0	4.5	0.14	13.0	1.9
4 BALTIMORE GAS & ELEC	0.75	2.88	9.9	5.0	3.5	5.5	0.30	13.0	3.8
5 BOSTON EDISON CO	0.55	2.55	11.0	2.5	1.5	5.0	0.26	13.5	3.5
6 CAROLINA PWR & LT CO	0.70	2.93	11.0	6.5	4.5	4.0	0.24	11.5	2.7
7 CENTRAL HUDSON GAS & ELEC	0.60	2.46	11.0	6.0	4.5	4.5	0.31	13.5	4.2
8 CENTRAL MAINE PWR CO	0.55	2.64	13.0	5.0	4.0	3.0	0.09	12.5	1.1
9 COMMONWEALTH EDISON CO	0.70	2.67	11.0	9.0	2.0	4.5	0.31	13.5	4.2
10 CONSOLIDATED EDISON NY	0.65	2.76	8.7	13.5	5.0	13.5	0.25	12.5	3.1
11 DELMARVA PWR & LT	0.65	2.82	10.0	5.0	3.0	5.5	0.19	14.0	2.7
12 DUKE POWER CO	0.65	2.89	11.0	6.5	4.0	5.5	0.33	13.5	4.5
13 DUQUESNE LT CO	0.60	2.52	13.0	1.5	1.0	3.5	0.06	12.5	0.8
14 EASTERN UTIL ASSOC	0.60	2.80	12.0	1.5	1.0	5.0	0.27	14.0	3.7
15 FLORIDA PROGRESS CORP	0.70	3.17	10.0	9.5	7.5	7.0	0.29	15.0	4.3
16 FLORIDA PWR & LT CO	0.70	2.61	9.9	14.0	11.0	8.0	0.27	13.5	3.7
17 LONG ISLAND LTG CO	0.55	2.35	13.0	4.0	3.0	4.0	0.26	14.0	3.7
18 NEW ENGLAND ELEC SYS	0.70	3.07	8.5	7.5	5.5	7.5	0.33	15.0	5.0
19 NEW YORK ST ELEC & GAS	0.60	2.75	12.0	4.5	3.5	5.0	0.30	13.0	3.9
20 NIAGARA MOHAWK PWR CP	0.65	2.92	12.0	5.5	4.0	4.5	0.26	12.5	3.2
21 NORTHEAST UTIL	0.60	2.81	12.0	3.0	2.0	6.0	0.25	14.0	3.5
22 ORANGE & ROCKLAND UTIL	0.65	2.93	10.0	5.0	3.5	6.0	0.27	13.5	3.6
23 PENNSYLVANIA PWR & LT	0.65	2.84	11.0	4.0	3.0	3.0	0.31	13.0	4.1
24 PHILADELPHIA ELEC CO	0.60	2.54	13.0	2.5	1.5	4.0	0.14	13.0	1.9
25 POTOMAC ELEC PWR CO	0.65	2.93	10.0	5.5	5.0	6.0	0.24	13.5	3.3
26 PUBLIC SVC CO N H	0.70	3.12	13.0	3.0	2.5	2.0	0.21	11.0	2.3
27 PUBLIC SVC ELEC & GAS	0.75	3.01	12.0	6.0	4.0	3.5	0.25	13.0	3.3
28 ROCHESTER GAS & ELEC CP	0.50	2.83	10.0	7.5	6.5	7.5	0.32	14.0	4.5
29 SAVANNAH ELEC & PWR CO	0.65	3.32	11.0	12.0	2.0	5.5	0.35	13.0	4.5
30 SOUTH CAROLINA ELEC & GA	0.70	3.11	11.0	3.5	3.5	4.5	0.15	13.0	1.9
31 SOUTHERN CO	0.65	2.54	11.0	2.5	2.5	3.5	0.33	14.5	4.8
32 TECO ENERGY INC	0.70	2.90	8.9	9.5	7.5	9.0	0.33	14.5	4.8
33 UNITED ILLUM CO	0.60	2.73	12.0	3.0	3.0	3.5	0.36	14.0	5.1
34 DOMINION RES (VEPCO)	0.60	2.65	12.0	3.5	2.5	4.5	0.21	11.5	2.4
AVERAGE	0.65	2.79	11.08%	5.41%	3.78%	5.21%	0.25	13.34%	3.43%
					4.60%				

TABLE 8-2 DCF COST OF EQUITY CAPITAL
COMPUTATIONS: 34 EASTERN ELECTRICS

ESTIMATE OF REQUIRED MARKET RETURN
ELECTRIC UTILITIES
HISTORICAL GROWTH

	Spot Dividend Yield	Adjustment Expectation	Expected Dividend Yield	Average Growth Rate	Return (3)+(4)
	(1)	(2)	(3)	(4)	(5)
Average of all companies	11.08	1.046	11.59	4.60	16.18%

ELECTRIC UTILITIES
GROWTH FORECAST

	Spot Dividend Yield	Adjustment Expectation	Expected Dividend Yield	Average Growth Rate	Return (3)+(4)
	(1)	(2)	(3)	(4)	(5)
Average of all companies	11.08	1.052	11.66	5.21	16.86%

ELECTRIC UTILITIES
RETENTION RATIO

	Spot Dividend Yield	Adjustment Expectation	Expected Dividend Yield	Average Growth Rate	Return (3)+(4)
	(1)	(2)	(3)	(4)	(5)
Average of all companies	11.08	1.034	11.46	3.43	14.88%

The same procedure is repeated only this time using the direct dividend growth forecasts provided by Value Line for each of the 34 utilities in the group, shown in Column 7 of Table 8-1. The average projected growth rate for the group is 5.21%, which produces a return on equity of 16.86%, as shown in the middle panel of Table 8-2.

The growth rate for the group can be estimated in yet another way. For each company in the group, Columns 8 and 9 of Table 8-1 show Value Line's expected retention ratio and expected book return on equity. The product of the two yields the growth rate for each company, shown in Column 10. In other words, the sustainable growth method whereby g = br is implemented for each company. The average growth for the group from this method is 3.43%. In the bottom panel of Table 8-2, the expected growth for the group is combined with the expected dividend yield for the group to arrive at a 14.88% estimate of the return on equity.

It should be pointed out that although electric utilities are being compared to The Southern Company in order to estimate the latter's cost of common equity, there is no circularity of logic in the analysis since the estimated required returns are based entirely on the actions of investors in a competitive market and not on regulatory decisions.

A second group of companies consists of all publicly traded electric utilities whose bond rating is the same as The Southern Company's, namely Baa by Moody's and BBB by Standard & Poor's, and with data availability on Value Line's Data Base. Holding companies with at least one subsidiary with a higher rating are excluded in order to preserve risk homogeneity. Twenty-three such companies survive the screen and are listed in Table 8-3. The average beta for the group is 0.64 which is almost identical to The Southern Company's beta of 0.65, and the average standard deviation of return for the group is 2.79%, compared to The Southern Company's 2.54%. These results confirm the risk similarity of The Southern Company and electric utilities with the same bond rating.

Application of the DCF formulation is shown in Table 8-4, and is developed in an identical fashion to that of the previous comparable group. The unadjusted average return on equity for the group is 15.63%. When the spot dividend yield is adjusted to obtain the expected dividend yield, the average cost of equity capital for the group is 16.1%. As in the case of the first comparable group, the same procedure is repeated using the direct dividend growth forecasts provided by Value Line for each of the 23 comparable risk utilities in the group. The average projected growth rate for th group is 4.46%, which produces a return on equity figure of 16.55%, as shown on the middle panel of Table 8-4.

Again as in the case of the first group, the growth rate for each company is estimated by multiplying Value Line's expected retention ratio and expected return on common equity. The product of the two yields the growth rate for each company, shown in Column 10 of Table 8-3. The average growth for the group is 3.55%, which combined with the expected dividend yield for the group produces a 15.54% return on equity estimate.

A third group of companies is defined as all those New York Stock Exchange publicly listed industrials, excluding utilities, whose risk is comparable to that of The Southern Company, as determined by the two objective risk measures. This reference group, shown in Table 8-5, includes all industrials whose beta lies between 0.60 and 0.80 and whose standard deviation of return is less than 4.25%, and with data availability on the Value Line Data Base; 26 companies survived the screens. The resulting companies are similar in risk to The Southern Company, as evidence by the group's average beta of 0.69 versus The Southern Company's 0.65 and the

TABLE 8-3 REQUIRED MARKET RETURN AND MEASURES OF RISK FOR 23 Baa/BBB ELECTRIC UTILITIES

COMPANY	BETA	STANDARD DEVIATION	CURRENT DIVIDEND YIELD	5-YEAR DIVIDEND GROWTH	10-YEAR DIVIDEND GROWTH	DIVIDEND GROWTH FORECAST	EXPECTED RETENTION RATIO	EXPECTED BOOK RETURN ON EQUITY	RETENTION RATIO GROWTH
(1)	(2)	(3)	(4)	(5)	(6)	(7)	(8)	(9)	(10)
ALLEGHENY PWR SYS INC	0.5	2.760	9.8	4.5	4.0	6.5	0.29	14.5	4.2
BOSTON EDISON CO	0.55	2.547	11.0	2.5	1.5	5.0	0.26	13.5	3.5
CONSUMERS PWR CO	0.65	2.800	13.0	3.5	2.0	2.5	0.30	13.5	4.1
DETROIT EDISON	0.65	2.667	11.0	2.5	1.5	3.5	0.17	13.0	2.2
EASTERN UTIL ASSOC	0.60	2.802	12.0	1.5	1.0	5.0	0.27	14.0	3.7
GULF STS UTILS CO	0.70	2.784	12.0	5.5	4.0	4.5	0.30	14.5	4.4
KANSAS CITY PWR & LT CO	0.65	2.850	9.8	4.0	3.0	4.0	0.26	13.0	3.4
KANSAS GAS & ELEC CO	0.60	2.540	11.0	4.0	3.5	2.5	0.25	14.0	3.5
LONG ISLAND LTC CO	0.55	2.346	13.0	4.0	3.0	4.0	0.26	14.0	3.7
MIDDLE SOUTH UTIL INC	0.75	2.852	11.0	4.0	5.0	4.5	0.30	14.0	4.2
NEVADA POWER CO	0.60	2.707	10.0	23.5	14.0	7.5	0.20	15.5	3.1
NEW YORK ST ELEC & GAS	0.60	2.748	12.0	4.5	3.5	5.0	0.30	13.0	3.9
NORTHEAST UTILS	0.60	2.810	12.0	3.0	2.0	6.0	0.25	14.0	3.5
OHIO EDISON CO	0.70	2.975	13.0	1.0	1.5	2.5	0.18	13.5	2.4
PACIFIC PWR & LT CO	0.70	2.911	9.8	4.0	4.0	4.0	0.30	14.5	4.4
PHILADELPHIA ELEC CO	0.60	2.543	13.0	2.5	1.5	4.0	0.14	13.0	1.9
PORTLAND GEN ELEC CO	0.65	2.969	12.0	1.0	2.5	4.0	0.34	14.0	4.8
PUBLIC SVC CO N H	0.70	3.120	13.0	3.0	2.5	2.0	0.21	11.0	2.3
PUGET SOUND PWR & LT	0.65	2.936	13.0	7.5	6.5	5.5	0.25	13.5	3.4
SAN DIEGO GAS & ELEC	0.60	2.941	9.9	6.5	4.0	7.0	0.27	15.5	4.2
SAVANNAH ELEC & PWR CO	0.65	3.320	11.0	12.0	2.0	5.5	0.35	13.0	4.5
TOLEDO EDISON CO	0.55	2.583	12.0	2.0	2.5	3.5	0.20	12.5	2.5
UNION ELECTRIC CO	0.60	2.651	12.0	3.0	2.0	4.0	0.28	14.5	4.1
AVERAGE	0.64	2.790%	11.58%	4.76%	3.35%	4.46%	0.26	13.72%	3.55%
					4.05%				

SOURCE: VALUE LINE DATA BASE, 9/1/1983
WALL STREET JOURNAL, 9/1/1983

TABLE 8-4 DCF COST OF EQUITY CAPITAL COMPUTATIONS: Baa/BBB ELECTRICS

ESTIMATE OF REQUIRED MARKET RETURN
ELECTRIC UTILITIES
HISTORICAL GROWTH

	Spot Dividend Yield	Adjustment For Expectation	Expected Dividend Yield	Average Growth Rate	Return (3)+(4)
	(1)	(2)	(3)	(4)	(5)
Average of all companies	11.58	1.041	12.05	4.05	16.10%

ELECTRIC UTILITIES
GROWTH FORECAST

	Spot Dividend Yield	Adjustment For Expectation	Expected Dividend Yield	Average Growth Rate	Return (3)+(4)
	(1)	(2)	(3)	(4)	(5)
Average of all companies	11.58	1.045	12.09	4.46	16.55%

ELECTRIC UTILITIES
RETENTION RATIO GROWTH

	Spot Dividend Yield	Adjustment For Expectation	Expected Dividend Yield	Average Growth Rate	Return (3)+(4)
	(1)	(2)	(3)	(4)	(5)
Average of all companies	11.58	1.036	11.99	3.55	15.54%

group's standard deviation of 3.07% versus the company's 2.54%. The majority of the industrial companies which survived the risk screens are in the food and consumer retail industries, traditionally regarded by investors as defensive stocks along with utilities.

Application of the DCF formulation is shown in Table 8-6, and is developed in an identical manner to that of the previous reference groups, using three proxies for expected growth. The average return on common equity for the group is 14.7%, 14.98%, and 15.38%, using historical growth, analysts' growth forecasts, and retention ratio growth respectively.

Table 8-7 summarizes the results from the nine DCF comparable

TABLE 8-5   REQUIRED MARKET RETURN AND MEASURES OF RISK FOR 24 INDUSTRIALS

COMPANY	BETA	STANDARD DEVIATION	CURRENT DIVIDEND YIELD	HISTORICAL HISTORICAL 5-YEAR DIVIDEND GROWTH	10-YEAR DIVIDEND GROWTH	PROJECTED DIVIDEND GROWTH	EXPECTED RETENTION RATIO	EXPECTED BOOK RETURN ON EQUITY	RETENTION RATIO GROWTH
(1)	(2)	(3)	(4)	(5)	(6)	(7)	(8)	(9)	(10)
1 AMERICAN BRANDS INC	0.70	3.204	7.1	9.5	7.5	9.00	0.51	18.50	9.44
2 ANCHOR HOCKING CORP	0.60	3.579	4.9	8.0	7.0	11.00	0.62	16.50	10.23
3 ARO CORP	0.60	3.468	4.3	5.5	4.5	1.00	0.70	11.50	8.05
4 BEATRICE FOODS	0.80	3.083	5.7	11.0	9.5	6.00	0.60	15.50	9.30
5 BORDEN INC	0.70	2.875	4.4	8.0	5.5	10.50	0.64	14.00	8.96
6 CAMPBELL SOUP	0.65	2.861	4.1	8.5	6.0	10.00	0.56	16.50	9.24
7 CARNATION CO	0.75	3.212	4.7	16.0	16.0	10.50	0.62	17.00	10.54
8 CONSOLIDATED FOODS C	0.60	3.322	5.4	6.5	5.0	9.00	0.60	17.50	10.50
9 DART & KRAFT INC	0.75	2.633	5.7	10.0	7.0	8.50	0.58	17.00	9.86
10 EQUIFAX INC	0.60	3.410	4.4	3.0	2.0	10.00	0.36	23.50	8.46
11 GENERAL FOODS CORP.	0.80	2.952	5.5	8.0	5.0	11.00	0.56	16.50	9.24
12 HARSCO CORP	0.65	3.139	5.3	12.0	11.0	9.00	0.63	16.50	10.40
13 JORGENSEN EARLE M DE	0.60	2.914	3.5	14.5	12.5	11.00	0.76	15.50	11.78
14 KELLOGG CO	0.75	3.135	5.9	8.5	11.5	7.50	0.51	22.00	11.22
15 LIBBEY OWENS FORD CO	0.70	2.841	3.2	-0.5	-3.0	14.00	0.64	14.50	9.28
16 MARSH & MCLENNAN COS	0.75	2.979	5.5	19.0	16.0	6.00	0.40	27.00	10.80
17 MERCANTILE STORES	0.75	3.117	2.0	15.5	9.0	18.50	0.81	16.00	12.96
18 NABISCO INC	0.80	3.038	6.0	7.5	4.5	11.00	0.58	19.00	11.02
19 NATIONAL SVC INDS IN	0.75	3.074	3.2	11.5	7.5	11.00	0.73	16.50	12.05
20 OAKITE PRODS INC	0.55	2.918	5.8	8.5	6.0	7.50	0.51	20.00	10.20
21 PROCTER & GAMBLE CP	0.70	2.499	4.5	12.0	10.5	11.00	0.57	18.50	10.55
22 UNILEVER N V	0.75	2.955	6.1	8.0	10.5	7.00	0.56	12.50	7.00
23 U.S. TOBACCO CO	0.75	3.293	3.6	16.5	15.0	14.00	0.50	23.50	11.75
24 WEIS MKTS INC	0.60	2.569	1.6	16.0	12.5	12.00	0.75	16.50	12.38
25 WESTCOAST TRANSMISSI	0.65	4.226	9.2	8.0	18.0	6.50	0.46	14.50	6.67
26 WINN DIXIE STROES IN	0.60	2.641	4.8	12.0	8.5	8.50	0.48	18.50	8.88
AVERAGE	0.69	3.07%	4.86%	10.12%	8.65% 9.38%	9.65%	0.59	17.50%	10.03%

SOURCE: VALUE LINE DATA BASE (9/83)
WALL STREET JOURNAL (9/1/83)

TABLE 8-6 DCF COST OF EQUITY CAPITAL COMPUTATIONS: 24 INDUSTRIALS

ESTIMATE OF REQUIRED MARKET RETURN
COMPARABLE RISK INDUSTRIALS
HISTORICAL GROWTH

	Spot Dividend Yield	Adjustment For Expectation	Expected Dividend Yield	Average Growth Rate	Return (3) + (4)
	(1)	(2)	(3)	(4)	(5)
Average of all companies	4.86	1.094	5.32	9.38	14.70%

ESTIMATE OF REQUIRED MARKET RETURN
COMPARABLE RISK INDUSTRIALS
GROWTH FORECAST

	Spot Dividend Yield	Adjustment For Expectation	Expected Dividend Yield	Average Growth Rate	Return (3) + (4)
	(1)	(2)	(3)	(4)	(5)
Average of all companies	4.86	1.097	5.33	9.65	14.98%

ESTIMATE OF REQUIRED MARKET RETURN
COMPARABLE RISK INDUSTRIALS
RETENTION RATIO

	Spot Dividend Yield	Adjustment For Expectation	Expected Dividend Yield	Average Growth Rate	Return (3) + (4)
	(1)	(2)	(3)	(4)	(5)
Average of all companies	4.86	1.100	5.35	10.03	15.38%

groups methodologies. The summary table shows the expected return obtained from each approach, along with the expected dividend yield component for that return. The dividend yield is conservatively adjusted for flotation cost by dividing by 0.95, following the discussion of flotation costs in Chapter 6, then added back to the growth component of return to arrive at the cost of common equity. The cost of common equity figure would be higher still if the quarterly timing of dividends was recognized. The average expected return obtained from the nine DCF methods is 16.19%. If the high and low estimates are removed from the computation of the average, the truncated mean expected return is 16.18%.

TABLE 8-7 SUMMARY OF COMPARABLE GROUPS DCF CALCULATIONS: SOUTHERN COMPANY

METHOD	RETURN	EXPECTED DIVIDEND YIELD COMPO- NENT	ADJUSTED DIVIDEND YIELD COMPO- NENT	GROWTH COMPO- NENT	COST OF EQUITY
EASTERN ELECTRIC UTILITIES					
1. HISTORICAL GROWTH	16.18	11.58	12.19	4.60	16.79
2. ANALYSTS FORECASTS	16.86	11.65	12.26	5.21	17.47
3. RETENTION RATIO	14.88	11.46	12.06	3.43	15.49
Baa - BBB ELECTRIC UTILITIES					
4. HISTORICAL GROWTH	16.10	12.05	12.68	4.05	16.73
5. ANALYSTS FORECASTS	16.55	12.09	12.73	4.46	17.19
6. RETENTION RATIO	15.54	11.99	12.62	3.55	16.17
COMPARABLE RISK INDUSTRIALS					
7. HISTORICAL GROWTH	14.7	5.32	5.60	9.38	14.98
8. ANALYSTS FORECASTS	14.98	5.33	5.61	9.65	15.26
9. RETENTION RATIO	15.38	5.35	5.63	10.03	15.66
		AVERAGE			16.194%
		TRUNCATED MEAN			16.185%

AT&T

The problem is to determine the expected rate of return for AT&T's particular risk class as of January 1983 (pre-divestiture). Three groups of companies are identified which are comparable in risk to AT&T. The first group of companies listed on Table 8-8 includes 24 high quality eastern electric utilities whose common shares are publicly traded, and whose financial strength is rated B++ or higher by Value Line.

Columns two and three of Table 8-8 show the beta and standard deviation risk measures as calculated by Value Line for each company. The

TABLE 8-8 REQUIRED MARKET RETURN AND MEASURES OF RISK FOR 24 HIGH-QUALITY ELECTRICS

COMPANY (1)	BETA (2)	STD. DEV. (3)	FINANCIAL STRENGTH (4)	CURRENT DIVIDEND YIELD (5)	DPS 5 YR GROWTH RATE (6)	DPS 10 YR GROWTH RATE (7)
Allegheny Pwr. Sys. Inc.	0.70	2.688%	A	9.6%	3.5%	3.5%
American Elec. Pwr. Inc.	0.65	2.348	B++	12.0	2.0	3.0
Atlantic City Elec. Co.	0.55	2.688	A	11.0	4.5	3.5
Baltimore Gas & Elec.	0.75	2.791	A+	9.5	4.5	3.5
Boston Edison Co.	0.55	2.519	A+	11.0	2.0	2.0
Carolina Pwr. & Lt. Co.	0.70	2.898	A+	11.0	6.0	4.0
Central Maine Pwr. Co.	0.55	2.617	B++	12.0	4.0	3.5
Duke Power Co.	0.65	2.818	A+	9.9	6.0	3.5
Duquesne Light Co.	0.55	2.385	B++	12.0	1.0	1.0
Florida Pwr. Corp.	0.70	N.A.	A+	N.A.	9.0	7.0
Florida Pwr. & Lt. Co.	0.70	2.613	A+	9.1	13.0	10.0
Long Island Ltg. Co.	0.55	2.346	B++	12.0	4.0	3.0
New England Elec. Sys.	0.70	3.005	A++	8.8	6.0	5.0
New York St. Elec. & Gas	0.60	2.672	A	9.7	4.0	3.0
Niagara Mohawk Pwr. Cp.	0.65	2.839	A	11.0	4.5	3.5
Pennsylvania Pwr. & Lt.	0.65	2.764	A	11.0	3.5	3.0
Philadelphia Elec. Co.	0.55	2.491	B++	12.0	2.5	1.0
Potomac Elec. Pwr. Co.	0.65	2.856	A	9.1	5.0	6.5
Public Svc. Elec. & Gas	0.75	2.904	A+	11.0	6.0	3.5
Rochester Gas & Elec. Cp.	0.55	2.692	A	10.0	6.5	6.0
South Carolina Elec. & Gas	0.70	2.983	A	11.0	3.0	3.5
Southern Co.	0.60	2.493	B++	11.0	2.5	2.5
Telco Energy Inc.	0.75	2.941	A	8.4	8.5	7.0
Virginia Elec. & Pwr. Co.	0.60	2.646	A	11.0	3.0	2.5
AVERAGE	0.64	2.70%		10.57%	4.77%	3.94%
					4.86%	
AT&T	0.65	2.00%	A++		8.1%	7.2%

SOURCE: VALUE LINE DATE BASE, NOVEMBER 1982
WALL STREET JOURNAL, JANUARY 11, 1983

data shows that AT&T's beta of 0.65 is very close to the 0.64 average beta for the group, and that its standard deviation of 2% is close to the group's average of 2.7%. Application of the DCF formulation is developed in an identical manner to that of the reference groups in The Southern Company case study. The expected return on common equity for the group is 15.39%.

The second group of companies includes 55 electric, gas, and non-Bell System telephone companies whose revenues are derived from the sale of electricity, gas, and telephone services. This group, shown in Table 8-9, contains all such companies that are in the Value Line Data Base, have common stock that is publicly traded, and have a Moody's bond rating of either Aaa or Aa and/or Standard and Poor's ranking of A + or A. The average beta for the group is 0.70 compared to AT&T's 0.65. The average standard deviation of return for the group is 2.95% compared to AT&T's 2%. Application of the DCF formulation is shown at the bottom of Table 8-9 and follows that of the previous reference group. The expected return on common equity for the group is 16.36%.

TABLE 8-9 REQUIRED MARKET RETURN AND MEASURES OF RISK FOR HIGH-QUALITY UTILITIES

HIGH-QUALITY UTILITIES

COMPANY	BETA	STD. DEV.	FINANCIAL STRENGTH	CUR-RENT DIV. YIELD	DPS 5-YR. GROWTH RATE	DPS 10-YR. GROWTH RATE
American Nat. Res. Co.	0.900	3.544%	A	8.3	5.000%	4.500%
Atlantic City Elec. Co.	0.600	2.686	A	11.0	4.500	3.500
Baltimore Gas & Elec.	0.700	2.839	A+	9.5	4.500	3.500
Central & So. West Corp.	0.700	3.030	A++	9.6	5.500	4.500
Central Ill. Pub. Svc. Co.	0.600	2.772	A	9.3	2.500	2.000
Cincinnati Gas & Elec.	0.650	2.988	A	12.0	4.500	3.000
Cleveland Elec. Illum.	0.650	3.088	A+	11.0	4.000	3.500
Commonwealth Edison Co.	0.700	2.640	A	12.0	2.500	2.000
Consolidated Nat. Gas	0.850	3.311	A	7.6	8.500	6.000
Consumers Pwr. Co.	0.650	2.776	B++	12.0	3.000	2.000
Duquesne Lt. Co.	0.550	2.458	B++	12.0	1.000	1.000
Enserch Corp.	1.150	4.370	A+	7.6	10.000	8.000
Florida Pwr. & Lt. Co.	0.700	2.692	A+	9.1	13.000	10.000
GTE Corp.	0.850	2.911	A+	7.1	8.500	6.000
Gulf Sts. Utils. Co.	0.700	2.753	B++	11.0	4.500	3.500
Hawaiian Elec. Inc.	0.600	2.638	A	9.6	8.000	6.000
Houston Inds. Inc.	0.700	2.778	A+	11.0	11.500	8.500
Houston Nat. Gas. Corp.	1.000	4.252	A+	4.6	24.000	22.500
Illinois Power Co.	0.700	2.777	A+	11.0	1.500	1.500
Indianapolis Pwr. & Lt.	0.650	3.012	A+	11.0	4.500	4.000
Iowa Ill. Gas & Elec. Co.	0.600	2.641	A	10.0	6.000	4.500
Iowa Pub. Svc. Co.	0.600	2.346	A	10.0	7.000	5.000
Iowa Southn. Utils. Co.	0.650	2.289	A	11.0	4.500	4.500
Kansas City Pwr. & Lt. Co.	0.650	2.831	A	11.0	3.500	3.000
Kansas Pwr. & Lt. Co.	0.650	2.795	A	12.0	6.000	5.000
Kentucky Utils. Co.	0.550	2.469	B++	10.0	3.500	3.000
Laclede Gas Co.	0.650	3.067	B++	10.0	4.000	3.500
Long Island Ltg. Co.	0.600	2.418	B++	12.0	4.000	3.000
Louisville Gas & Elec.	0.650	2.725	A+	11.0	2.500	3.000

COMPANY	BETA	STD. DEV.	FINANCIAL STRENGTH	CUR-RENT DIV. YIELD	DPS 5-YR. GROWTH RATE	DPS 10-YR. GROWTH RATE
Middle South Utils. Inc.	0.700	2.752	B++	11.0	4.500	5.000
Minnesota Gas Co.	0.450	2.757	A	N.A.	4.000	3.500
Nicor Inc.	0.900	3.171	A	10.0	6.000	4.500
Northern Ind. Pub. Svc.	0.700	3.061	B++	11.0	2.000	2.000
Northn Sts. Pwr. Minn.	0.700	2.841	A+	8.8	5.000	3.500
Okla. Gas & Elec. Co.	0.650	2.674	A+	9.9	3.000	3.500
Pacific Gas & Elec. Co.	0.600	2.403	A+	10.0	6.500	5.000
Pennsylvania Pwr. & Lt.	0.650	2.764	A	11.0	3.500	3.000
Peoples Energy Corp.	N.A.	3.243	A	9.9	8.000	7.000
Pioneer Corp. Tex.	1.300	5.403	A+	5.2	23.500	16.000
Public Service Co. Colo.	0.700	2.886	A	10.0	5.000	4.000
Public Svc. Co. Ind. Inc.	0.650	2.881	A++	11.0	6.500	5.500
Public Svc. Elec. & Gas	0.750	2.949	A+	11.0	6.000	3.500
Public Svc. N. Mex.	0.650	2.691	A	10.0	11.000	9.000
Rochester Tel. Corp.	0.700	3.199	A++	7.4	16.000	11.000
Southern Calif. Edison	0.650	2.537	A++	10.0	11.000	7.000
Southern Ind. Gas & Elec.	0.650	2.882	A	8.2	8.000	7.000
Southern Union Co.	0.950	4.378	B++	8.9	8.000	7.000
Southwestern Pub. Svc.	0.600	2.711	A+	9.7	8.000	6.500
Teco Energy Inc.	0.750	2.913	A	8.4	8.500	7.000
Texas Utils. Co.	0.700	2.853	A++	9.0	7.500	7.000
Toledo Edison Co.	0.550	2.557%	B++	12.0%	1.500%	2.500%
Utah Pwr. & Lt. Co.	0.700	2.684	A	11.0	9.500	7.500
Wisconsin Elec. Pwr. Co.	0.650	2.963	A+	8.3	5.500	5.500
Wisconsin Pub. Svc. Corp.	0.700	2.836	A+	8.9	5.500	4.500
Wisconsin Pwr. & Lt. Co.	0.600	3.297	A+	8.8	4.500	3.500
Average	0.70	2.949%		9.86%	6.55%	5.29%

5.92%

| AT&T | 0.65 | 2.00% | A++ | | 8.0% | 7.0% |

ESTIMATE OF REQUIRED MARKET RETURN HIGH-QUALITY UTILITIES

	Spot Dividend Yield		Adjustment For Expectation		Expected Dividend Yield		Average Growth Rate		Return (3)+(4)
	(1)		(2)		(3)		(4)		(5)
Average of All Companies	9.86%	x	(1 + 5.92%)	=	10.44%	+	5.92%	=	16.36%

SOURCE: MORIN (1983C)

A third group of companies consisted of 18 high-quality industrials which met strict quality requirements. This reference group, shown on Table 8-10, consists of all those industrials listed on the New York Stock Exchange, excluding utilities, with betas less than 1 and standard deviations less than 4%, had equity capital in excess of $100 million, had a Standard & Poor's stock rating of A+ and bond rating of AAA, and a Value Line safety rank of 1. In the case of companies with no bond rating from either Moody's or Standard & Poor's, the debt ratio had to be less than 10%. There were a total of 18 stocks which met all these stringent quality criteria, and for which corporate financial data were included in the Value Line Data Base.

TABLE 8-10 REQUIRED MARKET RETURN AND MEASURES OF RISK FOR 18 HIGH-QUALITY INDUSTRIALS

COMPANY	BETA	STD. DEV.	S&P STOCK RATING	S&P BOND RATING	MOODY'S BOND RATING	FINANCIAL STRENGTH	SPOT DIVIDEND YIELD	DPS 5-YR GROWTH RATE	DPS 10-YR GROWTH RATE	5-YR BK. RET. AVG. COM. EQUITY
(1)	(2)	(3)	(4)	(5)	(6)	(7)	(8)	(9)	(10)	(11)
American Home Prods	0.85	2.926%	A+	–	–	A++	5.0%	14.000%	12.500%	34.07%
Beatrice Foods Co.	0.85	3.013	A+	AAA	Aaa	A+	6.7	11.500	9.500	21.42
Bristol-Myers Co.	1.00	3.378	A+	AAA	Aaa	A++	3.1	14.000	10.000	23.65
Carnation Co.	0.75	3.183	A+	AAA	Aaa	A++	4.7	19.500	16.000	17.75
Coca-Cola Co.	0.85	3.305	A+	AAA	Aaa	A+	4.7	13.000	11.500	23.50
Donnelley (R R) & Sons	0.85	3.271	A+	–	–	A++	2.2	14.000	10.500	14.66
Eastman Kodak Co.	0.95	3.305	A+	AAA	Aaa	A++	3.5	9.500	9.500	18.87
Exxon Corp.	0.90	2.793	A+	AAA	Aaa	A++	9.7	14.500	10.500	18.17
Federated Dept. Stores	0.90	3.697	A+	AAA	Aaa	A++	4.6	7.500	6.000	14.16
General Electric Co.	0.95	2.840	A+	–	–	A++	3.4	12.500	8.500	19.76
Genuine Parts Co.	0.85	3.804	A+	AAA	Aaa	A++	2.9	18.500	15.000	19.94
IBM	0.95	2.990	A+	AAA	Aaa	A++	3.5	15.500	14.500	21.64
Kellogg Co.	0.70	3.193	A+	AAA	Aaa	A++	5.7	12.000	11.500	27.46
Merck & Co. Inc.	0.85	3.114	A+	AAA	Aaa	A++	3.2	10.000	8.000	22.91
Minn. Mng. & Mfg. Co.	0.95	3.107	A+	AAA	Aaa	A++	4.2	15.000	12.000	21.57
Procter & Gamble	0.75	2.423	A+	AAA	Aaa	A++	3.6	12.500	10.000	18.59
Timken Co.	0.80	3.323	A+	–	–	A++	3.4	9.500	6.000	13.74
Weis Markets, Inc.	0.60	2.347	A+	–	–	A+	1.9	17.000	12.000	19.83
AVERAGE	0.85	3.11%	A+	AAA	Aaa		4.22%	13.33%	10.75%	20.65%
								12.04%		
AT&T	0.65	2.00%	A+	AAA	Aaa		8.30%	8.0%	7.0%	

Source: VALUE LINE DATA BASE, NOVEMBER 1982
WALL STREET JOURNAL, JANUARY 11, 1983

Application of DCF formulation is depicted in Table 8-11, and proceeds as before. The average expected return on equity for the group of high quality industrials is 16.77%.

TABLE 8-11 ESTIMATE OF REQUIRED MARKET RETURN: HIGH-QUALITY INDUSTRIALS

	SPOT DIVIDEND YIELD	ADJUSTMENT FOR EXPECTATION	EXPECTED DIVIDEND YIELD	AVERAGE GROWTH RATE	RETURN (3) + (4)
	(1)	(2)	(3)	(4)	(5)
Average of All Companies	4.22%	x (1 + 12.04%) =	14.73%	+ 12.04% =	16.77%

Table 8-12 summarizes the final results after due allowance for flotation costs. The average cost of capital obtained is 16.63%.

TABLE 8-12 SUMMARY OF COMPARABLE GROUPS DCF CALCULATIONS: AT&T

METHOD	RETURN	EXPECTED DIVIDEND YIELD COMPONENT	ADJUSTED DIVIDEND YIELD COMPONENT	GROWTH COMPONENT	COST OF EQUITY
High-Quality Electrics	15.39	11.03	11.61	4.36	15.97
High-Quality Utilities	16.36	10.44	10.99	5.92	16.91
High-Quality Industrials	16.77	4.73	4.98	12.04	17.02
				AVERAGE	16.63%

Closer scrutiny of the risk measures for each of the three comparable groups suggests that AT&T's risk is slightly less than any of the three groups. This illustrates one potential problem with historically-estimated risk measures. The structural shift in the telecommunications industry's risk and in AT&T's risk in the beginning of the 1980's had not yet been fully reflected in the measured beta and strandard deviation, since these risk estimates are calculated using five years of past data using pre- and post-structural shift observations. As discussed in Chapter 4, beta and standard deviation risk measures are sluggish in detecting change. Thus, any difference between the expected return for AT&T common stock and for stocks in general might be expected to be lower than that implied by a comparison of beta and standard deviation alone. A recent change in a company's risk can be discerned by an examination of the time series of standard deviations implied by call option premium data on the company's common stock, provided that listed options are traded on that company's stock. Chapter 4 describes this technique.

8.2 SPECIAL SITUATIONS

A frequent deterrent to applying the DCF approach is the absence of investor-based market data. This situation usually prevails in the case of a utility company which is a subsidiary of a publicly listed parent company or in the case of a private unlisted company. Another deterrent is that the strategic assumptions of the DCF model are sometimes violated and the DCF model cannot be applied. Examples of violation include dividend interruption, severe financial distress, limited access to capital markets, or a structural shift in the fundamentals of the utility's operations. Remedies are available to salvage the DCF approach in such situations.

Use of Parent Company Data

In order to estimate a subsidiary's cost of equity with the DCF technique, one approach is to estimate the parent company's cost of equity based on market information. This is necessary for the DCF approach because the subsidiary's common stock has no separate market value and all new common equity for the subsidiary is frequently obtained by the parent company. The parent company's cost of equity is then assigned to the subsidiary's equity component. If the subsidiary conducts its own debt and preferred stock financing, the parent cost of equity is combined with the subsidiary's individual debt and preferred stock costs to arrive at a weighted average cost of capital. While this procedure accounts for the unique costs of the subsidiary's debt and preferred stock, it presumes the risk of the subsidiary to be similar to that of the consolidated parent company. If the subsidiary does not engage into any financing at all, the parent's consolidated weighted average cost of capital can be assigned to the subsidiary, again provided that the relative risks of the parent and subsidiary are similar.

In the case of an electric utility company which is a subsidary of an electric utility parent holding company, it is usually reasonable to assume that the subsidiary's risk and therefore its cost of equity is not substantially different from that of the consolidated parent company. The subsidiary's cost of common equity is not likely to change materially, although it may be higher, if it is not part of the parent company system. As a large multi-unit company, the parent company enjoys greater diversification than its individual operating subsidiaries. In effect, risks are pooled, so the risk of the whole is less than the sum of the risks of the parts because of diversification. Moreover, holding companies may be able to operate on a more cost effective basis by shifting energy resources in line with the relative supply-demand situation of the geographic areas of operation.

If the riskiness of all the subsidiaries in the system are the same, the assumption that a given subsidiary's risk, and therefore its cost of equity, is similar to that of the consolidated parent is viable. This condition can be verified by an empirical comparison of the relative bond ratings, coverage ratios, debt-to-equity ratios, and volatility of book return on equity for each subsidiary in the group over the past decade. Such comparisons will reveal whether the subsidiary's risk is greater, the same, or less than the average of the consolidated parent company.

To verify whether this assumption is met, a more formal study of the risk-return relationship between utility holding companies and utility operating companies in general can be performed as follows. The risks and returns of a sample of operating electric power companies, not part of a holding complex, and those of a sample of holding companies can be compared using beta and standard deviation as risk measures and the standard DCF model as a measure of return. The results of such a comparison should reveal whether the holding company arrangement improves earnings and reduces risk, and whether the cost of capital for firms in the group are reduced by diversification.[2]

Bond Rating Approach

Another approach is to apply the DCF model to a sample of utilities whose bond rating is similar to that of the utility in question, assuming that the subsidiary or company in question does in fact conduct its own debt financing and is rated by credit agencies. An example of this approach was actually provided in the case study discussed in the previous section where the second reference group of companies consisted of utilities whose bond rating matched that of The Southern Company. The assumption underlying this approach is that there is a one-to-one correspondence between a utility's equity risk and its debt risk. This is usually a plausible assumption as long as the proportion of preferred stock outstanding is comparable for each company in the reference group and that the regulatory risks confronted by each company in the group are similar, as revealed by regulatory climate rankings.

Bond Yield Spread Approach

In the absence of market data or in the case of clear violations of DCF assumptions, the following approach can be employed. First, the cost of equity is estimated for a group of typical utilities with the orthodox DCF method. Second, an appropriate risk increment is added to or subtracted from the equity return allowance, based on the bond and preferred yield relationships between the utility in question and the benchmark group of typical utilities. Two case examples will illustrate.

a. General Public Utilities

At the risk of oversimplification, the problem was to estimate the cost of equity in 1983 to The Metropolitan Edison Company and The Pennsylvania Electric Company, two subsidiaries of General Public Utilities, in the aftermath of the Three Mile Island nuclear accident in 1979.[3] None of the growth-estimating techniques in the DCF model were directly applicable as a result of the accident. Since no dividends were paid from 1979 until the time of this writing and since past and current earnings were severely depressed, the extrapolation of historical dividend growth rates into the future was unreasonable, and the retention ratio method of estimating growth was inoperative as well. The paucity of analysts' earnings and dividends forecasts and the wide divergence of opinion among analysts in the few forecasts which were available underscored the uncertainty and unreliability of such forecasts. The assumptions of constant perpetual growth and constant payout ratio were clearly not met. The dividend forecasts required for implementation of the non-constant growth model were also unreliable.

Since any estimate based on General Public Utilities corporate data was unreliable, an indirect two-step procedure was used. First, the cost of common equity was derived for three barometer group of companies: a group of 34 eastern electric utilities, a group of 7 electric utilities operating under comparable regulation, and a barometer group of industrial companies. This phase of the analysis proceeded in much the same way as in the earlier case example of The Southern Company. The average cost of equity figure for the three benchmark groups from all the DCF techniques was 16.75%[4].

Secondly, an appropriate risk increment was added to the DCF equity return for the reference utility groups. The magnitude of the risk increment was based on the amount by which the yields on the senior securities of the General Public Utilities Pennsylvania companies exceeded those of the groups of electric utilities. To illustrate, Figure 8-1 shows the yield spreads between Standard & Poor's BBB Bond Average and Metropolitan Edison and Pennsylvania Electric bonds in graphical form for eleven months in 1982. The bond yield spread fluctuated narrowly around 3% and 2.5% for the two companies respectively, with a current value of 2.5% and 2%. Similar patterns were uncovered for preferred stock yields. The 16.75% cost of capital estimate obtained by applying DCF to the reference groups was therefore conservatively adjusted upward by 2% and 1.5% to obtain Metropolitan Edison's and Pennsylvania Electric's cost of equity capital.

   b. Southern Bell

   The bond yield spread methodology was used to assess the relative risks of AT&T and the Bell operating companies following divestiture announcement in 1979. Prior to AT&T's divestiture, it was customary to estimate a Bell operating company's cost of equity capital by relying on AT&T market data. DCF estimates of AT&T's cost of equity were applied to

Figure 8-1

BOND YIELD SPREADS
MET-ED AND PENELEC COMPARED TO S&P'S BBB BOND
AVERAGE
JANUARY - NOVEMBER 1982

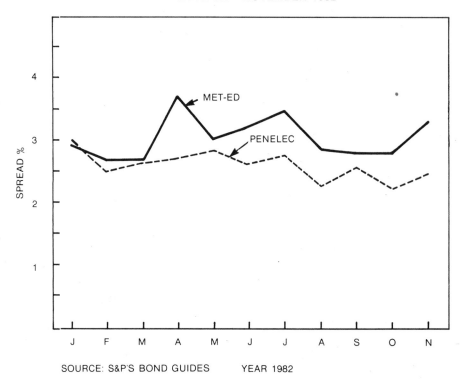

SOURCE: S&P'S BOND GUIDES   YEAR 1982

the operating companies on the grounds that the latter were at least as risky as the consolidated parent. This assumption became questionable following divestiture. The relative risk difference between AT&T and Southern Bell could no longer be assumed to be negligible.

Empirical evidence in capital markets pointed to increased risks of Southern Bell relative to AT&T, and hence increased cost of capital. Table 8-13 provides a yield comparison between AT&T and Southern Bell publicly traded bonds in the 1980 – 1982 period surrounding divestiture events. The first and second columns show the average yield on two representative Southern Bell bond issues and the average monthly yield on AT&T bonds of comparable coupon and maturity, respectively. Care was taken to compare bonds with similar characteristics in regard to maturity, coupon, and callability. The third column shows the yield spread between the two averages for the last three years. The average monthly spread over consecutive 6 – month intervals is shown in the last column of Table 8-13 and is displayed graphically on Figure 8-2. In that period, the yield spread steadily widened from 1980 to the first half of 1982, and declined somewhat in the latter part of 1982 to reach 52 basis points, attesting to increased investor risk perceptions of Southern Bell. During that period, investors perceived that Southern Bell's future revenue stream was riskier because of the increased business risk posed by network bypass threats from the competition, and the increased vulnerability to the regulatory process, following divestiture.

Based on comparative bond yields, the value of the incremental risk of Southern Bell over and above AT&T was approximately 50 basis points at that time. Therefore, the cost of equity capital estimate obtained from AT&T market data was adjusted upward by approximately 50 basis points in order to obtain Southern Bell's cost of equity.

Cluster Analysis

Vander Weide (1982) develops an interesting approach to estimate the cost of equity of a company whose stock is not publicly traded. He applies the DCF method to a group of publicly traded companies comparable in risk to the company in question, and uses the average DCF cost of equity for these companies as an estimate of equity costs.

Vander Weide selects the comparable companies on the basis of "closeness" to the company in question in terms of four risk variables: after-tax interest coverage, equity ratio, total capital, and predictability of operating income. After determining the location of each publicly traded firm on a graph whose coordinates are the four basic risk measures, he measures "closeness" by the length of a straight line between the point associated with the company in question and the points associated with each

TABLE 8-13 YIELD SPREAD SOUTHERN BELL
VS AT&T BONDS

Month/Year	Average Southern Bell Yield	Average AT&T Yield	Spread	Average
December, 1982	11.86	11.34	.52	
November	11.51	11.24	.27	
October	11.75	11.31	.44	
September	12.87	12.16	.71	.52
August	13.23	12.66	.57	
July	14.53	13.91	.62	
June	15.09	14.36	.73	
May	14.37	13.84	.53	
April	14.26	13.78	.48	
March	14.75	14.27	.48	.74
February	15.22	14.22	1.00	
January	15.64	14.43	1.21	
December, 1981	14.97	14.33	.64	
November	13.71	13.28	.43	
October	15.27	14.42	.85	
September	15.67	15.18	.49	.49
August	15.39	14.95	.44	
July	14.17	14.10	.07	
June	13.56	13.41	.15	
May	14.14	13.17	.97	
April	14.21	14.09	.12	
March	13.29	12.94	.35	.33
February	13.36	13.25	.11	
January	12.86	12.57	.29	
December, 1980	12.96	12.42	.54	
November	13.29	12.80	.49	
October	12.57	12.66	-.09	
September	12.63	12.32	.31	.29
August	11.95	11.80	.15	
July	11.46	11.12	.34	
June	10.55	10.42	.13	
May	10.90	10.81	.09	
April	11.64	11.18	.46	
March	13.17	12.78	.39	.13
February	12.22	12.75	-.53	
January	11.80	11.58	.22	

Source: Moody's Investor Services, Inc.

Figure 8-2

BOND YIELD SPREAD

SOUTHERN BELL v AT&T

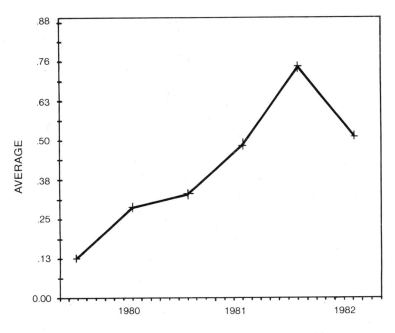

SOURCE: MORIN (1983C)

other firm. This measurement process is illustrated graphically on Figure 8-3 for two risk measures. Firm A has an interest coverage ratio of 3 and an equity ratio of 50%, and corresponds to point A on the graph. Firm A is closer to Firm B than to Firm C, despite its greater distance in terms of coverage alone. Vander Weide's measure of closeness considers the effect of all risk variables simultaneously.

Distances, or closeness, are measured mathematically as follows: If X and Y are two axes on a graph corresponding to two risk measures, and suppose there are two points on a graph with coordinates (X_1, Y_1) and (X_2, Y_2), then the distance between the two points is given by:

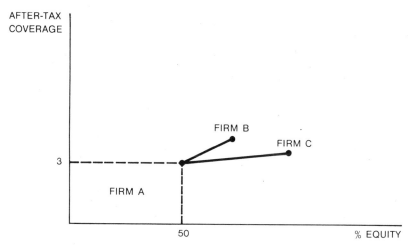

Figure 8-3

ILLUSTRATION OF DISTANCE MEASURE

SOURCE: VANDER WEIDE (1982)

$$\sqrt{(X_2 - X_1)^2 + (Y_2 - Y_1)^2} \qquad (8\text{-}1)$$

If the X and Y axes corresponding to the two risk variables are not measured in the same units, it is necessary to convert them to a common measure using the standard deviation of the sample as scale factors. If the X axis scale factor is S_1 and the Y axis scale factor is S_2, the distance formula becomes:

$$\sqrt{\frac{(X_2 - X_1)^2}{S_1^2} + \frac{(Y_2 - Y_1)^2}{S_2^2}} \qquad (8\text{-}2)$$

This process can be easily extended to include as many risk variables as desired. Vander Weide develops a comparable sample of firms by identifying publicly-traded firms which cluster closest to the company in question in terms of the four aforementioned risk variables on the basis of the distance measurement process described in Equation 8-2.

8.3   CLOSING COMMENTS ON DCF

The DCF method is firmly established as the standard method of measuring the cost of capital in the vast majority of corporate finance and investment textbooks, and is deeply entrenched in regulatory practice. The method is widely used by all parties in regulatory proceedings in most jurisdictions[5]. The method is solid conceptually, and controversy regarding the method generally centers on implementation and execution rather than on theoretical soundness.

It is clear from the material of the four chapters that have dealt with the DCF method that the permutations and combinations of estimates based on alternate time periods, measures, companies, models, statistical methodology are unbounded. The only solid generalization about DCF is that the final cost of equity recommendation is a judgment based on a wide variety of data and techniques. The important point is that judgmental estimates of equity cost rest on sound factual economic logic. Plausible and defensible DCF estimates within a narrow range can be developed, provided the tools of this and previous chapters are used intelligently and objectively.

The DCF method cannot be applied in a robotic mechanistic manner. The determination of expected growth is a judgmental exercise, since anticipated growth lies buried in the minds of investors, unobservable directly. Any inconsistency between historically-based growth estimates, analysts' growth forecasts, and sustainable growth estimates should be explainable by objective common-sense economic reasoning. The tools of this chapter provide diagnostic guides and calculating aids only. The vast arsenal of techniques described apply differently to different companies, or differently to the same company at different points in time. Each rate case possesses different circumstances. More than one cost of equity capital estimating must be consulted.

The need to broaden the sample and to extend the analysis to include comparable risk firms is evident in order to verify the reasonableness of the single-company estimate and to abide with the spirit of the *Hope-Bluefield* doctrines. Referencing data on other utilities and other unregulated companies will mitigate the circularity problem as well. Other cost of capital estimation techniques must be employed as an additional check on the reliability and reasonableness of the DCF estimate. These methods are the subject of subsequent chapters.

Several complications which arise in estimating the cost of equity are discussed in later chapters, such as the impact of capital structure and dividend policy. It is important to keep in mind that the DCF model does not explicitly supply any evidence as to what the cost of equity would be under different circumstances such as a different capital structure. The DCF model produces a cost of equity estimate predicated on current conditions. Alternate conditions may produce higher or lower growth rates, hence different equity cost estimates, depending on investor reaction to the change in conditions as manifested by the market price. Fortunately, the DCF model possesses a built-in compensatory mechanism which mitigates this problem; investor reactions to changes in expected growth are accompanied by changes in market prices which in turn alter the dividend yield in a direction opposite to that of the revised growth rate. In other words, the impact of any change in conditions on the dual components of the DCF model are at least partially self-correcting.

Notes

[1] If $\overline{\sigma}_i^2$ represents the average variance of the errors in a group of N companies, and $\overline{\sigma}_{ij}$ the average covariance between the errors, then the variance of the error for the group of N companies, σ_N^2, is given by:

$$\sigma_N^2 = \frac{1}{N} \overline{\sigma}_i^2 + \frac{N-1}{N} \overline{\sigma}_{ij}$$

If the errors are independent, the covariance between them is zero, and the variance of the error for the group is reduced to:

$$\sigma_N^2 = \frac{1}{N} \sigma_i^2$$

As N gets progressively larger, the variance gets smaller and smaller.

[2] Morin (1983) compared electric operating companies not part of a holding complex with holding companies in respect to risk and return to the common stock investor, using beta and standard deviation as measures of risk. The results were consistent with the notion that over the long run, the holding company arrangement improves earnings and reduces risk, and that the cost of capital for firms in the group may be reduced. The evidence indicated that on average an operating company is at least as risky as a holding company.

[3] See rate of return testimonies by Morin (1982) and Brigham (1982).

[4] From Morin (1983)

[5] In a comprehensive survey of the measures of equity costs utilized by public utility firms and regulatory commissions, Dukes & Chandy (1983) found that DCF methods are used by more respondents than any other technique. Use of the DCF technique was indicated by 92% of the utility firms and 97% of the commissions. The Risk Premium and Comparable Earnings techniques ranked second and third respectively with a 70% – 80% range of usage.

CHAPTER 9

RISK PREMIUM

The Risk Premium method of determining the cost of equity, sometimes referred to as the "stock-bond yield spread method" or the "risk positioning method", recognizes that common equity capital is more risky than debt from an investor's standpoint, and that investors require higher returns on stocks than on bonds to compensate for the additional risk. The general approach is relatively straightforward: First, determine the historical spread between the return on debt and the return on equity. Second, add this spread to the current debt yield to derive an estimate of current equity return requirements.

9.1 RATIONALE AND ISSUES

The basic idea behind the risk premium approach is portrayed graphically in Figure 9-1. The horizontal axis measures security risk; the further to the right a security lies, the greater its investment risk. U.S. government securities are shown at the origin since they are devoid of default risk. The vertical axis portrays the required returns. The straight line, labeled the capital market line (CML), shows at a point in time the risk-return tradeoff in capital markets, that is, the relationship between a security's risk and its required return. The term R_F, which stands for "risk-free", designates the rate of interest on default-free securities as measured by the rate of interest on U.S. Treasury bills. As discussed in Chapter 3, the risk-free rate can be decomposed into an inflation-free component, and a premium for expected inflation:

$$R_F = \textbf{real rate } + \textbf{ inflation premium}$$

Corporate bonds are riskier than U.S. Treasury securities, so their yields are higher. Typically, AAA corporate bonds yield from 50 to 100 basis points more than governments, and the risk premiums rise for lower quality corporate bonds. Therefore, the risks on corporate bonds are plotted higher than the risks of U.S. Treasury securities on the Capital Market Line, and their required returns are correspondingly higher. Common stocks are riskier than corporate bonds, and returns on stocks are correspondingly higher.

The Capital Market Line demonstrates the linkages between various segments of the capital market. Investor capital flows between the various markets depending on the risk-return relationship for each market segment, and the return for each type of capital increases with the risk of the security. Relative risk premiums, RP, corresponding to the slope and shape of the Capital Market Line at a point in time, exist for each type of security as follows:

$$
\begin{aligned}
\text{AAA Corporate bond yield} &= \text{U.S. Treasury bond yield} &+ RP_1 \\
\text{BAA Corporate bond yield} &= \text{AAA Corporate bond yield} &+ RP_2 \\
\text{Preferred Stock yield} &= \text{Baa Corporate bond yield} &+ RP_3 \\
\text{Common Stock Return} &= \text{Baa Corporate bond yield} &+ RP_4
\end{aligned}
$$

The magnitude of the relative risk premiums is determined by shifts in demand and supply in each capital market segment, which are in turn driven

Figure 9-1

THE RELATIONSHIP BETWEEN RISK AND
RETURN IN CAPITAL MARKETS

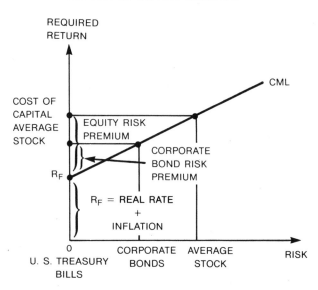

by investors' attitudes towards risk, and by the relative risk differentials perceived by investors between each type of security.

The risk premium approach to estimating the cost of equity derives its usefulness from the simple fact that while equity return requirements cannot be readily quantified at a given point in time, the returns on bonds can be assessed precisely at every instant in time. If the magnitude of the risk premium between stocks and bonds is known, then this information can be utilized to produce the cost of common equity.

Notwithstanding the simplicity of the concept, there are several specific problems which must be resolved before the method can be implemented:

Risk premium measurement

How should the general levels of these risk premiums be measured, or equivalently, how should the slope of the capital market line at a point in time be estimated? Several related questions must be answered. Over what historical period should the risk premium be established? Should the spreads be estimated using realized or expected returns? What specific debt and equity securities should be used?

Stability of the risk premium

The customary assumption which underlies the use of the risk premium technique is that shifts in interest rates have no significant impact on the required risk premium, that is, the slope of the capital market line remains unchanged even though the height of the line rises and falls in response to changes in interest rates. Are the risk premiums in fact constant? Do they fluctuate over time as the factors which determine the risk premium change? Expressed in another way, is investor risk aversion constant?

Risk adjustments

What is the relative size of the risk premium on utility and industrial stocks, and how is the return requirement derived from the risk premium method to be adjusted for the risk of a given utility? Some answers to those questions are offered in the remainder of this chapter.

9.2 RISK PREMIUM ESTIMATION: REALIZED RETURNS

One approach frequently used to estimate the risk premium is to examine the historical returns actually earned from investments in common equities and bonds. This approach can be expressed as follows:

$$K_e = K_d + \text{ historical bond-equity spread}$$
$$\text{where } K_e = \text{cost of common equity}$$
$$K_d = \text{incremental cost of debt}$$

Historical return data for common equities and bonds are compiled, and the historical mean return differential between stocks and bonds serves as the measure of risk premium. The best example of this approach is the landmark Ibbotson-Sinquefield (1982) study, which compared realized holding period annual returns on equities, government long-term and short-term securities, corporate bonds, and inflation from 1926 to 1981. Annual updates of the return results are published by Ibbotson- Sinquefield.

Application of the method proceeds directly from the historical results. Since the average return realized from investing in U.S. Treasury long-term bonds over the 1926–1981 period has been 3.1% while the mean historical return from investing in stocks during the same period has been 11.4%, then the average bond-stock spread over the total period was 8.3%. If long-term Treasury bonds are currently yielding 10% for example, then a reasonable estimate of the current equity return for the average stock is 10% + 8.3% = 18.3%.

Such a procedure is subject to three problems: the choice of time period, the choice of return computation method, and the realized return fallacy. First, time period. Realized risk premium results are dependent on the choice of time period over which the security return data are compiled. Both the length of the period and the choice of end points can make a substantial difference in the final results obtained. For example, Table 9-1 reports the realized returns on stocks and bonds obtained by Ibbotson-Sinquefield for the last 10, 20, 30, and 50 years ending in 1981. The resulting risk premium varies from 3.7% to 7.6%. Keeping the length of the period unchanged, and altering the end point by 2 years, the corresponding results for various periods ending in 1979 instead of 1981 show a risk premium varying from 0.4% to 8.5%.

Bond-stock spreads based on short time periods can be particularly volatile, changing with capital market conditions, inflationary expectations, and fiscal-monetary forces. The length of the period should at least be long enough to smooth out short-term aberrations, encompassing several business and interest cycles. A period covering a minimum span of 25 years

TABLE 9-1 THE INSTABILITY OF RISK PREMIUMS
COMPUTED FROM REALIZED RETURNS

PERIOD	STOCK RETURNS	BOND RETURNS	RISK PREMIUM
1972-1981	6.5%	2.8%	3.7%
1962-1981	6.8	2.6	4.2
1952-1981	9.9	2.3	7.4
1932-1981	10.6	3.0	7.6
1970-1979	5.9	5.5	0.4
1960-1979	6.8	3.5	3.3
1950-1979	10.8	2.3	8.5
1930-1979	8.2	3.0	5.2

Source: Ibbotson-Sinquefield (1982), Appendix B

should be employed when dealing with historical returns. Adjustment should be made for any significant trend in risk premium behavior. Such trends, if any, can be detected by visual inspection of the results, or more formally, by computing serial correlation coefficients. If risk premiums appear to fluctuate randomly around the mean, then historical averages over long periods can be valid estimates of current risk premiums. More on the issue of time period selection in the next section of this chapter.

The second problem in relying on historical return results is the arbitrary nature of the return computation. The analyst has wide latitude in his choice of stock and bond indices, weighting of securities in the indices, frequency of revision of the weights, and treatment of taxes, transaction costs, and dividends.

The third problem involves the distinction between expected and realized return. The historical risk premium approach fundamentally assumes that average realized return is an appropriate surrogate for expected return, or in other words that investor expectations are realized. Realized returns can be substantially different from prospective returns anticipated by investors, and therefore constitute an hazardous benchmark on which to base the risk premium between stocks and bonds.

Realized returns can be envisaged as the sum of an expected return plus a component of unanticipated return, which will be positive or negative depending on whether investors under- or overestimated expected future returns. Unless the mean unanticipated component of return on stocks equals that on bonds, historical spreads between stocks and bonds will not accurately reflect expected risk premiums. Only if investors do not systematically overestimate or underestimate future returns will spreads based on historical returns converge with those based on expected returns. For example, it is plausible that in recent years investors have consistently underestimated the phenomenal ascent in interest rates. The Federal Reserve's reversal in monetary policy in October 1979, whereby monetary aggregates are targeted instead of interest rates, was unanticipated by investors. The resulting gyrations in interest rates and increase in bond volatility in 1981–1982 led investors to expect higher returns from bonds, reducing the bond-stock spread somewhat. Reliance on historical returns would thus have produced an overestimate of the prevailing risk premium.

The *Hope* and *Bluefield* cases established the fundamental premise that investors should receive a return commensurate with returns currently available on comparable risk investments, and not that investors' be guaranteed a return coinciding with their initial return expectations. Consequently, the determination of a fair and reasonable return on equity should rest on investor expectations, and historical risk premiums should be based on expected returns rather than on realized returns.

All is not lost however, for over long periods, investor expectations and realizations should converge, or otherwise investors would not commit investment capital. Investors expectations are eventually revised to match historical realizations, as market prices adjust to bring anticipated and actual investment results into conformity. While forward-looking risk premiums based on expected returns are preferable, historical return studies over long periods provide a useful starting point as a guide for the future.

9.3   RISK PREMIUM ESTIMATION: EXPECTED RETURNS

A conceptually sound approach to assessing the risk premium is to estimate the expected rate of return on equity for a broad sample of companies for each of several years and subtract from these estimates the yields on newly issued debt for the corresponding year.

$$K_e = R_F + RP$$

where RP = Expected Equity Market Return – Bond Yield

To implement the method, several issues must be resolved. An appropriate debt security must be chosen, a representative selection of equity securities defined, the spread adjusted for comparable risk, and a proper time period selected. Each of those issues is discussed in turn.

Choice of Debt Security

With respect to the choice of debt security, three criteria should be met. First, in order to isolate the spread component of the return and avoid having to adjust the debt yield for default risk differentials, the yield should be risk-free, and should include a premium for anticipated inflation. Second, the maturity of the chosen instrument should match the period for which rates are being established. Third, debt securities issued by utilities should be excluded to avoid potential circularity problems.

Based on these considerations, the best surrogate for the risk-free rate is the yield on short-term Treasury bills, at least theoretically. But in practice, the T-Bill rate is highly volatile and dominated by short-term monetary and fiscal developments. Moreover, the T- Bill rate incorporates a premium for short-term inflationary expectations rather than a premium for the long-run inflationary expectations embedded in bond yields and stock returns. Yields on default-free long-term Treasury bonds would thus seem more appropriate. But long-term Treasury bonds are subject to interest rate risk and are therefore not riskless, especially in a period of volatile interest rates. Moreover, long-term bond yields embody investor expectations beyond the period for which rates will be in effect. An acceptable compromise is to select U.S. Treasury Notes with approximately 3 to 5 years in maturity. The latter are virtually riskless, are not issued by utilities, and have the appropriate remaining life. If data availability is prohibitive, long-term Treasury bonds provide an acceptable substitute.

If the yield curve beyond maturities of a few years is relatively flat, the choice between Treasury Notes and Treasury bonds is not crucial. An added incentive for selecting government securities is the presence of well-developed and active markets for interest rate futures contracts on government bonds. These markets contain market forecasts of rates on various Treasury securities.

Choice of Equity Securities

In order that the estimated risk premium be as stable as possible and be uncontaminated by the vagaries of a particular group of securities, the benchmark group of securities should be broadly representative and well diversified. There are several stock market indices on which comprehensive and easily accessible data are available. Value Line's Composite Market Index, Standard & Poor's 500 Index, and the Dow Jones Industrials Average are suitable proxies for the equity market portfolio. These indices are composed mainly of unregulated companies so that the potential circularity problem inherent in relying on a benchmark group of utility stocks is attenuated.

Method of Computing Returns

In the case of bonds, the yield to maturity serves as a proxy for expected return, and is a suitable measure of the return expected by bondholders who expect to hold the bond until maturity[1]. Yield to maturity data on government securities are widely available from the Federal Reserve Bulletin, Salomon Brothers' monthly "Analytical Record of Yields and Yield Spreads", and countless other published sources including commercially available computerized data bases.

Application of the standard DCF model to the market index as a whole can provide a reasonably precise estimate of the expected return for the market. The following example illustrates the methodology.

EXAMPLE

The aggregate expected market return is computed each year for the ten-year period 1972–1981, using data on Value Line's Composite Market Index by summing the dividend yields and the expected growth each year, as follows:

$$\text{Expected Equity Return}_t = \text{Expected Dividend Yield}_t + \text{Growth}_t$$
$$= \text{Spot Dividend Yield}_t \ (1 \ + \ g) + \text{Growth}_t$$
$$= \frac{D_o \ (1 + g)}{P_o} + g$$

Expected growth on the market aggregate is proxied by the historical 5-year growth in earnings per share on the composite index[2]. The Value Line Data Base provides the necessary data on the index. The year by year analysis of expected equity market returns and bond yields over the 1972–1981 period is shown on Table 9-2. An estimate of the risk premium on the average stock is obtained each year by subtracting the yields on the average corporate bond, proxied by Moody's New Issue Corporate Bond Yield Index, from the corresponding equity return. The results, depicted in Figure 9-2, indicate that the risk premium for the overall equity market averaged 4.32% over the last decade and 5.56% in the last five years over long-term corporate bonds. A similar and preferable analysis could be replicated using long-term Treasury bonds instead of corporate bonds. The corresponding risk premium results are 5.69% and 6.93%. These results are consistent with the results of a myriad of well-known academic and professional research studies published on the subject, using expected rates of return. See studies by Friend & Blume (1975), Malkiel (1979), Brigham & Shome (1982), and Brennan (1982) for example.

One potential problem in the above approach is that the method is only as good as the method of estimating expected returns. For example, historical growth may not be reflective of expected growth. This difficulty becomes acute after a deep recession, when growth prospects are revised upward while historical growth is depressed by the recession. Unfortunately, long-run growth forecasts are not readily available for composite market indices before 1981[3].

An alternate and potentially more accurate technique which circumvents this deficiency is articulated by Brigham & Shome (1982). For each company in the Dow Jones Industrials Index, excluding AT&T, they compute the equity return implicit in the Limited Horizon DCF model by solving the following equation for K (see Chapter 6.1, Equation 6-4):

$$P_o = \frac{D_i}{1+K} + \frac{D_2}{(1+K)^2} + \frac{D_3}{(1+K)^3} + \ldots + \frac{D_n}{(1+K)^n}$$

$$+ \frac{D_n(1+g)}{K-g} \times \frac{1}{(1+K)^n}$$

Brigham & Shome rely on Value Line's published forecast data for the year by year dividend forecasts and for the terminal year dividend. The long-run steady-state growth rate is computed by the sustainable growth method, whereby g = br, using Value Line's estimate of long-run expected return on book equity and long-run expected retention ratio for each firm in the index. Using the December 31st stock price, they solve the model for K for each company in the sample for each year, and calculate an average DCF return for the group, weighted by the market value of each company as a proportion of the total market value. Subtracting the December 31st long-term Treasury bond rate, a risk premium estimate is derived for each year.

One drawback to this approach is that the Dow Jones Industrials Average may not be representative of the overall equity market, and that a more diversified cross-section of American industry may be preferable. On the other hand, the data requirements for application of the Brigham-Shome approach to each company in a large diversified index are computationally prohibitive.

Risk Adjustments

The risk premium estimate derived from a composite market index must be adjusted for any risk differences between the equity market index

TABLE 9-2 RISK PREMIUM ANALYSIS: AGGREGATE RETURN DATA

RISK PREMIUM

YEAR (1)	AVERAGE SPOT DIVIDEND YIELD (2)	FIVE-YEAR GROWTH EARNINGS PER SHARE (3)	EXPECTED DIVIDEND YIELD (4)	EXPECTED EQUITY MARKET RETURN (5)	MOODY'S NEWLY ISSUED CORPORATE BONDS COMPOSITE (6)	RISK PREMIUM (7)
1972	2.28%	5.00%	2.39%	7.39%	7.50%	-0.11%
1973	2.55	6.50	2.72	9.22	7.90	1.32
1974	3.66	9.00	3.99	12.99	9.50	3.49
1975	3.60	10.00	3.96	13.96	9.80	4.16
1976	3.41	11.50	3.80	15.30	8.80	6.50
1977	4.13	12.00	4.63	16.63	8.40	8.23
1978	4.59	11.50	5.12	16.62	9.20	7.42
1979	4.71	11.50	5.25	16.75	10.40	6.35
1980	4.35	12.50	4.89	17.39	13.20	4.19
1981	4.92	12.00	5.51	17.51	15.90	1.61

AVERAGE RISK PREMIUM:

1977 – 1981: 5.56%

1972, 1981: 4.38%

Figure 9-2

BOND-STOCK RISK PREMIUM, 1972-1981

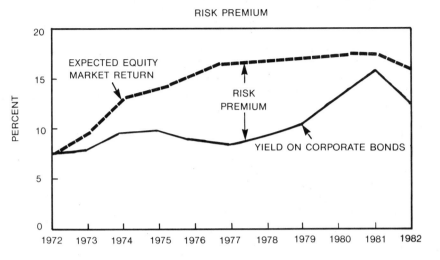

employed in deriving the risk premium and a specifed utility common stock.
Several methods can be used to effect the proper risk adjustment.

First, the beta for the subject utility or the beta of a group of
equivalent risk companies can serve as an adjustment device. The market
risk premium, RP_M, is multiplied by the beta of the utility, B_i, to find the
utility's own risk premium, RP_i:

$$RP_i = B_i \ RP_M$$

and the beta-adjusted risk premium is added to the utility's incremental
bond yield to arrive at the utility's own cost of equity capital. For example, if
the risk premium on the average stock is 5%, based on a broad-based index
such as Value Line's Composite Market Index, and the subject utility has a
beta of 0.60, the adjusted risk premium is 5% x 0.60 = 3%. This method is
in fact the Empirical Capital Asset Pricing Model approach in disguise.
Chapter 10 will address the CAPM in detail, pointing out its usefulness and
limitations.

A second risk adjustment approach is to scale the risk premium up or
down based on a comparison of the utility's risk relative to that of the overall
market. Any of the objective quantitative measures of risk described in

Chapter 3 are adequate for this purpose. For example, the ratio of the utility's standard deviation of returns to the average standard deviation of the individual component stocks of the index could be computed and serve as a basis for relative risk adjustment. Alternately, in the case of non-publicly traded utility stocks, the utility's average deviation around trend of earnings per share or of book return on equity relative to that of the market index could serve as the basis for the risk adjustment. The scaling can be also performed judgmentally on the basis of qualitative risk measures such as relative bond ratings, Standard & Poor's stock ratings, and Value Line's safety ratings.

Another way of tailoring the risk premium approach to a specific group of companies is to estimate a specialized risk premium for a subset of securities in a given industry, and then to base the risk premium for a specific company on the industry-wide risk premium. The disadvantage of this approach is that if the list of benchmark companies is over-specialized, then diversification may be insufficient to ensure the reliability of the risk premium estimate. An example of this approach is shown on Table 9-3 for a specific subset of stocks, namely Value Line's 34 Eastern Electrics Index. The analysis proceeds in a manner identical to that of Table 9-2, except that equity returns for this subset of securities are computed using aggregate data on the electric utility index, provided by Value Line. The mean risk premium over long-term government bonds for the ten-year period is 3.78%, and can be added to the utility's current bond yield to provide an estimate of its equity costs.

Another example of this approach is contained in the aforementioned Brigham & Shome (1982) study, where instead of using a broad market index, the expected equity return was computed individually for each security making up the Dow Jones Electrics index and then averaged to produce the overall equity market return for electric utilities. In order to reduce their exclusive reliance on Value Line forecasts, they expanded their analysis to include Salomon Brothers and Merrill Lynch forecasts on electric utilities as well as Value Line forecasts. Moreover, from 1980 onward, Brigham & Shome provide risk premium estimates on a monthly basis rather on an annual basis because of the need to track the risk premium more accurately in the turbulent bond market of 1981-1982.

Time Period

In the risk premium methodology, it is generally assumed that the average historical risk premium that prevailed over a period encompassing several years is a valid estimate of the current and prospective risk premium. There are situations where this assumption may be questionable, and corrective measures are necessary. If risk premiums exhibit a clear trend,

TABLE 9-3 RISK PREMIUM ANALYSIS: ELECTRIC UTILITY INDUSTRY

YEAR	SPOT DIVIDEND YIELD	DIVIDENDS PER SHARE	5 – YEAR DIVIDEND GROWTH	EXPECTED DIVIDEND YIELD	EQUITY RETURN	TREASURY BOND YIELD	RISK PREMIUM
(1)	(2)	(3)	(4)	(5)	(6) = (4) + (5)	(7)	(8) = (6) − (7)
1969	5.03	$1.30					
1970	6.30	$1.35					
1971	6.08	$1.37					
1972	6.35	$1.40					
1973	7.12	$1.44	2.07	7.27	9.33	6.97	2.36
1974	10.59	$1.40	0.73	10.67	11.40	7.93	3.47
1975	9.94	$1.47	1.42	10.08	11.50	8.04	3.46
1976	8.66	$1.53	1.79	8.82	10.61	7.86	2.75
1977	8.29	$1.61	2.26	8.48	10.73	7.62	3.11
1978	9.12	$1.69	3.84	9.47	13.31	8.42	4.89
1979	10.45	$1.76	3.67	10.83	14.50	9.24	5.26
1980	11.69	$1.81	3.42	12.09	15.51	11.29	4.22
1981	12.40	$1.92	3.58	12.84	16.43	13.69	2.74
1982	11.46	$2.04	3.84	11.90	15.74	13.07	2.67
1983	11.08	$2.20	4.6	11.59	16.19	10.98	5.21
					1974-1983	AVERAGE	3.78
					1979-1983	AVERAGE	4.02

then more reliance should be placed on the recent levels of the risk premium than on historical averages. Computation of a weighted average risk premium with a set of declining weights such that the recent past is weighted more heavily than the distant past will accomplish this.

Risk premiums tend to fluctuate with changes in investor risk aversion. Such changes can be tracked by observing the yield spreads between different bond rating categories over time. If risk premiums are unstable over a given period, emphasis should be placed on more current risk premium information. Significant changes in the relative taxation of returns received from stocks and bonds can also alter risk premiums; measured risk premiums will in fact incorporate investor adjustments to relative taxation rates, since it is pre-tax risk premiums that are measured from capital market data rather than post-tax quantities.

The detailed month-to-month results of the Brigham-Shome risk premium study indicate that during periods of capital market turbulence and interest rate volatility such as 1981-1982, current risk premiums are more appropriate than long-run historical risk premiums. In September 1979, the Federal Reserve Board announced a shift in monetary policy from an interest rate emphasis to a money supply growth emphasis. The result was increased volatility in the bond market and a temporary shrinkage of the risk premium. In periods of relative stability, risk premiums are restored to their normal long-run historical levels.

9.4   RISK PREMIUM ESTIMATION: BOOK RETURN METHOD

Another variation of the relative risk premium method is to estimate the relationship between book returns on equity and bond yields over some reference period, and apply the resulting relationship to a specified utility's current borrowing costs.

In order to ensure that realized book returns reflect expected returns, only those public utilities which have succeeded in issuing common stock without diluting shareholders' equity should be studied. To apply the method, all publicly-traded public utilities with a market-to-book ratio in excess of 1.05 and less than 1.2 should be retained. This particular range allows for flotation cost coverage and is sufficiently broad so as to contain a reasonable number of companies. In other words, the sample should consist of all utilities earning a return equal to their cost of capital including an allowance for underpricing costs. The reference period should be the most current year if the estimated risk premium is to be representative of current conditions. If the sample size is too small, the period can be expanded to include additional years.

As an illustration, for each of the years from 1978 to 1981, the Value Line Data Base was screened to obtain all the electric, gas, and telephone utilities with a market-to-book ratio in excess of 1.05. The risk premium was calculated by subtracting the appropriate Moody's bond yield on similarly-rated corporate bonds for that year from the return on average common equity for that company in the same year. For the period 1978-1981, 42 risk premium observations were obtained, as shown on Figure 9-3. The average risk premium for the sample was 3.82% calculated by adding each individual risk premium in the sample and dividing the result by 42. The frequency distribution of risk premiums on Figure 9-3 can serve as a check on the risk premium obtained from other risk premium estimation techniques. For example, if the aggregate risk premium based on some stock market index was 5%, which when multiplied by the utility's beta of 0.60 gave a risk premium of 3%, the reasonableness of the 3% can be gauged by reference to Figure 9-3. Of the total of 42 companies, 27 have risk premiums greater than or equal to 3%, attesting to the reasonable nature of the 3% estimate. If a specified utility's publicly held bond issues were currently yielding 13%, a return on common equity of 16% would be indicated.

9.5   RISK PREMIUM ESTIMATION: COMPARATIVE TECHNIQUES

The actual historical relationship between risk premiums and the risk of a large population of common stocks can be observed over a long time period and used to estimate the appropriate risk premium for a given utility. The utility's cost of equity is then estimated as the yield on long-term Treasury bonds plus the estimated risk premium. To illustrate, Litzenberger (1979) estimated the actual relationship between risk premiums and betas on common stocks over a long time period, and used this historical relationship to estimate the risk premium on AT&T's common equity, on the grounds that over long time periods, investors' expectations are realized.

Litzenberger obtained monthly rates of return for all common stocks listed on the New York Stock Exchange over the period 1926-1979 from the CRISP data tapes. Five-year betas were computed for each month for each company. For each month, the securities were assigned to one of 10 portfolios on the basis of ranked betas, from the lowest to the highest beta. Monthly returns for each of the portfolios were compounded to produce annual rates of return on each of the 10 portfolios from 1931 to 1979. Litzenberger then calculated historical risk premium on each of the ten portfolios by averaging for the 49 year period 1931-1979 the difference between the portfolio's annual rate of return and the one-year government

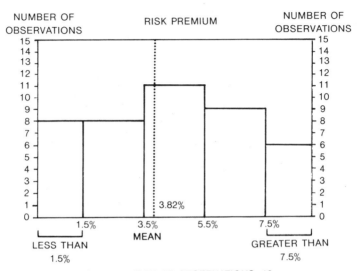

Figure 9-3

RISK PREMIUM ANALYSIS FOR UTILITIES WITH A
MARKET-TO-BOOK RATIO IN EXCESS OF ONE

TOTAL NUMBER OF OBSERVATIONS: 42
AVERAGE SAMPLE RISK PREMIUM: 3.82%

bond yield. The following relationship between the risk premium and the portfolios' betas was obtained:

Risk Premium = 4.21% + 3.94% x Beta

The relationship is portrayed on Figure 9-4. Using AT&T's beta of 0.60 at that time, the risk premium for AT&T is:

4.21% + 3.94% x 0.60 = 6.6%

A long-term cost of equity capital estimate for AT&T is obtained by adding the risk premium of 6.6% to the current yield on long-term Treasury bonds or to the projected long-term yield implied by the closing prices on the Treasury bond futures contract traded on the Chicago Board of Trade. The latter measures the consensus long-term interest rate expectation of investors[4]. A similar procedure could be developed based on the standard deviation of return rather than on beta as risk measure.

Figure 9-4

THE RELATIONSHIP BETWEEN RISK PREMIUM
AND BETA, 1931-1979

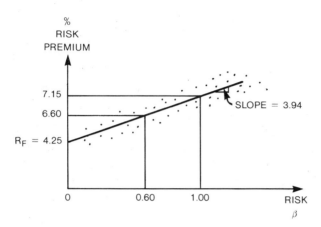

The technique, whether based on beta or standard deviation, can also be used to check the reasonableness of a cost of equity estimate derived from DCF techniques. From Figure 9-4, if the DCF-derived equity cost is 18%, versus the 17.6% measure obtained from the risk premium method, confidence in the reliability of the DCF measure is enhanced. Since the end result of the technique is an earnings rate for a given utility commensurate with the earnings rate of comparable risk companies based on a broad sample of companies, the method is directly consistent with the *Hope* and *Bluefield* doctrines of fair return.

9.6   RISK PREMIUM ESTIMATION: COMPANY SPECIFIC APPROACH

Instead of relying on an aggregate stock market index or an industry-specific index, the risk premium can be estimated by focusing on company-specific data directly.

Under this approach, a forward-looking risk premium can be estimated by computing the required market rate of return for the company's stock based on the DCF method for each month, or quarter, over a specified period, and then subtracting from these returns the spot yield on the utility's bond at the end of the same month or quarter. Computation of the expected equity return is based on the standard DCF model, whereby the expected dividend yield is added to the long-run expected growth rate for each month. The latter can be proxied by a simple average of stock analysts' estimates of the long-term growth rate of the company's earnings and/or dividends during the past six months if such forecasts are available, or else on historical growth. The company's own risk premium is obtained for each month by subtracting from the equity return estimate the yield to maturity of its bonds for that month. The monthly risk premiums are averaged to produce the mean historical risk premium for the company.

One drawback of this approach is that the risk premium estimate is only as good as the DCF estimate of equity return used in deriving it and is thus susceptible to the singular vagaries of that particular company. An abnormally low or high risk premium can result from a biased DCF estimate. For example, a negative risk premium can arise from a low or even negative historical growth rate, caused in turn by an inadequate earnings level, or by a low dividend yield component. The reverse conditions may cause an upward-biased risk premium. The estimated risk premium may be illusory because of the inability to measure accurately the equity return on the company's stock.

If the risk premium is based on the company's own bond yields rather than on Treasury bond yields, distortions can occur due to characteristics of the company's bonds. For example, the spread between Treasury bond yields and Bell System bond yields in the volatile 1979-1982 period widened because of call provision effects. Long-term Bell System bonds are normally callable after five years from the issue date versus a 25 year non-callable period for long-term Treasury bonds. When investors expect falling interest rates, the relative probability of recall on Bell System bonds is thus increased, and a greater yield premium is required from Bell System bonds.

Another potential drawback of the approach is that rate of return witnesses sometimes use the approach as a check on their DCF estimate; this is circular logic, since the risk premium computation relies in turn on the DCF estimate of equity return

9.7 NEGATIVE RISK PREMIUM

In the 1980-1981 era of turbulent capital markets and volatile interest rates, several cost of capital experts testifying in regulatory proceedings advanced the notion that utility debt securities had become riskier than equity securities, and that the bond-stock risk premium had become negative. This section will review the arguments underlying this view.

The notion of a negative risk premium refers to the situation where the expected market return of common equity is less than that of the bonds of the same issuer. Expressed in another way, the debt securities having prior claims are more costly to the issuer than the securities having residual claims.

Such a view is not consistent with the basic precepts of finance, economics, and business law. By simple legal fact, common shareholders are residual claimants to a company's earnings and assets, while bondholders are priority claimants on corporate assets and earnings. The interest payments to bondholders take precedence and must be serviced first, before any distribution of dividends to common shareholders can be contemplated. It follows that the basic business risks of a company will fall much more heavily upon the earnings available to shareholders than upon the earnings available to service the priority claims of bondholders, and that therefore stocks are riskier than bonds.

Financial theory has always asserted that the greater a security's risk, the greater the return required from that security, with risk defined as the uncertainty of the return. Setting aside the question of bankruptcy and default which by itself makes stocks riskier investment vehicles than bonds, the return on a bond, represented by fixed interest payments and repayment of principal, is contractual in nature. But there is no such guarantee in the case of common stocks. Dividend payments are not guaranteed, and the shareholders' claim on assets and earnings is junior to that of the bondholders. Bondholders expect that they will earn the prevailing coupon rate or yield-to-maturity when they purchase a bond, and shareholders expect a return made up of dividends and capital gains. To subscribe to the idea of a negative risk premium is synonymous with believing that investors price securities such that they assign a higher probability of earning the stock's non-contractual return than of earning the bond's guaranteed return, which seems highly unlikely.

If the expected return on bonds were to momentarily exceed the expected return on common equity, rational profit-maximizing and risk-averse investors could both enhance the yield of their portfolios and reduce the risk of their holdings by simply switching out of common stocks and into bonds. Such portfolio-switching behavior would lower stock prices and increase bond prices, thereby raising the yield on stocks and lowering the yield on bonds. This portfolio substitution of bonds for stocks would continue until a normal positive risk premium was restored. The existence of a negative risk premium could not persist for any length of time in efficient capital markets.

The allegation of a negative risk premium sometimes rests on empirical studies of historical "realized" risk spreads of stocks over bonds as opposed to the study of "expected" risk premiums. Clearly, during depressed stock market periods, common stocks do worse than bonds, and realized stock returns are lower than realized bond returns. The realized return of bonds has in fact exceeded the return on stocks in several instances in the past, but this only shows that investor expectations simply were not realized for those periods. In a forward-looking sense, expected stock returns will exceed expected bond returns. Risk premium studies should always be conducted on the basis of expectations, and not on the basis of realizations.

Outstanding bonds are in fact exposed to interest rate risk, that is, the risk that interest rates will rise and bond prices will fall, inflicting a capital loss on bondholders. This risk can rise substantially in periods of volatile interest rates, such as the 1980-1981 period. It should be kept in mind however that some stocks, utility stocks in particular, are highly interest-sensitive. These stocks provide a return to their holders predominantly in the form of dividend yield, which is interest-rate sensitive. There is a well-known bond theorem which states that the longer the maturity of a security, the greater its price volatility. It is also a fact that common stocks do not mature, and therefore have a longer maturity than bonds. If interest rates fall, the price of a public utility's stock would increase more than the price of its bonds. But the converse is also true. If interest rates were to rise, the common stock price would fall more. And this is precisely why interest-sensitive common stocks would be riskier than bonds.

Leaving aside the interest-sensitivity argument, negative risk premiums can only prevail if the interest rate risk of bonds exceeds the combined business risk and financial risk of stocks. Advocates of negative risk premiums argue that such a situation indeed exists during inflationary periods. During such periods, utility stocks are safer investments than bonds since equity returns can be increased by regulators while bond returns are fixed. In other words, utility common shareholders are not subject to interest rate risk because regulators will increase allowed common equity returns as inflationary pressures intensify. The dollar returns received by bondholders are fixed and cannot be adjusted for inflation, whereas the returns received by shareholders are indexed to inflation by the regulatory process itself. This argument is often characterized as the "hedging" argument whereas bonds are poor inflation hedges and stocks are a good hedge against inflation.

The hedging advantage of bonds over stocks argument is misstated right from the start. While bonds are not hedged against unanticipated inflation, they are hedged against anticipated inflation since bond yields increase in step with anticipated inflation. So if bonds are indeed superior hedges, it is against the unanticipated component of inflation only.

Theoretically, equity investments represent claims against physical assets whose real returns should remain unaffected by inflation. In reality, equities have not provided a hedge against inflation. Up until 1982, the stock market indices had not progressed substantially since the upward inflationary spiral started in the late 1960's, and declined severely in real inflation-adjusted terms. The view that equities are a hedge against inflation is unsupported by the facts. The tax system erroneously taxes inflation profits, and historical cost-based depreciation charges do not cover replacement costs adequately in inflationary times. Inflation increases financing requirements at the very time that such financing is expensive, depressing earnings.

As far as utilities are concerned, several studies by both practitioners and academicians have documented the fact that the average returns on common equity for the utility industry have not kept pace with inflation[5]. Even casual empiricism will reveal that despite increases in equity return allowances, the equity returns actually earned by utilities have not increased commensurately. The record of the last decade indicates that the returns earned by utilities cannot be readily adjusted in response to adverse interest rate changes.

In fact, even if stocks in general were inflation hedges, utility stocks are likely to be poor hedges. During the period of regulatory lag, which is likely to lenghten during inflationary periods, the utility shareholder is not protected against changes in expected inflation. Compared to unregulated companies, the utilities have few of the characteristics which would make them good inflation hedges; they are more capital intensive, enjoy relatively little pricing flexibility, and have more rigid financing requirements.

To mitigate further the argument that interest rate risk affects bonds more than stocks, a subtantial fraction of bond market participants, usually institutional, are able to attenuate interest rate risk by hedging this risk either through appropriate positions in financial futures contracts, or by pursuing so-called immunization strategies. Institutional bondholders neutralize the impact of interest rate changes by matching the maturity of a bond portfolio with the investment planning period, or by engaging in hedging transactions in the financial futures markets. The merits and mechanics of such strategies are well documented by both academicians and practitioners[6]. Stocks are not so easily immunized, being of infinite maturity. Moreover, the mechanisms and market techniques for minimizing the effects of interest rate risk on stock portfolios are still embryonic in nature, compared to similar techniques for bond portfolios.

To further assess the likelihood of negative risk premiums, Brigham & Shome (1982) argue that if negative risk premiums do exist, they should be associated with sharply upward sloping yield curves. If investors are deeply concerned with inflation, the maturity premium of long-term bonds over short-term bonds should expand, compressing the stock-bond risk premium. In fact, the reverse situation usually prevails in times of interest rate volatility. The yield curve is negative, with short-term rates higher than long-term rates. This is inconsistent with negative yield spreads.

Some analysts contend that after-tax return factors can justify the existence of a negative risk premium. By applying tax adjustments to the raw returns on stocks and bonds, a negative risk premium emerges. The adjustments reflect the favorable tax treatment accorded to the capital gains component of stock returns and the tax incentives available for dividend income received from electric utilities. Such adjustments are unnecessary as they are already impounded in stock prices. To the extent that such advantages exist, investors are willing to pay higher market prices, and accept lower expected returns. Any forward-looking cost of capital calculation already embodies tax effects since investor price securities on the basis on after-tax returns.

The existence of a negative risk premium is highly unlikely, as it is at serious odds with the basic tenets of finance and law. Using proper definitions for equity and debt expected rates of return, the preponderance of the evidence indicates that the negative risk premium does not exist. Several risk premium studies cited in Section 9.3 of this chapter have found positive risk premia well in excess of 3% over the last decade. Risk premiums do narrow during unusually turbulent and volatile interest rate environments, but then return to normal levels. They are most unlikely to ever become negative.

9.8   CONCLUSION

The risk premium method is conceptually sound, firmly rooted in the conceptual framework of Capital Market Theory, the subject of the next chapter. Data requirements to implement the method are not prohibitive. The methodology provides a useful complement to the DCF technology, in view of its responsiveness to changes in capital market conditions. The method is a timely signalling device for current interest rate trends, in contrast to the DCF method which may be sluggish in detecting changes in return requirements, especially when based on historical data. For example, a DCF estimate anchored on historical growth trends may actually decline during a steep rise in interest rates. The high costs of borrowing erode utility earnings, producing low earnings growth rates, and a downward-biased DCF estimate. The reverse scenario occurs in a period of declining interest costs, producing upward-biased DCF estimates.

Notes

[1] The yield to maturity of a bond is the return promised to the bondholder so long as the issuer meets all interest and principal obligations and the investor reinvests coupon income at a rate equal to the yield to maturity. See Homer & Leibowitz (1972) for a full discussion of bond return computations and of the pitfalls of yield to maturity as a valid return measure.

[2] The growth in earnings is used instead of the growth in dividends because several stocks which make up the Value Line Composite Index do not pay dividends. In any event, for an index made up of a large number of companies, dividend growth and earnings growth are likely to coincide over the long-run, since in the aggregate dividend policies are stable.

[3] As a proxy for the expected growth on the overall market, the average five-year earnings growth forecast of analysts reported by IBES for a large number of publicly-traded stocks is suitable.

[4] The average market forecasts of rates in the form of interest rate Treasury securities futures contracts data can be used as a proxy for the expected risk-free rate.

[5] Several studies have documented the poor performance of common stocks as inflation hedges. See Reilly (1979) for a discussion and review of these studies.

[6] See McEnally (1980) and Kolb & Gay (1983) for a discussion of immunization strategies for bond portfolios.

CAPITAL ASSET PRICING MODEL

This chapter describes the Capital Asset Pricing Model (CAPM) approach to cost of capital estimation, and explores the model's applicability to public utilities. Conceptual, empirical and computational issues are raised. The first section provides a succinct conceptual background of the model. Formal theoretical development of the model is only briefly considered; comprehensive and detailed presentations of the theory are generously available in most finance or investment textbooks[1]. The second section examines the CAPM's consistency with public utility regulation. The third section discusses the practical usefulness of the model, problems in application, and potential remedies. The fourth section summarizes the empirical evidence on the CAPM's validity, and the fifth section explores extensions of the model in light of its conceptual and empirical limitations, setting the stage for the Arbitrage Pricing Model in Chapter 11.

10.1 CONCEPTUAL BACKGROUND

The concept and measurement of risk were treated extensively in Chapters 3 and 4. Risk was defined as the variability of outcomes around an expected result. For an undiversified investor who views a security in isolation, the standard deviation of realized returns provides a valid estimate of the security's risk.

An underpinning of the CAPM is that an investor diversifies by combining risky securities into a portfolio such that the risk of the portfolio is less than any of its parts through diversification effects. Diversification reduces portfolio risk because security returns do not move perfectly together. Complete elimination of risk is impossible however since securities all move together to a certain extent because of the influence of pervasive market-wide forces.

A security's total risk can be partitioned into "specific risk", the portion unique to the company, and "market risk", the nondiversifiable portion related to the general movement of security markets. The core idea of the CAPM is that investors can eliminate company-unique risks by appropriate diversification, and should therefore not be rewarded for bearing this superfluous risk. Diversified risk-averse investors are only exposed to market risk, and are therefore rewarded with higher expected returns for bearing only market-related risk. Beta is a measure of market risk, and captures the extent to which a security's returns move in tandem with the returns of the overall market.

Risk-averse investors demand higher returns for assuming additional risk, and higher-risk securities are priced to yield higher expected returns than lower-risk securities. The CAPM quantifies the additional return required for bearing incremental risk, and provides a formal risk-return relationship anchored on the basic idea that only market risk matters, as measured by beta. Securities are priced such that:

Expected Return = Risk-free Rate + Risk Premium
= Risk-free Rate + Relevant Risk x Market Price of Risk
= Risk-free Rate + Beta x Market Price of Risk

$$K = R_F + \beta(R_M - R_F) \qquad (10\text{-}1)$$

Equation 10-1 is the seminal CAPM expression; a formal derivation of the model can be found in Appendix 10-A. The CAPM asserts that an investor expects to earn a return, K, that could be gained on a riskless investment, R_F, plus a risk premium for assuming risk, proportional to the security's market risk, β, and the market price of risk, $R_M - R_F$.

The CAPM risk-return relationship, often referred to as the Security Market Line (SML), is portrayed graphically in Figure 10-1. The intercept of the line is the expected risk-free rate R_F which has a beta of zero, and the slope is the expected market return, R_M, less R_F. The expected return on the market has a beta of one by definition. Utility X on the graph has a beta less than one and thus an expected return (cost of capital), K_x, less than R_M, while Utility Y has a beta greater than one and an expected return K_Y greater than R_M.

The CAPM can be viewed as a equilibrium pricing schedule for capital of varying risk, depicting the going rate of return prevailing in capital markets on investments of varying risk. The model states that in well-functioning capital markets, the expected risk premium on each investment is proportional to its beta. This implies that each security should lie on the security market line. Competition in capital markets among investments of differing risk produces the CAPM risk-return relationship. Any security selling at a price low enough to yield more than its appropriate return on the SML attracts profit-maximizing investors who bid up its price until its

Figure 10-1

THE SECURITY MARKET LINE

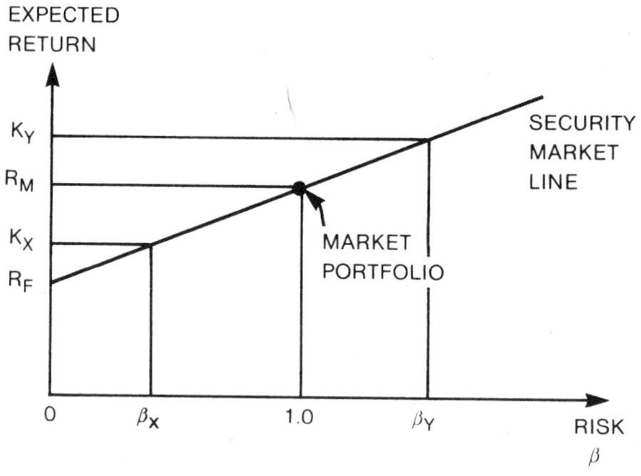

expected return falls to its appropriate position on the SML. Conversely, investors will dispose of any security selling at a price high enough to put its expected return below the SML, exerting downward pressure on price until the security's return rises to the level justified by its beta.

A multitude of assumptions are required to obtain the CAPM. Two general assumptions overshadow the others. The first general assumption is that capital markets are competitive and efficient, whereby information is freely available to all investors and rapidly impounded in security prices such that security prices can be trusted to represent the best estimate of the true value of a security at a point in time. A massive body of empirical evidence amassed by researchers generally points to a high degree of efficiency in capital markets[2]. The second general assumption is that investors are rational profit-maximizers who pursue their monetary self-interests, and in the process demand higher returns for higher risks and drive expected returns toward their levels predicted by the SML.

The remaining assumptions are more stringent and specialized. Investors hold diversified portfolios and operate in capital markets unencumbered by transaction costs, taxes, and restrictions on borrowing and short-selling. Investors possess homogeneous expectations, thereby agreeing on the likely prospects of securities over a common time horizon. Finally, investor preferences and the statistical nature of security returns follow rigid definite patterns.

In spite of the lack of realism of some of these assumptions, the true test of the CAPM is whether the model possesses explanatory power and forecasting ability. According to the "end result" doctrine of the Hope case, and according to the dictates of economic positivism, a model should be judged by its ability to predict and explain rather than by the robustness of its assumptions. Several extensions of the basic CAPM have been developed, relaxing the assumptions, without tarnishing the fundamental nature of the model. It is worthwhile asking whether the assumptions underlying the CAPM are any less confining than those underlying the constant growth DCF model.

The CAPM is not a static once-and-for-all relationship. The height and slope of the SML fluctuate in response to macroeconomic forces and changes in investor behavior. For example, Figure 10-2 shows the new SML following an increase in expected inflation from 0% to 6%. At every level of risk, the real inflation-free cost of capital rises by 6% to adjust to its new nominal level. Figure 10-2 also demonstrates the higher risk premium which results from a steepening of the slope of the SML in response to a higher degree of investor risk aversion.

Figure 10-2

INFLATION, RISK AVERSION, AND
THE RISK-RETURN TRADEOFF

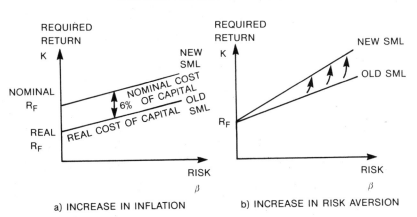

a) INCREASE IN INFLATION   b) INCREASE IN RISK AVERSION

10.2   CAPM, DCF, AND RISK PREMIUM INTERRELATIONSHIP

It is useful at this point to spell out the link between the three broad approaches to cost of capital estimation. The interrelationships between DCF, risk premium, and the CAPM are configured on Figure 10-3. DCF Valuation theory defines the value of an equity security as the discounted present value of its future stream of dividend payments. Given the market price of the security and its forecast dividend stream, the implicit *expected return* from the security can be derived. The Risk Premium approach holds that the expected return for a security can be derived by adding to the risk-free return an appropriate premium return to reflect the asset's risk. The latter is empirically derived. The CAPM also asserts that the expected return depends on the risk-free rate and the risk premium, but formally quantifies the risk premium as a linear function of market risk, or beta. Thus, given forecasts of future dividends, the risk-free rate of return, and an estimate of beta, the security's expected rate of return can be assessed.

10.3   THE CAPM AND PUBLIC UTILITY REGULATION

The cornerstone of public utility rate of return regulation is the legal principle enunciated in the *Hope* case that "the return to the equity owner should be commensurate with returns on investments in other enterprises having corresponding risk". The CAPM presents a conceptual framework which meets the legal criteria for the establishment of a fair return, and which operationalizes the *Hope* doctrine. The concept of commensurate return is the return which investors expect when they purchase other equity shares of comparable risk. The *Hope* decision requires consideration of relative risk which can be measured by beta. Provided that estimates for the relevant risk and attendant return quoted in the *Hope* doctrine can be obtained, the CAPM relationship can be used to determine a fair and reasonable return.

In the *Bluefield* decision, the U.S. Supreme Court also required that the allowed return be sufficient to assure a utility's financial soundness, which implies that market returns be considered. The CAPM-based cost of capital is the rate of return prevailing in capital markets on investments of similar risk, and is therefore the return necessary to attract capital to investments of a given risk, consistent with the soundness criterion of *Bluefield.*

In a 1981 survey, Harrington (1981) reported that the CAPM experienced increased usage by regulatory commissions. Prior to 1981, CAPM estimates of cost of capital were reasonably consistent with estimates derived from DCF and Risk Premium techniques. With interest rates soaring

Figure 10-3

RELATIONSHIP BETWEEN DCF, RISK PREMIUM,
AND CAPM

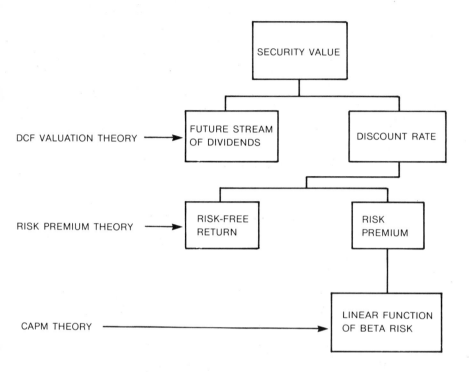

after 1981, the CAPM dwindled in popularity, partly because it yielded unreasonable estimates of equity costs, and partly in response to the academic community's growing disenchantment with the CAPM, challenging its veracity on both conceptual and empirical grounds.

While the CAPM provides a valid and rigorous conceptual framework to determine capital costs, the implementation problems are formidable. None of the inputs to the CAPM are known with certainty so that only estimates of equity costs are obtained. The true equity return is unobtainable. It is possible however to develop a range of estimates based on the application of several methodologies supplemented by the exercise of informed judgment throughout the estimation process.

10.4 CAPM APPLICATION

At first glance, the CAPM appears simple in application. Estimates of the future values of the CAPM's three input parameters, R_F, B, and R_M, are estimated, and inserted into the CAPM formula to produce the cost of equity estimate, or used in reading directly the cost of equity from the SML. A numerical example is shown in Figure 10-4. Assuming a 9% risk-free rate, and a 16% market return, the cost of equity estimates for Utilities X, Y, and Z are 13.2%, 14.6%, and 16.7% respectively, corresponding to their respective betas of 0.60, 0.80, and 1.10.

Despite the CAPM's conceptual appeal and mechanistic simplicity, operationalizing the CAPM to estimate a fair return on equity presents several practical difficulties. From the start, the model itself is an expectational forward-looking model. To stress this point, the following equation restates the CAPM formula with expectational operators attached to each input variable:

Figure 10-4

ESTIMATES OF UTILITY COST OF CAPITAL USING THE
CAPM: A NUMERICAL ILLUSTRATION

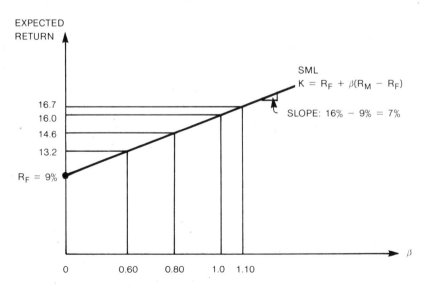

$$E(K) = E(R_f) + E(B) \times [E(R_M) - E(R_F)] \qquad (10\text{-}2)$$

where $E(K)$ = expected return, or cost of capital
$E(R_F)$ = expected risk-free rate
$E(B)$ = expected beta
$E(R_M)$ = expected market return

The CAPM model is an expectational model while only historical data are available to match the three theoretical input variables: expected risk-free return, expected beta, and expected market return. None of the input variables exist as separate identifiable entities. It is thus necessary in practice to employ different proxies, with different results obtaining with each set of proxy variables. Each of the required inputs to the CAPM is examined below. Mullins (1982), Rhyne (1982), and Malko (1983) discuss the practical difficulties in implementing the CAPM model. The following draws on and extends their contributions.

Risk-free Rate

Theoretically, the yield on 90-day Treasury Bills is virtually riskless, devoid of default risk and subject to a negligible amount of interest rate risk. But the T-Bill rate fluctuates widely, leading to volatile and unreliable equity return estimates. Moreover, 90-day Treasury Bills typically do not match the equity investor's planning horizon. Equity investors generally have an investment horizon far in excess of 90 days. Finally, short-term Treasury Bills yields reflect the impact of factors different from those influencing long-term securities such as common stock. The premium for expected inflation impounded into 90-day Treasury Bills is likely to be far different than the inflationary premium impounded into long-term securities yields. On grounds of consistency alone, the yields on long-term Treasury bonds match more closely with common stock returns. But long-term Treasury yields are exposed to substantial interest rate risk, and so are not truly riskless.

A compromise solution is to utilize the yields on intermediate Treasury securities, three to five years in maturity. This is reinforced by the fact that a risk-free rate based on a 3 to 5-year time frame more closely matches the time period over which rates will be in effect. If the yield curve is expected to be relatively flat, the choice of an appropriate Treasury security becomes academic.

While the spot yield on intermediate Treasury securities provides a reasonable proxy for the risk-free rate, the CAPM specifically requires the expected spot yield. Recently, market forecasts of rates on Treasury securities in the form of interest rate futures contracts yields have become available, and can be employed as proxies for the expected yields on Treasury securities.

Over the last 50 years, the Treasury Bill rate has approximately equaled the annual inflation rate [see Fama (1975) and Ibbotson-Sinquefield (1982)]. Refined techniques to forecast inflation based on the current shape of the yield curve could thus be employed to obtain the expected risk-free rate[3]. Alternately, the consensus inflation forecast over the requisite horizon by economists could be employed to derive the risk-free rate estimate. None of these techniques is likely to provide superior estimates than supplied by current yield data however. The complexity ar.d computational costs are likely to outweigh their marginal usefulness.

In practice, sensitivity analyses employing various input values for the risk-free rate can produce a reasonably good range of estimates of equity costs. For example, for a risk-free rate range of 8% to 9%, a market return of 16%, the CAPM cost of equity for a public utility with a beta of 0.80 ranges from 14.4% to 14.6%. This is shown graphically in Figure 10-5.

Figure 10-5

CAPM ESTIMATES OF CAPITAL COST WITH
DIFFERENT RISK-FREE RATE ESTIMATES

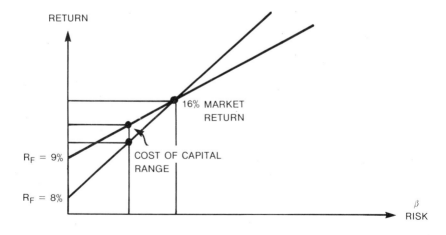

Beta Estimate

In Chapter 4, it was argued that beta is a useful simple objective measure of risk when used to gauge the relative risks of securities. The relative risk ranking of securities is relatively immune to the beta estimation method. The situation is quite different when the objective of estimating beta is to obtain an absolute estimate of cost of equity for an individual security. In this case, the reliability of the beta-estimation technique has a direct effect on the confidence in the estimate of equity cost.

A useful starting point is the utility's historical beta. Historical price and dividend data are easily accessible and statistical regression techniques which gauge the past variability of the utility's stock relative to the market can estimate the utility's beta. Or, beta books can be consulted; several investment firms supply betas, the most noteworthy being Value Line and Merrill Lynch. Published betas have the advantage of being already adjusted for their natural tendencies to revert to one. If the utility's past market risk seems likely to continue, based on an examination of company fundamentals, historical beta calculations can be used to estimate the cost of equity.

Historically estimated betas are notoriously unstable and sensitive to the estimation technique. The CAPM was initially developed in the context of portfolio theory and was aimed at portfolio management practices, and not at utility cost of equity estimation. When portfolios of securities are considered, the statistical estimation errors for each individual security's beta cancel out, so that historically estimated betas for portfolios are reliable and constitute reliable predictors of the portfolio's future beta. But when using the CAPM to estimate a utility's cost of capital, only one security is considered, accentuating the statistical estimation problem. One remedy is to rely on an industry beta instead of a one-security sample, whereby a portfolio of securities in the same industry is used to derive the beta estimate.

The perils and biases of relying on historical beta as a proxy for the true fundamental future beta were documented in Chapter 4, and several remedies were offered. Since betas change over time as both company fundamentals and capital structures change, examination of possible future changes in company fundamentals can reveal the future likely trend and value of beta. Clues to such changes can be obtained by studying the behavior of key accounting variables, such as payout ratios, capital structure ratios, and earnings stability trends. Comparison of historical betas with "fundamental betas" can reveal changes in the utility's risk fundamentals. "Accounting betas" which essentially arise out of the observed correlation between company fundamentals and historical betas are also useful in signalling changes in future beta.

If listed call options are traded on the utility's stock, a time series of the standard deviation implied in daily call options premiums can reveal on a timely basis whether investor risk perceptions are changing and whether beta is changing in some predictable manner.

The final CAPM estimate of equity cost should be sensitized over a range of beta estimates to produce a range of estimates of the cost of equity. A 95% confidence interval, based on the standard error of estimate, around the best estimate of the beta coefficient, could be utilized. For example, for a risk-free rate of 8%, a market return of 16%, the CAPM estimate of equity cost for a utility with a beta of 0.80 is 14.4%; if the standard error of estimate of beta is 0.15, beta estimates range from 0.65 to 0.95, with a corresponding range of equity cost of 13.2% to 15.6%. See Figure 10-6.

Market Return

The last required input to the CAPM is the expected return on the market, R_M. Some analysts estimate the market return directly, others use the concept of the risk premium which is the difference between the market return and the risk-free rate.

The former can be achieved by applying the DCF methodology to a representative market index, such as the Standard & Poor's 500, Value Line Composite, or the New York Stock Exchange Index. For reasons of consistency, the market index employed should be the same as the market index used in deriving estimates of beta. The previous chapter outlined the specifics of the methodology to measure the aggregate market return based on the DCF method.

Figure 10-6

CAPM ESTIMATES OF CAPITAL COST WITH DIFFERENT BETA ESTIMATES

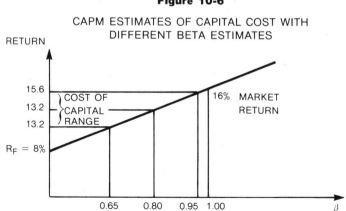

Another technique of estimating expected market return is based on a procedure described in detail by Ibbotson-Sinquefield (1982) which relies on the analysis of the current yield curve. Ibbotson-Sinquefield present forecasts of stocks, bonds, bills, and inflation rates based on the current yield curve. Essentially, the forward rates implied in the current curve are computed each year into the future. Forecasts of the nominal riskless rate are derived by subtracting the expected maturity premiums from the 1982 forward rates. Adding the historical equity risk premium to the riskless rate forecasts gives the common stock nominal return. The advantage of the method is that equity return forecasts are directly obtained, and that is what the CAPM requires. The disadvantage is the relative complexity and burdensome computational requirements of the method.

The second broad approach is to obtain directly the expected equity risk premium $R_M - R_F$, based on historically-derived risk premiums. A common recipe is to assume that investors anticipate about the same risk premium in the future as in the past. From 1926 to 1981, the risk premium on the Standard & Poor's 500 Index averaged 8.3%, based on the Ibbotson-Sinquefield historical return series. If the expected T-Bill rate is 8%, a benchmark estimate of 8.3% for the risk premium implies an estimated R_M of 16.3%. As pointed out in the previous chapter, the method assumes that investors anticipate the same risk premium in the future as in the past, which may be questionable in times of capital market agitation. A similar procedure only this time based on expected return series rather than on historical return series would be a preferable alternative. If risk premiums are volatile, the former procedure of directly measuring R_M is preferred; subtracting the current risk-free rate from that estimate results in a current valid risk premium.

As in the case of the beta estimate and risk-free rate estimate, a sensitivity analysis of possible CAPM cost of capital estimates should be conducted for a specified utility using a reasonable range of estimates for the market return. See Figure 10-7 for an illustration.

The range of cost of capital estimates obtained using a separate range for each of the three input variables to the CAPM can be combined to produce an overall sensitivity analysis for the cost of equity value. This is illustrated in Figure 10-8, where the range of estimates obtained is 12.55% to 16.65%, with a midpoint value of 14.6%. See Rhyne (1982) for a similar illustration.

The broad range of estimates obtained is typical of CAPM application, and the CAPM has been criticized for this. The results obtained will vary depending upon the statistical methodology selected. Efforts to fine-tune the estimates and rescue the CAPM from this limitation are described in the following section.

The following example, extracted from an actual 1982 rate case,

Figure 10-7

CAPM ESTIMATES OF CAPITAL COST WITH
DIFFERENT EXPECTED MARKET RETURNS

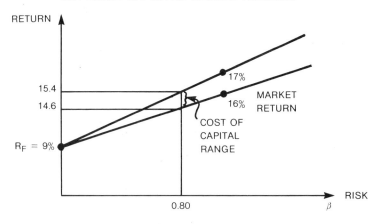

Figure 10-8

RANGE OF CAPM COST OF EQUITY
CAPITAL ESTIMATES

β RANGE	R_F RANGE	R_M		
		15%	16%	17%
	8%	12.55	13.20	13.85
0.65	9%	12.90	13.55	14.20
	10%	13.25	13.90	14.55
	8%	13.60	14.40	15.20
0.80	9%	13.80	14.60	15.40
	10%	14.00	14.80	15.60
	8%	14.65	15.60	16.55
0.95	9%	14.70	15.65	16.60
	10%	14.75	15.70	16.65

RANGE: LOW   12.55%
MID   14.60%
HIGH 16.65%

illustrates one approach to estimate the market return. The object was to calculate the required return (cost of capital) for the average stock in the U.S. as of mid-1982.

EXAMPLE

The year by year analysis of expected equity market returns and bond yields over the period 1972-1981, described in Section 9.3 of the last chapter, indicated that the risk premium for the overall equity market as represented by Value Line's Composite Market Index averaged 5.69% over the last decade and 6.93% in the last five years over long-term Treasury bonds. Table 10-1 shows the return on 20-year Treasury bonds, the rate of inflation, and the returns on the aggregate equity market for each of the last 10 years. The latter is reproduced from Table 9-2 in Chapter 9. The real rate of interest, defined as the difference between the nominal Treasury bond rate and the inflation rate is computed in the fifth column. The risk premium on the stock market, computed as the difference between the expected return on equity and the Treasury bond rate, is shown in the sixth column.

Table 10-2 provides an historical perspective on the cost of equity. The cost of equity is defined as the nominal return on a riskless asset, taken as the return on 20-year Treasury bonds, plus a risk premium. The risk-free rate can in turn be further subdivided into two components, the rate of inflation and the real rate of interest:

Equity Market Return = Risk-free Rate + Risk Premium
= Real Rate + Inflation Rate + Risk
Premium

Table 10-2 shows that the average cost of equity over the last two 5-year periods has risen because of increases in the inflation rate and the real rate. If the current yield (mid-1982) on 20-year Treasury bonds is 11%, adding the 10-year average risk premium of 5.69% to the nominal Treasury bond rate, the implied cost of equity for an average stock market investment is 16.69% for 1982.

TABLE 10-1 HISTORICAL YIELDS AND RISK PREMIUMS ON THE AGGREGATE MARKET

YEAR	YIELD ON 20-YEAR TREASURY BONDS	RATE OF INFLATION	COST OF EQUITY HISTORICAL PERSPECTIVE EXPECTED EQUITY MARKET RETURN	REAL YIELD ON TREASURY BONDS	RISK PREMIUM STOCKS OVER TREASURY BOND RATE
(1)	(2)	(3)	(4)	(5)	(6)
1972	5.82%	3.30%	7.39%	2.52%	1.57%
1973	6.97	6.23	9.22	0.74	2.25
1974	7.93	10.97	12.99	-3.04	5.06
1975	8.04	9.14	13.96	-1.10	5.92
1976	7.86	5.77	15.30	2.09	7.44
1977	7.62	6.45	16.63	1.17	9.01
1978	8.42	7.66	16.62	0.76	8.20
1979	9.24	11.26	16.75	-2.02	7.51
1980	11.29	13.52	17.39	-2.23	6.10
1981	13.69	10.37	17.51	3.32	3.82

TABLE 10-2 COST OF EQUITY CAPITAL:
AN HISTORICAL PERSPECTIVE

	1972-76	1977-81
Rate of Inflation	7.08%	9.85%
+		
Real Yield on Treasury Bonds	0.24	0.20
=		
Risk-free Rate	7.32	10.05
+		
Risk Premium	4.45	6.93
=		
Cost of Equity	11.77%	16.98%

10.5 EMPIRICAL VALIDATION

The last section showed that the practical difficulties of implementing the CAPM approach are surmountable. Serious conceptual and empirical problems remain however.

At the conceptual level, the CAPM has been submitted to a barrage of criticisms by academicians and practitioners alike. Roll (1977) argues that the CAPM has never been tested properly and that it can never be tested. Barring this criticism, conceptual difficulties remain. Investors may not act according to the precepts of the CAPM's assumptions. Investors may choose not to diversify, and bear company-specific risk if abnormal returns are expected. In a survey of individual investor portfolios, Friend & Blume (1975) report that a substantial percentage of individual investors are inadequately diversified. Short selling is somewhat restricted, in violation of CAPM assumptions. Factors other than market risk may influence investor behavior such as taxation, firm size, and restrictions on borrowing. Attempts to enrich the CAPM's conceptual content and improve its applicability are discussed in the next section of this chapter. The use of the CAPM in regulatory proceedings has not escaped criticism. See for example Malko and Einhorn (1983), Chartoff, Mayo, and Smith (1982), and the Autumn

1978 issue of *Financial Management*, where several prominent finance scholars address the use of the CAPM in regulatory proceedings.

There have been countless empirical tests of the CAPM to determine to what extent security returns and betas are related in the manner predicted by the CAPM[4]. The results of the tests support the idea that beta is related to security returns, that the risk-return tradeoff is positive, and that the relationship is linear. The contradictory finding is that the empirical SML is not as steeply sloped as the predicted SML. That is, low-beta securities earn returns somewhat higher than the CAPM would predict, and high-beta securities earn less than predicted. This is shown in Figure 10-9. The slope is less than predicted by the CAPM, and the intercept term is greater than the risk-free rate. This result is particularly crucial for public utilities whose betas are typically less than one. A CAPM-based estimate of cost of capital underestimates the return required from such securities, based on the evidence.

The empirical evidence also demonstrates that the SML is highly unstable over short periods, and differs significantly from the long-run relationship. This evidence underscores the potential for error in cost of capital estimates which apply the CAPM using historical data over short time periods. The evidence[5] also shows that the addition of specific company risk, as measured by standard deviation, adds explanatory power to the risk-return relationship.

Roll (1977) argues that the CAPM has never been tested and that such a test is infeasible. Roll argues moreover that the market index proxy used in emprical tests of the CAPM is inadequate; since a true comprehensive market index is unavailable, such tests will be biased in the direction shown

Figure 10-9

THEORETICAL VS EMPIRICAL ESTIMATE
OF THE CAPM

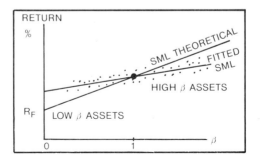

by the actual empirical results. Deviations of empirical results from the predictions of the CAPM does not necessarily mean that the CAPM is misspecified but rather that the market index used in testing is inefficient. Roll's conclusion is that the CAPM is not testable unless the exact composition of the true market portfolio is known and used in the tests.

Moreover, the CAPM is a forward-looking expectational model, and to test the model it is necessary to predict investor expectations correctly. Any empirical test of the CAPM is thus a test of the joint hypothesis of the model's validity and of the function used to generate expected returns from historical returns.

In short, the currently available empirical evidence indicates that the simple version of the CAPM does not provide an accurate description of the process determining security returns. Explanations for these results include the following:

1. The CAPM excludes other important variables which are important in determining security returns.

2. The market index used in the tests excludes important classes of securities, such as bonds, mortgages, and business investment.

3. Constraints on investor borrowing exist contrary to the assumption of the CAPM.

Each of these explanations produces a SML which is flatter than the CAPM prediction, and this result is inconsistent with the simple version of the CAPM used in several rate cases to estimate equity costs. Corresponding to each explanation, revised CAPM models have been proposed, each varying in complexity, each attempting to inject more realism in the assumptions. Ross (1978) presents a complete survey of the various asset pricing theories and related empirical evidence. The next section addresses the more tractable extensions to the CAPM which possess some applicability for public utility regulation.

10.6 CAPM EXTENSIONS

In light of the CAPM's empirical deficiencies, several attempts to enrich the model's conceptual validity and to salvage the model's applicability have been advanced. In this section, extensions of the CAPM and pragmatic solutions to safeguard the model's applicability are discussed.

The first explanation of the CAPM's inability to explain security returns satisfactorily is that beta is insufficient, and that other systematic risk factors affect security returns. The effects of these other independent variables should be quantified and used in estimating the cost of equity capital. The impact of the supplementary variables can be expressed as an additive element to the standard CAPM equation.

Letting 'a' stand for these other effects, the CAPM equation becomes:

$$K = R_F + a + B(R_M - R_F) \qquad (10\text{-}3)$$

To capture the variables' impact on the slope of the relationship, a coefficient 'b' is substituted for the market risk premium. The revised CAPM equation becomes:

$$K = R_F + a + b \times Beta \qquad (10\text{-}4)$$

The constants 'a' and 'b' capture all the market-wide effects which influence security returns, and must be estimated by econometric techniques.

Factors purported to affect security returns include dividend yield, skewness, and size effects.

Dividend Yield Effect

Empirical studies by Litzenberger & Ramaswamy (1979), Litzenberger *et al.* (1980) and Rosenberg & Marathe (1975) find that security returns are positively related to dividend yield as well as to beta. These results are consistent with after-tax extensions of the CAPM developed by Breenan (1973) and Litzenberger & Ramaswamy (1979) and suggest that the relationship between return, beta, and dividend yield should be estimated and employed to calculate the cost of equity capital.

The dividend yield effects stem from the differential taxation on corporate dividends and capital gains. The standard CAPM does not consider the regularity of dividends received by investors. Utilities generally maintain high dividend payout ratios relative to the market, and by ignoring dividend yield, the CAPM provides biased cost of capital estimates. Since taxable investors demand higher returns from the more heavily taxed high-yielding stocks, high-yielding stocks must offer investors higher pre-tax returns[6]. The heavier taxation on dividend income relative to capital gains causes investors to require higher pre-tax returns in order to equalize the after-tax returns provided by high-yielding stocks with those of low-yielding stocks.

The traditional return-beta relationship described by the SML fails to recognize the dividend yield dimension. But the two-dimensional SML can be expanded into a three-dimensional security market plane (SMP) by adding a dividend yield line as in Figure 10-10, which portrays the relationship between return, beta, and dividend yield. The positive effect of yield on return can be seen on the graph. The Wells Fargo Bank has in fact implemented the SMP approach for actual investment management decison-making, in effect recommending for purchase undervalued securities situated above the SMP.

Skewness Effects

Empirical studies by Kraus & Litzenberger (1976), Friend, Westerfield, & Granito (1978), and Morin (1981) found that, in addition to beta, skewness of returns has a significant negative relationship with security returns. This result is consistent with the skewness version of the CAPM developed by Rubinstein (1973) and Kraus & Litzenberger (1976). Once more, this may be particularly relevant for public utilities whose future profitability is constrained by the regulatory process on the upside and relatively unconstrained on the downside in the face of socio-political realities of public utility regulation. The traditional CAPM provides down-ward-biased estimates of cost of capital to the extent that these skewness effects are significant. A security market plane (SMP) similar to that envisaged in the case of dividend yield effects can be imagined, substituting a skewness line for the dividend yield line.

Figure 10-10

THE RELATIONSHIP BETWEEN RETURN, BETA
AND DIVIDEND YIELD

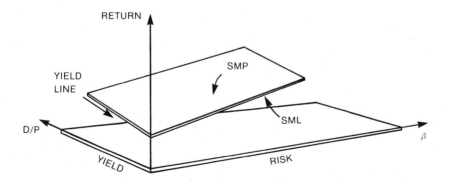

Size Effects

Empirical studies by Banz (1981) and Reinganum (1981A) have found that investors in small-capitalization stocks require higher returns than predicted by the standard CAPM. Ibbotson-Sinquefield's historical returns confirmed this finding; for the period 1926-1981, the average small stock premium was 6% over the average stock. One plausible explanation for the size effect is the higher information search costs incurred by investors for small companies relative to large companies. This effect is likely to be negligible for all but the very small public utilities. Moreover, Roll (1981) has recently questioned the evidence on the small firm effect.

Missing Assets

Empirical studies to validate the CAPM invariably rely on some stock market index as a proxy for the true market portfolio. The exclusion of several asset categories from the definition of market index misspecifies the CAPM and biases the results found using only stock market data. See Kolbe and Read (1983) for an illustration of the biases in beta estimates which result from applying the CAPM to public utilities. Unfortunately, no comprehensive and easily accessible data exist for several classes of assets, such as mortgages and business investments, so that the exact relation between return and stock betas predicted by the CAPM does not exist. This suggests that the empirical relationship between returns and stock betas is best estimated empirically rather than by relying on theoretical and elegant CAPM models expanded to include missing assets effects. In any event, stock betas may be highly correlated with the true beta measured with the true market index.

Constraints on Investor Borrowing

One of numerous versions of the CAPM developed by researchers is the so-called zero-beta, or two-factor, CAPM which provides for a risk-free return in a market where borrowing and lending rates are divergent. The model has the following form:

$$K = R_Z + B(R_M - R_F) \qquad (10-5)$$

The model, christened the zero-beta model, is analogous to the standard CAPM, but with the return on a miminum risk portfolio which is unrelated to market returns, R_Z, replacing the risk-free rate, R_F. The model has been empirically tested by Black, Jensen, and Scholes (1972), who found a flatter than predicted SML, consistent with other researchers' findings.

The zero-beta CAPM cannot be literally employed in cost of capital projections, since the zero-beta portfolio is a statistical construct. Attempts to estimate the model are formally equivalent to estimating 'a' and 'b' in Equation 10-4.

Empirical CAPM

Whatever the explanation for the flatter than predicted SML, whether it be dividend yield, skewness, size, missing assets, or constrained borrowing effects, the general suggestion is that the empirical relationship between returns and betas should be estimated empirically rather than asserted on an a priori basis. Equation 10-4 has gradually evolved to become known as the Empirical Capital Asset Pricing Model (ECAPM), and represents a pragmatic solution to the problems of the standard CAPM, whether it be data limitations, unrealistic assumptions, or omitted effects. All the vagaries of the model are telescoped into the two constants 'a' and 'b', which must be estimated econometrically from market data. The technique is formally applied by Litzenberger, Ramaswany, and Sosin (1980) to public utilities in order to rectify the CAPM's basic deficiencies. Not only do they summarize the criticisms of the CAPM insofar as they affect public utilites, but also described the econometric intricacies involved and the methods of circumventing the statistical problems. Essentially, the average monthly returns over a lengthy time period on a large cross-section of securities grouped into portfolios, are related to their corresponding betas by statistical regression techniques; that is, Equation 10-4 is estimated from market data. The utility's beta value is substituted into the equation to produce the cost of equity figure. Their own results demonstrate how the standard CAPM underestimates the cost of equity capital of public utilities on account of their high dividend yield and return skewness.

It was only natural that the next generation of CAPM models formally account for the presence of several factors influencing security returns. A new finance theory has been proposed to replace the CAPM which extends the standard CAPM to include sensitivity to several market factors other than market risk. Proponents of the Arbitrage Pricing Model (APM) contend that APM provides better results than does the CAPM and is not plagued by the shortcomings of the CAPM, while retaining its basic intuition. The next chapter discusses this latest paradigm in financial theory, and explores its pertinence in cost of capital determination.

10.7 CLOSING COMMENTS

The CAPM provides a powerful conceptual framework to understand the process of determining security returns. It is a useful pedagogic and expository device to explain the relationship between risk and return. Like all models in the social sciences, it is nevertheless an abstraction from reality, analogous to the model of perfect competition in economics. Applying the model to social problems is an uncomfortable and difficult task. As in the case of the DCF model, the CAPM is more than just an equation in which arbitrary numbers are inserted, and requires detailed and logical analysis for each of its component supplemented by enlightened judgment.

On the positive side, as a tool in the regulatory arena, the CAPM is a rigorous conceptual framework, and is logical insofar as it is not subject to circularity problems, since its inputs are objective market-based quantities, largely immune to regulatory decisions. The data requirements of the model are not prohibitive, although the amount of data analysis required can be substantial, especially if CAPM extensions are implemented.

On the negative side, the input quantities required for implementing the CAPM are difficult to estimate precisely. These problems are not insurmountable however, provided that a strong dose of judgment is exercised and that the logic underlying the methodology is well supported. The techniques outlined in this chapter should prove helpful in this regard. Sensitivity analysis over a reasonable range of risk-free rate, market return, and beta is strongly recommended to enhance the credibility of the estimates.

The raw form of the CAPM must be used with extreme caution. There is strong evidence that the CAPM is an incomplete description of security returns, especially for public utilities. Beta is helpful in explaining security returns only when complemented with other risk indicators, such as dividend yield, size, and skewness variables. Rather than theorize on the effects of such extraneous variables, a more expedient approach to estimating the cost of equity capital is to estimate directly the empirical relationship between return and beta, and let the capital markets speak for themselves as to the relative impact of such variables. The empirical form of the CAPM provides an adequate model of security returns. If a utility's beta can be estimated for a given period, then by knowing the empirical relationship between risk and return, the security's expected return, or cost of capital, can be estimated. Here again, the cost of capital estimates produced by a ECAPM procedure should be sensitized to produce a range of estimates. The range of cost of equity capital estimates can serve as a check on the estimates derived from the DCF and Risk Premium methodologies.

The CAPM is one of several tools in the arsenal of techniques to determine the cost of equity capital. Extreme caution, rigorous training in finance and econometrics and judgment are required for its successful execution, more so than DCF or Risk Premium methodologies.

Notes

[1] For a complete development of the CAPM, see Brealey & Myers (1984), Sharpe (1981), Copeland & Weston (1983); Hagin (1979) presents a straightforward non-mathematical treatment of the model.

[2] Reilly (1979) presents a synthesis of the empirical evidence on market efficiency.

[3] See Ibbotson-Sinquefield (1982) for a description of the methodology of forecasting future security yields based on yield curve analysis.

[4] For a summary of the empirical evidence on the CAPM, see Jensen (1972) and Ross (1978). CAPM evidence in the Canadian context is available in Morin (1981).

[5] See Friend, Granito, and Westerfield (1978) and Morin (1976).

[6] The strength of the tax effect on yield is diluted by non-taxable institutional ownership and by the personal tax exemption on dividend income from electric utility stocks.

APPENDIX 10-A

Capital Asset Pricing Model

If a fractional investment of x_1 is invested in the market portfolio, and $(1-x_1)$ in a risk-free security, the expected return on the combined portfolio is given by:

$$E(R_p) = x_1 E(R_M) + (1 - x_1)R_f \qquad (1)$$

The portfolio's beta is, by definitions

$$\beta_p = \frac{cov(R_p, R_M)}{\sigma^2(R_M)} = \frac{\sigma_{pM}}{\sigma_M^2} \qquad (2)$$

Substituting for R_p in (2):

$$\beta_p = \frac{cov(x_1 R_M + (1 - x_1)R_f, R_M)}{\sigma_M^2}$$

$$= \frac{x_1 \sigma_M^2 + (1 - x_1)\sigma_{fM}}{\sigma_M^2}$$

Since the return on the risk-free security is certain; $\sigma_{fM} = 0$.

Thus,
$$\beta_p = \frac{x_1 \sigma_M^2}{\sigma_M^2} = x_1 \qquad (3)$$

Substituting (3) into (1)

$$E(R_p) = \beta_p E(R_M) + (1 - \beta_p)R_f \qquad (4)$$

Rearranging:

$$E(R_p) = R_f + \beta_p(E(R_M) - R_f) \qquad (5)$$

Equation (5) is the CAPM. A similar expression can be shown to hold not only for portfolios, but for each risky security in the market portfolio (see Sharpe (1981)):

$$\boxed{E(Ri) = R_f + \beta_i[E(R_M) - R_f)]} \qquad (6)$$

CHAPTER 11

ARBITRAGE PRICING THEORY

The Arbitrage Pricing Model (APM) developed by Ross (1976) preserves the intuitive appeal of the CAPM, yet is more flexible, and eliminates some of the conceptual problems and troublesome aspects of the CAPM. The idea that higher risk is associated with higher return, the idea of partitioning security risk into a diversifiable and a non-diversifiable risk component, the notion of market-wide systematic influences on security returns, and the concept of a risk-free rate and risk premium are preserved by the APM. The inability to test the CAPM adequately and the somewhat artificial nature of the model are somewhat circumvented by the APM.

The APM is essentially a multiple-factor CAPM. The CAPM suggests that investors should only be recompensed for market risk, namely beta. But what if systematic elements of risk are more complex than can be captured by beta? Other plausible risk elements which permeate across all securities include changes in economic activity, changes in inflationary expectations, or changes in interest rates. For example, securities with low traditional betas such as public utilities may very well possess high systematic risk with respect to inflation, given their capital intensive nature. So, even if a security has a beta of one, it may not track overall stock market returns when inflationary expectations intensify.

The APM rests on two central notions, explored in the next section of this chapter: first, that security returns are influenced by several economy-wide systematic factors, unlike the CAPM which recognizes only one such component, and by a specific company-related component. Second, that assets which are close substitutes will sell for the same price. The next section describes the conceptual underpinnings of the APM. The empirical evidence and practical implications are presented in a subsequent section.

11.1 CONCEPTUAL BACKGROUND

The first of the APM's two conceptual building blocks is that security returns are a linear function of an unknown number of unspecified factors.

Investors predict individual security returns based on predictions of a variety of changes in the economy which systematically affect all securities. If the predictions are correct and if the process which converts the factor predictions into security return predictions is also correct, then investor predictions are fulfilled. But if there are unanticipated changes in the economy, then returns realized by investors will deviate from what was expected. It is therefore possible to envisage realized returns as the sum of the return initially expected by investors and a deviation component, or surprise effect, caused by inaccurate factor predictions. Moreover, the extent of the discrepancy will depend on the security's own response to the economic factors.

Suppose, for example, that inflation and industrial production are the only two economic factors impinging on security returns. Then, actual returns will consist of the predicted returns plus the surprise effects, caused by the unanticipated deviations of interest rates and inflation from expectation. The magnitude of the surprise effect will depend on the security's own sensitivity to inflation and interest rates:

Actual Return = Expected Return
+
Inflation Surprise × Sensitivity to Inflation
+
Interest Rate Surprise × Sensitivity to Interest Rates

In equation form,

$$R = E(R) + B_1F_1 + B_2F_2 \tag{11-1}$$

where R = actual return
$E(R)$ = expected return
B_1 = sensitivity to factor 1
B_2 = sensitivity to factor 2
F_1 = economic factor 1
F_2 = economic factor 2

For example, suppose that a utility has a sensitivity of 2 to inflation. Investors were predicting an inflation rate of 8%, but the actual inflation rate turned out to be 10%, then actual returns will deviate by 4% from prediction. The 2% surprise in inflation is magnified into a 4% discrepancy between actual and expected return. The sensitivity factor can be thought of as an inflation beta of 2. A similar "factor beta" exists for interest rate effects, and for any other systematic economic factors acting pervasively upon all security returns. The higher the security's factor sensitivity, the greater its exposure risk to that factor.

Actual security returns are also influenced by factors unique to the company, factors unrelated to macroeconomic developments. These forces were referred to as "specific risk" in earlier discussions of the CAPM. An additional term must be added to the actual return equation above in order to recognize the impact of unexpected company specific events.

$$R = E(R) + B_1F_1 + B_2F_2 + e \qquad (11\text{-}2)$$

where e = return on specific factors

As was the case with the CAPM, company specific risks can be eliminated by diversification, whereby the impacts of specific events on a portfolio will cancel out by virtue of the law of large numbers. The returns on portfolios will be dominated by systematic factors and will be largely immune to company specific effects. It follows that the only risk of concern to investors will be the exposure to factor risks.

Equation 11-2 represents the first fundamental assumption of the APM, and describes the process which is assumed to generate security returns. While the existence of two factors was assumed for expository convenience, empirical research by Roll & Ross (1980) suggests the existence of at least 3 or 4 important factors. Expression 11-2 can be generalized to accommodate any number of factors:

$$R = E(R) + B_1F_1 + B_2F_2 + B_3F_3 + \ldots + B_k F_k + e \qquad (11\text{-}3)$$

In summary, APM asserts that security returns are generated by the multi-factor model of Equation 11-3. In words, the equation says that for each security investors have an expected return in mind, but that certain economic forces, or factors, may lead to actual results which differ from initial investor expectations. This feature of the APM is reasonable and quite consistent with the prevailing practice by investment managers of fitting securities into different behavioral groups.

The second conceptual building block underlying the APM is that there must be a particular relationship between expected return (cost of capital) and the systematic risk measures for a given security if no riskless profit opportunities are to be found in capital markets. This relationship is developed as follows.

If there is a risk-free asset with no systematic exposure to economic factors, then investors will require at least this much return from a security plus a premium for compensation to factor risks:

Expected Return = Risk-free Return + Factor Risk Premiums

Only the risks of exposure to unanticipated changes in the economic factors are systematic and thus deserve compensation. All other risks can be eliminated by diversification. The amount of extra return for a given risk factor will depend on the security's exposure to that factor, as measured by its sensitivity to that factor, and on the price of risk associated with the factor. Going back to the initial example of two systematic factors, namely inflation exposure and interest rate exposure, the expected return on a security can be represented as:

Expected Return = Risk-free Return
+
Sensitivity to Inflation × Risk Premium for Inflation
+
Sensitivity to Interest Rates × Risk Premium for Interest Rates

In equation form,

$$E(R) = R_f + B_1[F_1 - R_f] + B_2[F_2 - R_f] \tag{11-4}$$

Equation 11-4 asserts that a security's expected return will be a linear function of the security's sensitivity to the two common factor movements. Generalizing to the case of 'n' factors, and letting r_i stand for the market price for risk related to factor 'i', the fundamental APM relationship emerges:

$$E(R) = R_f + B_1r_1 + B_2r_2 + \ldots + B_nr_n \tag{11-5}$$

EXAMPLE

Consider the three-factor APM model:

$$E(R) = R_f + B_1r_1 + B_2r_2 + B_3r_3$$

The risk-free return is 8%, and a public utility has the following risk coefficients with respect to the three factors: $B_1 = 0.40$, $B_2 = 0.10$, $B_3 = 0.80$. The risk premiums are 7%, 2%, and 5% for each of the three factors respectively. The cost of capital is then computed by substituting the requisite values in the above equation:

$$K = 8\% + 0.40 \times 7\% + 0.10 \times 2\% + 0.80 \times 5\%$$
$$= \underline{15\%}$$

The crux of the APM is that an arbitrage process ensures that Equation

11-5 will prevail. The term arbitrage refers to the buying and selling pressures exerted on security prices by investors. These arbitrage forces will enforce the APM relationship of Equation 11-5. If returns deviate from what the equation predicts, profit-seeking investors step in and buy undervalued securities and sell overvalued securities thereby causing the equation to be true. To see how this arbitrage principle operates, consider for expository convenience the simple case of only one factor, say the market factor, shown in Figure 11-1. Since there is only one factor, Equation 11-5 becomes:

$$E(R) = R_f + B_1 r_1$$

which is the equation of a straight line, as depicted on Figure 11-1.

Consider 3 well diversified portfolios A, B, C, with respective factor betas of 0.80, 0.90, 1.00 and expected returns of 14%, 17%, and 18% respectively, as shown on Figure 11-1. Portfolio C is mispriced and lies above the APM risk-return relationship, presenting investors with an opportunity for arbitrage profits. By combining portfolio A and B into a new portfolio D, investors can create a new portfolio with the same risks as C. The risks of D will be a weighted average of the risks of A and B, and the expected return on D will also be a weighted average of the expected returns

Figure 11-1

A ONE-FACTOR ARBITRAGE PRICING MODEL

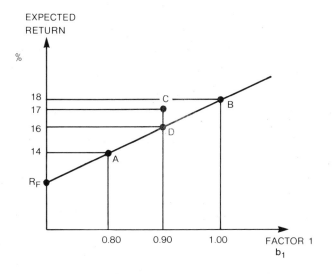

on A and B. If portfolio D consists of equal dollar amounts of A and B, the expected return on D will 16%, the average of the returns on A and B. The risk of D will be 0.90, the average of A and B's risks.

Investors will note that security C has the same risk as D, namely 0.90, but offers a higher return, 17%. Investors can capture a riskless arbitrage profit by selling short D, which is a combination of A and B, and by using the proceeds of the short sale to buy C. In doing so, investors will drive up C's price, and drive down A and C's prices, lowering the expected return on C and increasing the expected returns on A and B. The buying and selling will continue until all securities are located on the straight line. At this point, equilibrium is reached and each security's return will be a linear function of its systematic risk.

The important point in the above example is that the arbitrage profit is achieved with no net dollar outlay by investors and with no risk, since the long and short positions are perfectly offsetting. The APM equilibrium pricing relationship must prevail because riskless and costless arbitrage profit opportunities cannot exist in an efficient market.

The same idea can be extended to the case of more than one factor. In the case of two factors, each security's return will be a linear combination of its systematic risks with respect to the two factors. Each security will plot on a plane in final equilibrium, as illustrated schematically on Figure 11-2. All security returns will adjust until riskless arbitrage profits are eliminated, and all returns reside on plane ABCD. In the case of more than two factors, one can visualize each security as plotting on an "hyperplane" with the appropriate number of dimensions.

11.2 CAPM versus APM

The APM relationship embodied in Equation 11-5 asserts that the return on any risky security is equal to the risk-free rate plus a linear combination of risk premiums. Each risk premium is the expected return in excess of the risk-free rate associated with an asset that has a systematic risk with respect to that factor only. The CAPM is a special case of the APM if only one factor influences security prices, and if that factor happens to be the market portfolio. Under this circumstance, the APM collapses into the CAPM, and Equation 11-5 reduces to the CAPM with the coefficient B_1 transformed into the traditional security beta.

The assumptions underlying the APM are far less stringent than the assumptions required for the standard CAPM to obtain. The APM derives from two major assumptions: that security returns are linear functions of several economic factors as per Equation 11-2, and that no profitable

Figure 11-2

A TWO-FACTOR ARBITRAGE PRICING MODEL

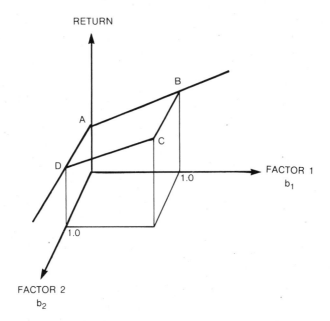

arbitrage opportunities exist since investors are able to eliminate such opportunities through riskless arbitrage transactions. The other assumptions required by the APM are that investors are greedy, risk averse, that they can diversify company-specific risks by holding large portfolios, and that enough investors possess similar expectations to trigger the arbitrage process.

The market portfolio plays no special role in the APM; it may or may not be one of the relevant factors affecting security prices. As such, the APM is immune to Roll's critique that the CAPM is inherently untestable. Unlike the CAPM, the APM has a more general theoretical structure. It does not require the assumptions of a single holding period and can easily be extended to a multiperiod framework. Nor does it require unrestricted borrowing and lending at the risk-free rate, and that investors select portfolios solely on the basis of their expected returns and standard deviation of returns. The APM makes no explicit assumptions about the empirical distribution of asset returns. The APM is a statement about the relative pricing of any subset of securities, and therefore one need not measure the entire universe of securities in order to test the model.

The chief attraction of the APM is that it allows security returns to depend on more than one factor, not just beta. The APM can easily accommodate the effect of changes in several economic factors on security returns. For example, it is quite plausible that a public utility has a different pattern of sensitivities to underlying economic forces than the average industrial stock. But since the traditional CAPM beta of a utility only measures how sensitive the utility is to the particular mix of economic factors in an aggregate stock index such as the Value Line Composite Index, the CAPM provides a distorted estimate of a utility's cost of capital. It could very well be that utilities are more inflation-sensitive and less GNP- sensitive than the average stock. An APM-based cost of capital estimate would recognize this differential sensitivity, while a CAPM-based estimate would ignore it.

Chen (1981, 1983) performed a direct empirical comparison of the APM and the CAPM by fitting both models to historical return data. The unexplained residual portion of the returns explained by the CAPM was statistically related to the APM's factor coefficients; similarly, the unexplained residual portion of the returns explained by the APM was statistically related to the CAPM coefficients. The results showed that the APM could explain a significant portion of the CAPM's unexplained return portion but that the CAPM could not explain the APM return residual. Chen concluded that the APM was a more potent model for explaining security returns.

Fogler (1982) addressed the more general question of whether the APM is really any different from the more general multiple-factor extensions of the CAPM enunciated in the previous chapter, and concluded that the severity of the required assumptions and the testability requirements favor the APM. Whether one subscribes to the APM or to the multiple-factor CAPM, Fogler argues correctly that although the theoretical framework of the models differ, the empirical issue boils down to identifying the factors and developing the indexes necessary to capture the systematic sources of security returns.

In summary, the APM is based on less stringent assumptions than the CAPM, does not require the identification of the true market portfolio, and is not restricted to a single holding-period. The disadvantage of the APM is that the number or identity of the factors are unspecified.

11.3 EMPIRICAL EVIDENCE

Studies by Gehr (1975), Roll & Ross (1980), Reinganum (1981) and Chen (1981, 1983) have tested the APM using historical daily return data on publicly listed common stocks. These studies are generally supportive of the

APM. These studies typically employ a statistical technique known as "factor analysis" to establish if multiple factors explain security returns better than a single factor. Factor analysis determines the number of variables driving a given series of observations, here security returns, based on the observed covariance relationships between series of observations. The number of factors and their sensitivity coefficients are statistically derived from the data itself, rather than postulated as predetermined economic phenomena, based on the ability of the factors to reproduce the covariance structure observed within a set of historical returns. The results obtained by Gehr and Roll & Ross indicate that there are 3 and possibly 4 factors that systematically influence security prices. In most of these studies, addition of specific company variables such as size or standard deviation risk did not add significantly to the explanation of security returns, consistent with the APM. The only exception is Reignanum who refutes the APM on the grounds that it cannot account for the effect of company size on security returns.

For cost of capital estimation purposes, the important issue is to identify the actual factors at work. Ross & Roll's (1980) own research suggests that 3 of the most important underlying economic forces are unanticipated movements in inflation, in industrial production, and in the general cost of risk bearing. Based on innumerable empirical studies, it is safe to assert that the market portfolio is one of the factors, and that the traditional beta is a plausible factor loading for that factor. An industry effect was found by King (1966) and Farrell (1974). The results of Banz (1981) and Reinganum (1981) indicate a company size effect, and studies by Reinganum (1981A) and Basu (1977) indicate that Price/Earnings Ratios may be a factor for pricing securities. Dividend yield effects were documented in the previous chapter. A considerable amount of research is currently being conducted to expand knowledge of the specific macroeconomic forces influencing security returns.

Paradoxically, it is important to point out that identification of the factors is not necessary to use the APM as a cost of capital determination device, as long as the number of factors is known. The relationship between security returns and the associated factors can be expressed in terms of observable portfolios of securities. Since portfolio returns are dominated by systematic factors, different portfolios can be carefully selected in such a way that they each have different sensitivities to the systematic factors, and these portfolios can be used as indices for the factors. An example from Roll & Ross (1983) will illustrate. Suppose that there are two unknown factors which systematically influence returns. To estimate the cost of capital for a particular company, we need only find two large imperfectly correlated portfolios. If the two portfolios are not perfectly correlated, it follows that one is more heavily weighted towards one of the two unknown economic factors than the other. So, to determine a company's cost of capital, it is only necessary to calculate the security's sensitivity to each of these proxy or "mimicking" portfolios and use these sensitivities to calculate the cost of capital

11.4 APM AND UTILITY COST OF CAPITAL

At the time of this writing, the only APM empirical study specifically directed at public utilities' cost of capital is the study by Roll & Ross (1983). Using a three-factor model, Roll & Ross calculated the difference between the average historical monthly return and the return obtained by the standard CAPM for each of a sample of 131 regulated utility companies over the period 1925-1980. Consistently positive differences were obtained, indicating that the CAPM consistently underestimated the cost of capital for the sample utilities relative to their historical costs. They also calculated the difference between historical returns and the returns using the APM. The differences between actual capital costs and those predicted by the APM model were much smaller and essentially random, neither predominantly positive nor negative. The estimated costs of capital were on average significantly greater for the APM than for the CAPM. Roll & Ross conclude that by including additional forces which influence security risks, the APM does a superior job of explaining security returns than the CAPM. The CAPM is unable to capture the greater sensitivity of utility stocks to unanticipated inflation compared to unregulated companies, while the APM recognizes the sensitivity to inflation as a risk for which investors require compensation.

While the APM provides a superior method from both a conceptual and practical perspective for computing the cost of equity capital, the final verdict on the APM is still pending. It is still early to proclaim the APM as the natural successor to the CAPM. Considerable empirical problems remain, and much work remains to be done.

One troublesome aspect of the APM at this time is the inability to specify precisely the identity of the explanatory factors. Voluminous research on factor identification and on providing economic content to the APM is currently in progress. Of course, the CAPM is even more vulnerable in this regard, given the inability to find an acceptable proxy for the true market portfolio.

The process of delineating factors must extend beyond statistical estimation. The danger of developing statistically estimated factors based on the factor analysis approaches is that they may represent statistical artifacts devoid of economic meaning. Even if economically meaningful factors could be located, the question of their stability over time must be resolved. One important criterion in the search for relevant factors and indexes is that they remain stable in order of importance from period to period if they are to be used for predictive purposes. For example, if inflation sensitivity is found to be a crucial factor based on an analysis of the 1973-1981 period, and inflation abates in the 1982-1986 period because of consistent monetary and fiscal policies, the question arises as to whether an inflation index remains relevant for explaining security returns. The question also arises as to whether the covariance relationships between factors remain stable under a changed economic environment. Some initial evidence by Arnott (1980) indicates that factor betas are more stable than the CAPM betas.

The APM literature is burgeoning, following the same path the CAPM did over the last two decades. The identity of the factors, the method of calculating the factors, the stability of such factors are being explored. Controversies as to the testability and logical consistency of the APM are being raised, for example by Shanken (1982). Replies, rejoinders, and retaliations by academicians follow suit. Already, extensions to the APM are being formulated to enrich the content of the theory. It is only a matter of time before cost of capital witnesses before regulatory proceedings introduce the APM in cost of capital testimony. Pending the results of current research, the ECAPM provides a viable temporary alternative, with the impact of the systematic factors buried in the estimated coefficients.

CHAPTER **12**

COMPARABLE EARNINGS

12.1 RATIONALE

The comparable earnings standard has a long and rich history in regulatory proceedings, and finds its origins in the fair return doctrine enunciated by the U.S. Supreme Court in the landmark *Hope* case. The governing principle for setting a fair return decreed in *Hope* is that the allowable return on equity should be commensurate with returns on investments in other firms having comparable risks, and that the allowed return should be sufficient to assure confidence in the financial integrity of the firm, in order to maintain credit worthiness and ability to attract capital on reasonable terms. Two distinct standards emerge from this basic premise: a standard of capital attraction and a standard of comparable earnings. The capital attraction standard focuses on investors' return requirements, and is applied through market value methods described in prior chapters, such as DCF, CAPM, or Risk Premium. The Comparable Earnings standard uses the return earned on book equity investment by enterprises of comparable risks as the measure of fair return.

The Comparable Earnings approach stems from the traditional and widely accepted interpretation of the *Hope* language that returns are to be defined as book rates of return on equity of other firms. Book return on common equity is computed by dividing the earnings available to common shareholders by the book common equity. The approach rests on a particular notion of opportunity cost, namely that a utility should be allowed to earn what it would have earned had its capital been invested in other firms of comparable risk. A goal of fairness is said to be achieved by this. As pointed out by Myers (1972), this legal interpretation of returns stands in sharp contrast to financial theory which interprets returns as forward-looking market-determined returns, derived from the capital gains and dividends expectations of investors relative to stock prices.

To implement the approach, a group of companies comparable in risk to a specified utility is defined, the book return on equity is computed for each company, and the allowed return is set equal to the aggregate return on book value for the sample. The reference group of companies is usually made up of unregulated industrial companies of similar risk. The rationale of the method is that regulation is a duplicate for competition. The profitability of unregulated firms is set by the free forces of competition. In the long run, the free entry of competitors would limit the profits earned by these unregulated companies, and, conversely, unprofitable ventures and product lines would be abandoned by the unregulated companies. Aggregating book rates of return over a large number of unregulated companies would even out any abnormal short run profit aberrations, while averaging over time would dampen any cyclical aberrations. Thus, by averaging the book profitability of a large number of unregulated companies, an appropriate measure of the fair return on equity for a public utility is obtained[1].

12.2   ADVANTAGES OF COMPARABLE EARNINGS

The Comparable Earnings standard is easy to calculate, and the amount of subjective judgment required is minimal. The method avoids several of the subjective factors involved in other cost of capital methodologies. For example, the DCF approach requires the determination of the growth rate contemplated by investors, which is a subjective factor. The CAPM requires the specification of several expectational variables, such as market return and beta. In contrast, the Comparable Earnings approach makes use of simple readily available accounting data; return on book equity data is widely available on computerized data bases for most public companies and for a wide variety of market indices.

The method is easily understood, and is firmly anchored in regulatory tradition. The method is not influenced by the regulatory process to the same extent as market-based methods such as DCF and CAPM. The base to which the comparable earnings standard is applicable is the utility's book common equity, which is much less vulnerable to regulatory influences than stock price which is the base to which the market-based standards are applied. Stock price can be influenced by the actions of regulators.

12.3   PRACTICAL DRAWBACKS

To implement the Comparable Earnings standard, all that is required is a sample of comparable risk companies and an appropriate time period over which book equity returns are measured. The apparent simplicity of the method is overshadowed by several practical difficulties encountered in executing the method, some of which are more illusory than real.

Risk Comparability

One frequent objection to the Comparable Earnings approach is that the search for companies of comparable risk is a difficult task. The arsenal of quantitative and qualitative measures of risk described in Chapter 4 provides a solid basis for identifying firms in a comparable risk class. For example, a list of comparable companies comparable in risk to a specified utility might be screened from a computer data base according to the following criteria: (1) they should have a standard deviation of market return and/or beta as close as possible to the subject utility; (2) they should be publicly traded companies to ensure data availability; (3) they should have a given Value Line rating indicating a degree of safety similar to the subject utility; (4) they should have a given Standard & Poor's quality rating, comparable to the subject utility; and (5) the companies should be non-regulated industrials so as to avoid circularity problems. Any of a myriad of risk screening criteria can be used, such as bond ratings, and various accounting ratios. It is probably easier to generate a set of comparable risk companies than it is to measure accurately the input quantities required in alternate cost of capital estimating techniques, such as DCF and CAPM.

It is sometimes alleged that the Comparable Earnings method matches accounting book rates of return with market-based risk techniques, and is thus inconsistent. To circumvent this objection, risk measures based on accounting returns can be used such as the variability of book return on equity over a certain time period or its average deviation around trend. Market-based risk measures are nevertheless valid, for the relevant risk of a share of common stock is the risk to which its shareholder is exposed, and this is best measured by market-based variables.

Circularity

In defining a population of comparable risk companies, care must be taken not to include other utilities in the sample, since the rate of return on other utilities depend on the allowed rate of return. The book return on equity for regulated firms is not determined by competitive forces but instead reflects the past actions of regulatory commissions. It would be hopelessly circular to set a fair return based on the past actions of other regulators, much like observing a series of duplicate images in multiple mirrors. The rates of return earned by other regulated utilities may very well have been reasonable under historical conditions, but they are still subject to tests of reasonableness under current and prospective conditions.

Time Period

Historical returns on equity vary from year to year, responding to the cyclical forces of recession and expansion and to economic, industry-specific and company-specific trends. The choice of time period may thus exert a marked influence on the outcome of the comparable earnings standard. Aggregating returns over a large number of comparable risk unregulated firms averages the abnormally high and low rates of profitability in any given year. Furthermore, to remove the cyclical peaks and troughs in profitability, an average over several time periods should be employed. If there is a time trend in the average returns of the sample, a time trend normalized return would be more appropriate.

A useful rough-and-ready variant of this approach, which could be labeled as "real comparable earnings" analysis, consists of examining the adequacy of unregulated companies' current book returns in relation to varying inflationary environments. For example, say that a given utility has the same degree of risk as the average stock market investment. The Standard & Poor's 400 Industrials Index provides a ready-made comparable risk group of companies. If from 1964-1983, the book equity returns of the S&P 400 averaged 15%, and the rate of inflation over the corresponding period was 6%, then annual real return must have averaged 9%. If the current or forecast inflation rate is 5%, an average prospective return on book equity for the S&P 400 index of 14% would be required to maintain a real return comparable to past experience.

A theoretically superior method of assessing real returns is to work with formal inflation-adjusted financial statements where reported earnings and equity book values are adjusted for inventory profits, replacement cost depreciation, and for the monetary gains of debt financing. Holland & Myers (1979) have studied the real returns of U.S. corporations using the national income accounts. The complexity and data requirements involved in applying these methods are probably not worth the practical benefits. Inflation accounting remains a controversial topic. More importantly, accounting rates of return possess conceptual blemishes which far outweigh any the benefits of applying formal inflation adjustments. This is discussed in the next section.

Some analysts confine their return study to the most recent time period. One difficulty with this approach is the lag in the availability of accounting data. Frequently, the most recent accounting data available is already one year old, notwithstanding the fact that rates will not become effective until an even later date. Another difficulty with this approach is that in the short run reported book profitability frequently moves in the opposite direction to interest rates and to investors' required returns. For example, a period of disinflation and falling interest rates will increase company earnings and earned equity returns, while investors' return requirements are falling, and conversely.

Measurement Error

Despite the umbrella of generally acceptable accounting principles, intercompany comparisons of book rates of return are computationally misleading because of differences in intercompany accounting. Major areas of difference include the treatment of inventory valuation, depreciation, investment tax credits, deferred taxes, and extraordinary items. The lack of accounting homogeneity is exacerbated by the necessity of studying nonregulated companies, which are likely to exhibit greater accounting differences. As a practical matter, such differences pale in comparison to the problems of risk estimation and time period discussed earlier, and may be somewhat attenuated by employing reasonably diverse aggregates in the reference group. If the companies in a particular reference group have clear identifiable differences in accounting treatment, the latter should be used as an additional screening criterion to eliminate such companies, or the accounting rates of return should be restated on a consistent comparable basis.

12.4   CONCEPTUAL SHORTCOMINGS

Accounting rates of return are not based on opportunity cost in the economic sense, but reflect the average returns earned on past investments, and hence reflect past regulatory actions. The denominator of accounting return, book equity, is an historical cost-based concept, which is insensitive to changes in investor return requirements. Only stock market price is sensitive to a change in investor requirements. Investors can only purchase new shares of common stock at current market prices, and not at book value. If book value per share coincides with market price, the market-to-book ratio is one, indicating that the utility is earning its cost capital; there is no need for a regulatory hearing, and the issue is moot.

Another way of expressing the above argument is that the Comparable Earnings standard ignores capital markets. If interest rates go up 2% for example, investor requirements and the cost of equity should increase commensurately, but if regulation is based on accounting returns, no change in equity cost results. Investors capitalize expected future cash flows, and not current earnings, and what was earned on book value is not directly related to current market rates.

Another conceptual problem is that when the utility's current book rate of return is compared to that of firms of comparable risk, it is assumed that there is a fundamental theoretical relationship between accounting returns and risk. But no such relationship exists in financial theory. The risk-return tradeoff found in financial theory is expressed in terms of market values rather than in terms of accounting values. Only if long time periods are examined and broad aggregates are used can an empirical relationship between risk and accounting return be found. In those circumstances, accounting return will act as a valid proxy for investor expectations since over long time periods, investor expectations are realized.

One of the fundamental assumptions of the Comparable Earnings method is that the comparable risk firms' accounting returns are equal to their cost of capital, or in other words, that realized book returns are an adequate surrogate for expected returns. To visualize this assumption more clearly, one can think of the problem in terms of Figure 12-1, which represents a probability distribution of returns envisaged by investors. What the Comparable Earnings standard is attempting to measure is the return expected (cost of capital), or the mean of the distribution. But the actual realized return in any given time period represents but a single outcome on the distribution, which may be far removed from initial investor expectations. This problem is not unique to the Comparable Earnings method. Any method which relies on historical data is vulnerable to this deficiency. To maximize the possibility that historical results will match expectations, the sample of companies studied should be large enough so that deviations from the mean return will cancel out. But such deviations will only cancel out if there are no systematic economy-wide effects acting upon all companies at the same time such as recession or expansion cycles. The remedy is to average actual book returns over long periods of time over several economic cycles.

It is sometimes alleged that if the average market-to-book ratio for the group of comparable risk companies is reasonably close to one, and if the standard DCF model is applicable to the companies in the group, then the sample companies are earning their cost of capital. If the average market-to-book ratio deviates markedly from one, then the group's average book return is not an adequate measure of cost of capital. This argument is valid only if actual realized book returns are in fact reflective of expected book returns. The market-to-book argument refers to expected book returns, and not to actual book returns. If realized book returns over a large aggregate of comparable risk companies over long time periods are taken as valid surrogates for expected book returns, then it is appropriate to compute market-to-book ratios in order to gauge whether these companies are expected to earn an amount more, less, or equal to their cost of capital.

To maximize the possiblity that the average book returns of the reference companies are in fact reflective of their cost of capital, a specified

Figure 12-1

PROBABILITY DISTRIBUTION OF RETURNS:
EXPECTED VS REALIZED OUTCOME

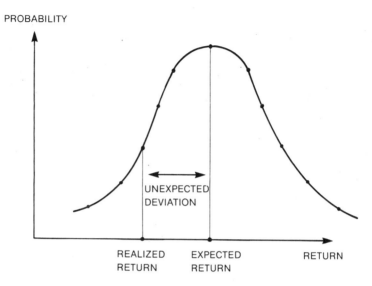

market-to-book ratio range should be applied on the sample companies as an additional screening criterion. It is sometimes difficult to identify unregulated companies comparable to utilities because unregulated companies with risk characteristics similar to that of utilities are often found in monopolistic or oligopolistic sectors of the economy. Such companies have market-to-book ratios in excess of one, as investors expect them to earn an amount in excess of their cost of capital. One way to circumvent this problem is to eliminate from the sample industries characterized by high concentration ratios.

More fundamentally, the basic premise of the Comparable Earnings approach is that regulation should emulate the competitive result. It is not clear from this premise which is the proper level of competition being referenced. Is the norm the perfect competition model of economics where no monopolistic elements exist, or is it the degree of competition actually prevailing in the economy?

Another fundamental assumption inherent in the Comparable Earnings standard is that accounting rates of return are in fact accurate measures of true economic rates of return. In times of variable inflation, it is obvious that this is not the case as was noted earlier in the inflation-accounting discussion. What is less obvious is that accounting returns are generally not valid measures of economic returns even in non-inflationary environments.

Book returns can be poor measures of true economic returns. The relationship between the two rates is a complex function of the age structure of a firm's assets, the company's growth, depreciation policy, and inflation. As a crude illustration, the book return of a utility with aged assets will exceed that of a company with relatively new assets, all else remaining constant.

Several academic studies, notably by Solomon (1970), Solomon & Laya (1967), Fisher & McGowan (1981), have confirmed the strong disparity between accounting and true economic return and that the biases inherent in book returns are systematic and do not cancel out in the averaging process. To avoid the circularity problem, it was suggested earlier that the reference group of companies be made up of unregulated companies. But, given that rates are set on the basis of a book value rate base in most jurisdictions, the economic value of a utility is likely to be in closer concordance with its book value. Thus, the biases in book returns of unregulated firms are inherently more serious than the biases for regulated firms.

All of the conceptual flaws in the Comparable Earnings standard discussed in this section boil down to a repudiation of the core assumption that accounting rates of return are valid proxies for opportunity costs. The Comparable Earnings test does not rest well with economic theory. But if the basic purpose of comparable earnings is not to determine the true economic return, then all the arguments of this section evaporate. If regulation considers a fair return as one which is equal to the book rates of return earned by comparable risk firms rather than one which is equal to the cost of capital of such firms, the Comparable Earnings test is relevant. This narrow definition of fairness, rooted in the traditional legalistic interpretation of the *Hope* language, validates the Comparable Earnings test.

If regulation is a substitute for competition, and if the cost of capital is to play the same role in utilities as in unregulated industries, then the allowed rate of return should be set in excess of the cost of capital. The reason, as articulated by Friend (1983), is that the economic criterion employed by corporations in their investment decisions is that the expected marginal return on new projects be greater than the cost of capital. Corporations rank investment projects in descending order of profitability, and successively adopt all investment projects to the point where the least attractive project has a return equal to the cost of capital. The average return on all new investment projects will then exceed the cost of capital. If the average, rather than the marginal, return is set equal to the cost of capital as is the case with Comparable Earnings, the implication is that a company also accepts investment projects which are less profitable than the cost of capital, so that the average return on all projects accepted is equal to the cost of capital. Corporate investment would largely cease under such a scheme. Moreover, if unregulated companies were to pursue such an investment policy, a serious misallocation of economic resources would ensue.

Notes

[1] For illustrative implementation of the Comparable Earnings approach, see Morin (1983), Litzenberger (1979), and Nathan (1982).

CHAPTER 13

MARKET-TO-BOOK AND Q-RATIOS

This chapter discusses the practical applications of Market-to-Book Ratios in the determination of equity capital cost. The first section establishes the formal relationship between the allowed return on equity, the cost of equity, and the Market-to-Book Ratio (P/B). This relationship can be used to find the cost of equity consistent with the observed P/B ratio, given investors' return on equity expectations. The second section demonstrates how the DCF cost of equity figure is transformed into an appropriate allowed return on equity, based on a target P/B ratio. The importance of maintaining a P/B slightly in excess of one is underscored. The third section discusses the estimation of cost of equity capital based on the multivariate statistical analysis of the determinants of P/B ratios. The fourth section describes the Q-Ratio approach to determining the cost of equity capital. The last section discusses the use of coverage ratios in determining equity costs.

In Chapter 1, it was suggested that if regulators set the allowed rate of return equal to the cost of capital, the utility's earnings will be just sufficient to cover the claims of the bondholders and shareholders. No wealth transfer between ratepayers and shareholders will occur.

The direct financial consequence of setting the allowed return on equity, r, equal to the cost of equity capital, K, is that share price is driven towards book value per share. Intuitively, if r > K, and is expected to remain so, then market price will exceed book value per share since shareholders are obtaining a return in excess of their opportunity cost. But if r < K, and is expected to remain so, market price will be below book value per share since the utility is failing to achieve its opportunity cost. A simple idealized example will illustrate this important point.

EXAMPLE

Consider a utility with a book value of equity per share of $10, and let us say that the market's required return on equity is 18% for firms in that risk class. If the $10 book value of equity is allowed to earn $1.80 per share, or 18%, the market price will set at $10, since the market's required return at that price will be also $1.80 / $10, or 18%. If, on the other hand, the $10 book equity per share is allowed to earn say only 9%, the market price has to fall to $5.00 in order for the market's required return to be 18%, that is, $0.90 / $5, or 18%. A public utility's market value will equal book value only if it consistently earns a book return equal to the cost of equity.

13.1 MARKET-TO-BOOK RATIOS AND THE COST OF CAPITAL

The relationship between r, K, P/B and the circumstances under which share price and book value are equal can be articulated from a simple manipulation of the standard DCF equation. Starting from the seminal DCF model:

$$P_0 = D_1 / K-g \qquad (13\text{-}1)$$

and expressing next year's dividend, D_1, as next year's earnings per share, E_1, times the earnings payout ratio, $(1-b)$, we have:

$$D_1 = (1-b)E_1 \qquad (13\text{-}2)$$

Substituting the latter equation into Equation 13-1:

$$P_0 = \frac{E_1(1-b)}{K-g} \qquad (13\text{-}3)$$

But next year's earnings per share, E_1, are equal to the expected rate of return on equity, r, times the book value of equity per share, B, at the end of the current year:

$$E_1 = rB \qquad (13\text{-}4)$$

Substituting Equation 13-4 in Equation 13-3:

$$P_0 = \frac{rB(1-b)}{K-g} \qquad (13\text{-}5)$$

Dividing both sides of the equation by B, and noting that $g = br$:

$$P_o/B = \frac{r(1-b)}{K-br} = \frac{r-br}{K-br} \qquad (13\text{-}6)$$

From Equation 13-6, it is clear that the market-to-book ratio, P/B will be unity if $r = K$, will be greater than unity if $r > K$, and less than unity if $r < K$:

$$P/B \gtrless 1 \text{ as } r \gtrless K \qquad (13\text{-}7)$$

For a given company, the relationship between P/B and return on equity embodied in Equation 13-6 is graphed on Figure 13-1 for a given K, and for different retention ratios. The graph shows that if the true cost of equity is known, and a return on equity equal to K is allowed and investors expect this return to be earned, then the P/B ratio will equal one. If the allowed return is less (more) than K, the P/B ratio will be less (more) than one. The exact shape of the graph in Figure 13-1 varies with the retention ratio and with K; the graph becomes steeper with rising retention ratios, with the effect depending on the value of the return on equity. Issuance of additional shares of stock also steepens the graph, indicating lower P/B ratios if K is greater than the expected book return on equity, and conversely. As pointed out by Brigham, Shome & Bankston (1979), the graph is approximately a straight line over a reasonable range of K and allowed return on equity.

An observed disparity between market value and book value for a particular utility suggests that realized rate of return on the book value of common equity, or the expected magnitude of the latter, differs from the market cost of common equity, for whatever reason. Solving Equation 13-6 for K, a basic measure of cost of equity adjusted for the prevailing P/B ratio is obtained:

$$K = \frac{r(1-b)}{P/B} + br \qquad (13\text{-}8)$$

In words, Equation 13-8 demonstrates that finding the cost of equity reconcilable to the book return on common equity requires that the latter be increased/decreased by the market-to-book ratio in proportion of the fraction of income distributed as dividends. Equation 13-8 provides a method of finding the cost of equity capital that is consistent with the observed P/B ratio.

EXAMPLE

The market value of a utility's common stock has fallen to 75% of its

Figure 13-1

THE RELATIONSHIP BETWEEN THE MARKET-TO-BOOK
RATIO AND THE ALLOWED RATE OF RETURN

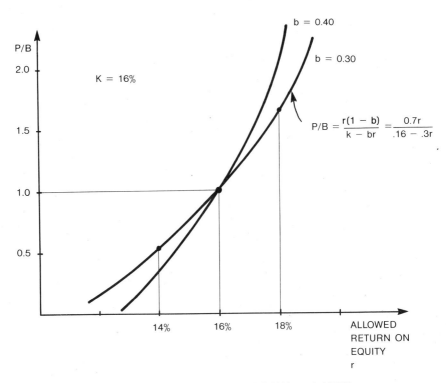

SOURCE: ADAPTED FROM BRIGHAM, et al. (1979)

book value. Realized return on book equity expected by investors is 15%. Earnings are divided evenly between dividends and retentions.

$$b = .50 \ = \ (1 - b)$$
$$r = .15$$

The cost of common equity reconciliable with the observed P/B ratio is:

$$K = \frac{r(1 - b)}{P/B} + br$$

$$= \frac{.15 \times .50}{0.75} + 0.50 \times .15$$

$$= .10 + .075 = .175 \text{ or } 17.5\%$$

This method provides a useful check on the results obtained from other methods. One cautionary note is that the *expected* return on book equity rather than the *currently allowed* return on equity must be used, because the P/B ratio is determined by what investors expect regulators to do, and not by what the regulators did in the past. A serious circularity problem may arise if the current allowed return on equity is used because the numerator of the P/B ratio is stock price, which reflects the expected allowed return and not the currently allowed return. Applying the approach to a sample of comparable risk firms in the same industry will mitigate the circularity problem somewhat.

While straightforward application of the DCF approach will drive share price toward book value per share, it must be true that the utility can actually be expected to earn the rate set for regulatory purposes. Several factors can cause the utility to earn more or less than is nominally allowed. Delay in instituting new regulatory proceedings, or regulatory lag, can cause the utility to earn more or less than is prescribed. If cost trends deviate from expectations in the case of a forward test year jurisdiction, or if unexpected future changes in cost and output levels occur, regulatory lag will cause the utility to earn more or less than is allowed.

Other external factors will impinge on the market-to-book ratio. Diversification into nonregulated fields may cause the ratio to deviate from one, even though the profitability of the regulated portion is restricted. Even if all the firm's activities are regulated, if assets are excluded from rate base, or if CWIP does not appear in rate base and no AFUDC is allowed on CWIP, rate base will not equal net book value, and the market-to-book ratio will not equal one. In summary, in order for the market-to-book ratio to converge to unity, the actual return that investors expect the utility to earn on its rate base must equal its cost of capital, not the allowed rate of return.

13.2 TARGET MARKET-TO-BOOK RATIOS AND THE COST OF EQUITY

The previous section developed a method of estimating the cost of equity based on observed market-to-book ratios. The process is now reversed. This section demonstrates how the cost of equity figure obtained from standard DCF can be translated into an appropriate allowed rate of return on book equity to take into account any sanctioned difference between market price and book value. The magnitude of the adjustment will depend on the choice of target P/B ratio. The technique is labeled the Target Market-to-Book Method.

Various arguments can be made to the effect that allowed rates of return on book equity should be sufficient to sustain a given market price. For example, continued access to the equity capital market requires a market price at, or somewhat above, book value to insure salability of new equity issues. Duplication of the result that would obtain in an unregulated competitive environment requires a market-to-book premium similar to that which prevails for unregulated firms.

Capital Attraction and Market-to-Book Ratios

A strong case can be made for a market price at least equal to book value. One of the fundamental indicators of a utility's financial integrity is the ability to raise equity capital under favorable conditions. This is especially crucial in the case of public utilities whose needs for external equity are frequent, inflexible, and large. It is a well known fact noted by several finance scholars that if a company sells stock at less than book value, the book value of the previously outstanding shares will be diluted, and so will the earnings per share, dividends per share, and earnings growth. Moreover, it becomes increasingly difficult to distribute the same dollar dividends on an increased number of shares outstanding, and investors will become increasingly reticent in accepting any further stock issues.

In Commonwealth of Massachusetts. *New England Telephone and Telegraph Co.* v. *Department of Public Utilities*, 354 N.E. 2d 860, 867. (Mass. 1976), the Massachusetts State Supreme Court ruled:

> "If new stock yields net proceeds less than book value, the equity of existing shareholders is diluted; and forced dilution is confiscation..." (p. 860)

> "We conclude that a market-to-book ratio of 1.2 to 1 is the minimum necessary to compensate the Company adequately for selling costs and market pressure." (p. 867)

The following numerical example illustrates the adverse consequences for both ratepayers and stockholders of selling stock below book value.

EXAMPLE

Consider a utility with $500 of plant investments, all equity-financed, with 20 common shares outstanding. The book value per share is therefore $500 / 20, or $25. The allowed rate of return is 10%, and the market's required return is 20%.

Earnings will total 10% x $500 = $50, and earnings per share will be $50 / 20 = $2.50. The stock price is therefore $2.50 / .20 = $12.50, or half of the book value per share since the allowed return is one half of the required return. The market-to-book ratio is P/B = 0.50.

What happens if the utility requires an additional $500 of assets to be financed by a $500 stock issue with each share selling for $12.50? The company is allowed to earn an additional $50 on this incremental investment (.10 x $500), for a total earnings figure of $100. To finance an amount of $500 at $12.50 per share requires the issuance of 40 additional shares, bringing the total number of shares from 20 to 60. Earnings per share decline to $100 / 60 = $1.67, and the price of each share drops to $1.67 / .20 = $8.55 in order for shareholders to continue earning 20%. The book value per share drops from $25 to $1000/60 = $16.67. Summarizing the results in tabular form:

	BEFORE	AFTER
Equity capital	$500	$1000
Number of shares	20	60
Book value per share	$25	$16.67
Earnings (10% of equity)	$50	$100
Earnings per share	$2.50	$1.67
Market price (20% return)	$12.50	$8.35
Market-to-book ratio	0.50	0.50

Therefore, sale of stock when the P/B ratio is less than one dilutes the share in ownership of the original holders of the 20 shares. The book value for each share they own declines from $25 to $16.67, since the new equity capital base is now shared among 60 shares. The market price drops by 52% as a consequence of the equity dilution.

The above example does not imply that utilities cannot in fact raise capital when share prices are below book value, but that they can only do so at the expense of existing shareholders. When expected earnings are less than investors' requirements and a sale of stock occurs, new shareholders can only expect to gain their return requirement at the expense of the old shareholders. The market recognizes the potential dilution impact and reprices the shares downward as protection of the required return.

A regulatory policy of setting the allowed return such as to obtain a P/B ratio of at least one avoids such deliberate economic confiscation and abides by the financial integrity criterion of the *Hope* case and the financial soundness criterion of the *Bluefield* case. Such a policy is also in the interests of ratepayers. Systematic dilution of equity imposed on shareholders, because of deficient earnings, endangers the success of the next stock issue. Investor uncertainties as to whether reasonable earnings will be allowed are raised, thereby increasing the cost of debt and equity.

EXAMPLE

The effects of selling stock below, and above, book value, are illustrated by the following example. The allowed return is assumed to be 15%, and the dividend payout 60%. The financial data before any contemplated stock issue are as follows:

	BEFORE
Current equity	$500
Shares	20
Book Value per share	$25
Return on Equity (15%)	$75
Earnings per share	$3.75
Dividends per share (60%)	$2.44
Total dividends	$48.80

Assume that $50 of new common stock is sold at 80% of book value, or $20 per share.

	AFTER
New Equity	$50
Price per share	$20
New shares	2.5
Total shares outstanding	22.5
(20 initial + 2.5 new)	
Total equity (500 + 50)	$550
New book value per share	$24.44
(550 / 22.5)	
Return on equity (15% of 550)	$82.5
Earnings per share (82.5 / 22.5)	$3.66
Total Dividends (2.44 × 22.5)	$54.9

The detrimental effects of selling stock below book to both shareholders and ratepayers are noteworthy. The sale of stock below book value requires a higher rate of return on equity just to stay even. To maintain original earnings per share of $3.75 after the sale of common shares below book value, the company must now have earnings of $84.4: 22.5 shares outstanding x $3.75 = $84.4. To earn $84.4 however, the company must have a rate of return on equity of 15.34%: $550 x 15.34% = $84.4.

Conversely, let us assume the stock can be marketed at 120% of book value.

	AFTER
New equity	$50
Price per share	$30
New shares	1.7
Total shares outstanding	21.7
(20 initial + 1.7 new)	
Total equity (550 + 50)	$550
New book value per share	$25.35
(550 / 21.7)	
Return on equity (15% × 550)	$82.5
Earnings per share	$3.80
($82.5 / 21.7)	
Total dividends ($2.44 × 21.7)	$52.9

It is noteworthy that the company will seek more in rates from the customer if the stock is sold below book than if the stock is sold above book value, because of the added dividend burden imposed by an increased number of shares. Thus, if the stock is sold at 20% below book value compared with selling at 20% above book value the ratepayer will be asked to pay the company $2 more in rates. This can be a substantial amount in practice given the tens of millions of dollars typically involved in a utility's equity base.

The costs of floating common stock, including the underwriter spread, market pressure, and allowance for market break, have been ignored thus far. The nature and magnitude of issue costs were addressed extensively in Chapter 6. A market price sufficiently above book so that the net proceeds after costs of issue from the sale of new stock are greater than book value, will enable a company to attract capital on terms which do not dilute the value of existing shares. The return allowed by the regulator should be such that neither confiscation of old equity nor dilution of new equity occurs.

Adjustment for Target Market-to-Book Ratio

The adjustment to the cost of equity capital to obtain an allowed return on book equity revised to account for any sanctioned difference between market price and book value is obtained from the standard DCF equation. Solving Equation 13-6 for 'r':

$$r = P/B \ (K - g) + g \qquad (13\text{-}9)$$

Equation 13-9 defines the return on book value required to be earned such that the investor will receive his required rate of return and the target P/B ratio will be maintained.

EXAMPLE

The cost of equity for a utility is 15%, as determined by the standard DCF process. The growth component of that return is 5%. The commission which regulates the utility is on record as stating that its regulatory intention is to allow a rate of return such that the utility's stock will sell at 1.1 times book value to avoid dilution. The allowed return on book equity follows from Equation 13-9:

$$r = 1.1(.15 - .05) + .05 = .16 \text{ or } \underline{16\%}$$

To illustrate yet another use of the general DCF formula, the next example combines the Target Market-to-Book Ratio approach with the Finite Horizon model enunciated in the first section of Chapter 6.

EXAMPLE

A regulatory commission advocates a market-to-book ratio of 1.1. This fact is known to investors, but, at present, the stock is trading at book value exactly. It is assumed that current dividends are $5, book value per share is $76.43, the long-run expected growth is 7%, and that investors expect the recovery of stock price to take place in one period. In other words, regulatory lag lasts one period. From the general Limited Horizon model of Equation 6-2 in Chapter 6:

$$P_o = \frac{D_o(1 + g)}{1 + K} + \frac{1.10 \ B_o(1 + g)}{1 + K}$$

$$(13\text{-}10)$$

$$\$76^{43} = \frac{\$5 \ (1 + .07)}{1 + K} + \frac{1.10 \times \$76.43 \ (1 + .07)}{1 + K}$$

from which $K = 25\%$. Alternate assumptions on length of the recovery period can easily be handled by the general model of Equation 6-2.

13.3 ECONOMETRIC MODELS OF THE MARKET-TO-BOOK RATIO

Another approach to measure the cost of equity capital consists of statistically estimating the market-to-book ratios for a sample of companies as a function of several explanatory variables, one of which is the expected book return on equity. Using the statistically-estimated relationship, the expected book return on equity which causes the P/B ratio to be one is the estimate of cost of equity capital.

Equation 13-6 is the conceptual departure point for the statistical model. From Equation 13-6, the P/B ratio is approximately a linear function of the expected book return on equity, 'r'. At first glance, it seems reasonable to relate statistically the P/B ratios and book equity returns for a sample of companies by the following linear relationship:

$$P/B = a_o + a_1 r \qquad (13\text{-}11)$$

where a_o and a_1 are constants.

Equation 13-11 is the basis for the so-called Comparable Earnings Pricing Technique (CEPT) employed by some analysts. The CEPT method assumes the market-to-book ratio achieved by a company is a function of the return on equity actually earned by that company. To implement the technique, Equation 13-11 is estimated statistically by regression techniques over a large sample of unregulated companies. From the estimated relationship, the return on equity which produces a market-to-book ratio of slightly above 1.00 is the cost of equity capital.

The technique has several flaws, both conceptually and empirically. The simplistic linear relation assumed between P/B and r does not fully explain the P/B ratios of the companies in a given sample. A simple regression of P/B ratios on return on equity is inappropriate because it presumes that every company in a given sample has the same risk, and growth rate. Additional variables are needed to fully explain actual P/B ratios. Studies which use the empirical relationship between return on equity and P/B ratios to infer the return necessary to produce a P/B ratio of 1 are misleading because they assume a constant invariant relationship between P/B ratios and equity returns for all firms, irrespective of their risk, growth, and dividend yield. Empirically, the regression relationship can be falsified by outlying points which distort the regression line away from the trends set by most of the points. The technique can also be criticized for failing to include other risk measures in addition to the P/B ratio in its selection of comparable companies. A wide range of returns may correspond with a specified range of P/B ratio.

A more realistic and general explanatory equation would take the form:

$$P/B = a_o + a_1 r + a_2 F_2 + a_3 F_3 + \ldots a_n F_n \qquad (13\text{-}12)$$

This equation asserts that a company's P/B ratio is a linear function of several explanatory factors, F_1, F_2, $F_3 \ldots F_n$, including the expected book return on equity. The magnitude and direction of the variables' effects on

P/B ratios are measured by the factor coefficients, a_1, a_2, ...a_n. Typical explanatory variables include growth, dividend yield, beta, standard deviation, and proxies for earnings quality, regulatory climate, and accounting convention. Multiple regression techniques are applied to Equation 13-12 over a sample of companies to produce estimates of the magnitude of these effects. Three examples will illustrate the methodology

EXAMPLE

Brigham, Shome, and Bankston (1979) specify the following P/B model for the domestic telephone industry:

$$P/B = a_o + a_1 \text{ (Book yield)} + a_2g + a_3 \text{ (Dummy)} \quad (13\text{-}13)$$

where Book Yield = Common dividends/Book equity
   g = expected growth rate
   Dummy = dummy variable = 1 for Bell companies
                    = 0 for non-Bell companies

Book yield is measured by multiplying the expected book return on equity, r, by the expected dividend payout rate, 1-b; growth is measured by the retention ratio method as 'br'. The required data for 13 domestic telephone companies were collected from 1978 annual reports, and the coefficients of the above equation were estimated by multiple regression techniques. The resulting equation was:

$$P/B = -0.4725 + 16.62 \text{ Book Yield} + 1.99 \text{ g} - 0.0425 \text{ Dummy}$$

The explanatory power of the regression, as measured by R^2, was 88%, which indicates a high degree of accuracy on the part of model's ability to explain P/B ratios. The coefficients all had the anticipated signs; companies with high book yields and high growth rates had higher P/B ratios; the dummy variable had a negative coefficient, indicating that Bell System telephone companies sell for higher P/B ratios than non-Bell companies.

Inserting a specified company's actual values for the explanatory variables in the fitted equation, the cost of equity is obtained by solving the fitted equation for the level of book equity return that makes the P/B ratio one. For example, if AT&T's 1978 dividend payout of 59% and retention ratio of 41% are inserted into the fitted equation, AT&T's cost of equity is found by solving the equation for 'r':

$$1 = -0.47 + 16.62 [r(1-b)] + 1.99 \text{ br} - .0425 \text{ Dummy}$$
$$1 = -0.47 + 16.67 [.59 r] + 1.99 (.41r) - .0425 \text{ x } 0$$

Solving for r, r = 13.78%. If the estimated equation is valid for AT&T, and if the target P/B ratio is 1, then regulators should set the allowed equity return at 13.78%.

EXAMPLE

Brigham, Shome, and Bankston estimate a slightly more complex equation to explain electric utilities' P/B ratios. The regression equation they used was:

$$P/B = a_0 + a_1(\text{Book yield}) + a_2 g + a_3(\text{Equity Ratio}) + a_4(\text{AFUDC}) + a_5 (\text{Flow-through Dummy}) + a_6(\text{Commission Ranking})$$

The equity ratio variable was added as a measure of financial risk, and the percentage of net income made up of AFUDC was added as a measure of earnings quality. A dummy variable to distinguish among utilities' regulatory climate, and a dummy variable to differentiate flow through from normalizing companies were also added. The model was estimated for 100 electric utilities with 1978 data. The fitted equation was:

$$P/B = -0.10 + 9.39 \ (\text{Book yield}) + 1.32g + 0.36 \ (\text{Equity Ratio}) - 0.04 \ (\text{AFUDC}) - 0.00 \ (\text{Flow-through Dummy}) + 0.08 \ (\text{Commission Ranking})$$

$$R^2 = 74\%$$

Inserting the 1978 values for Wisconsin Public Service, a 13.51% cost of equity was obtained by solving the above equation for the value of 'r' which produced a P/B ratio of 1.

EXAMPLE

Copeland (1979) develops a convenient and easy to use econometric model of the cost of equity for firms in a given risk class also derived in the traditional DCF mode. Solving for 'r' in Equation 13-6 , the valuation equation for a given firm in a sample of 'n' firms becomes:

$$r = br + (K - br) (P/B) \tag{13-14}$$

Copeland argues that expressing 'r' as a function of P/B rather than the other way around has the practical advantage of alleviating the measurement error in 'r', since the true expected book equity return can only be measured with error. To allow for interfirm variations in dividend yields, D/P, and expected growth rates, Copeland specifies the following two additional equations:

$$br = a_0 + a_1(D/P) \tag{13-15}$$

$$(k - br) = a_2(D/P) \tag{13-16}$$

These two equations together imply that if 'br' is a valid estimate of expected growth, then $(K - br)$ will equal D/P and a_2 will equal one, and thus a_0 will equal K, and a_1 will equal -1. The coefficients a_0, a_1, and a_2 should theoretically equal K, -1, and 1 respectively. Substituting the latter two equations into Equation 13-14 produces Copeland's basic model:

$$r = a_0 + a_1(D/P) + a_2(D/P)\ (P/B) \tag{13-17}$$

$$= a_0 + a_1(D/P) + a_2(D/B) \tag{13-18}$$

Equation 13-18 can either be estimated by the usual regression techniques or the following simple linear model can be estimated across a sample of comparable risk firms. The two approaches are equivalent.

$$r = a_0 - D/P + D/B \tag{13-19}$$

Copeland expresses a strong preference for the latter method on two grounds: first, econometric complications from the dependence between D/P and D/B are avoided; and second, the computations required to estimate the cost of equity, a_0, are extremely simple. Since the linear model must go through the point of averages for the variables, the cost of capital estimate follows simply and directly from the sample estimates of the average expected return on equity $\bar{r}$, average dividend yield, $\overline{D/P}$, and average book yield for the sample $\overline{D/B}$:

$$K = a_0 = \bar{r} + \overline{D/P} - \overline{D/B} \tag{13-20}$$

Copeland estimated the cost of equity from the above equation for a sample of 45 electric utilities for the years 1961-1976. The model provided a strong degree of explanatory power, and the cost of equity estimates were reasonable in that the implied risk premiums over bond yields were stable and plausible. One drawback of the Copeland method is that it is restricted to firms of comparable risk.

Like all other cost of capital estimation methods, P/B-based econometric models of equity costs have advantages and shortcomings. On the positive side, such models are firmly anchored on the foundations of DCF theory. The data required to implement the models are easily accessible in computer-readable form. The method makes the required judgment explicit, in contrast to other methods; econometric techniques facilitate the specification of confidence limits which can be used to establish a range of reasonableness for ratemaking purposes. The major contribution of the models is that they allow the user to make cost of capital comparisons between firms, while holding all the factors which differentiate firms from one another constant.

On the negative side, the method is vulnerable to "curve fitting" excesses. The temptation is strong to include a multitude of explanatory variables which may or may not have any economic validity. The inclusion of explanatory variables should rest on strong defensible economic arguments, rather than on empirical elegance and spectacular explanatory power.

Another drawback of the approach is that the user requires a solid understanding of econometric estimation techniques. It is important that the assumptions of linear regression techniques be well understood and verified for possible violation. Checks for multicollinearity between the explanatory variables, measurement error biases, omitted variables biases, and scale effects should be conducted. The stability of the coefficients over time is also necessary if the econometric model is to be useful for forecasting equity costs.

One common error in specifying P/B models is to use the currently allowed book return on equity, rather than the expected return, as one of the explanatory variables. The stock price which appears in the numerator of the P/B ratio reflects the return expected by investors to be granted, and not the return currently allowed or currently earned. If the model is estimated using actual return, the estimated coefficient for that variable will be biased, since the actual P/B ratio will be different from what is justified by the current return on equity. The coefficient of return on equity will thus be invalid, and use of the method to infer the cost of equity capital will lead to distorted values of equity costs.

The earlier caveat that share price will only be driven toward book value if the utility can actually be expected to earn the rate set for regulatory purposes deserves reiteration.

13.4 THE Q-RATIO

Overview

Briefly, the Q-ratio is used to establish a target P/B ratio for a company. The Q-ratio is defined as the ratio of the market value of a firm's securities to the replacement cost of its assets. A control group of comparable unregulated companies is used to establish an appropriate Q-ratio. This ratio is multiplied by the replacement cost value of equity-financed assets in a subject utility to obtain a target market price which measures the replacement cost market value of the equity. The target P/B ratio employs the target market price, and the return on book equity required to support the target P/B ratio is computed from the transformation relationship of Equation 13-9:

$$r \ = \ P_Q/B \ (K - g) \ + \ g$$

where P_Q = target market price computed from the target Q-ratio.

Rationale

The market value of a firm's securities clearly exerts an important influence on the firm's incentive to invest in capital projects. If the market value of a firm's stocks and bonds exceeds the cost of establishing productive capacity, there is an incentive to raise capital and establish new productive capacity, since such investments increase stock price. Conversely, if the market value of a firm's securities is less than the current cost of establishing productive capacity, there is a disincentive to invest in new plant, since such investments would decrease stock price, and investors could exercise the option to liquidate the firm's assets at a value in excess of the equity value.

In the long-run, for a competitive industry, the possibility of free entry and exit of firms in a competive industry would ensure that the market value of a firm's securities equals the replacement cost of its assets. Otherwise, the possibility of entry and exit into the industry would trigger the addition or deletion of further production, thereby altering product prices, profits, and finally market values until such an equality prevailed.

The relationship between the market value of a firm's securities and the replacement cost of its assets is embodied in the Q-ratio, first developed by Tobin & Brainard (1971). The Q-ratio is defined as follows:

$$Q \ = \ \frac{\textbf{Market Value of a Firm's Securities}}{\textbf{Replacement Cost of Firm's Assets}}$$

If $Q > 1$, a firm has an incentive to invest, and if $Q < 1$ a firm has a disincentive to invest in new plant. In final long-run equilibrium, the Q-ratio is driven to one.

The Q-Ratio and Regulation

The language of the *Hope* decision strongly suggests that the objective of regulation is to target a utility's profits at a level commensurate with the profits earned by competitive firms of comparable risk. Since in the unregulated sector, competitive forces will assure that over long periods of time the Q-ratio will be one, regulators should provide public utilities with a return sufficient to realize an expected average Q-ratio of one.

In the short-run, temporary disequilibriums occur so that unregulated firms will not necessarily achieve Q-ratios of one. Consistent with the comparable earnings doctrine and the capital attraction standard of *Hope*, a utility's profits should be targeted at a level commensurate with the actual profits earned by firms of similar risk. By this standard, the end result of the rate setting process is a stock price that implies a Q-ratio equal to the aggregate Q-ratio for a sample of comparable risk unregulated firms. In other words, under the Q-ratio standard, the allowed return should be set so that the market values of regulated and unregulated firms of comparable risk have the same ratio to their replacement costs.

It may be useful to view the Q-ratio standard in the following terms. Earlier in this chapter, it was argued that the cost of equity should be translated into an allowed rate of return such that the P/B ratio will be slightly in excess of one in order to prevent dilution of book value when new stock is sold. But these considerations only related to dilution of nominal book value. The Q-ratio extends this argument to include protection from dilution in real terms. In an inflationary period, the replacement cost of a firm's assets may increase more rapidly than its book equity. To avoid the resulting economic confiscation of shareholders' investment in real terms, the allowed rate of return should produce a P/B ratio which provides a Q-ratio of 1 or a Q-ratio equal to that of comparable firms.

To implement the standard, the cost of equity derived from DCF, CAPM, Risk Premium technologies, is translated into the fair equity return consistent with a Q-ratio equivalent to that of comparable unregulated firms. In other words, the cost of book equity is the return required to be earned on the utility's book equity such that the investor will receive the required return (K) and the stock price maintains a Q-ratio equal to that of comparable firms.

Data Considerations

The U.S. Council of Economic Advisers in the Economic Report of the President (1979) and Von Furstenberg (1977) have developed aggregate estimates of the Q-ratio for the corporate sector as a measure of the incentive for corporate investment in plant and equipment. These aggregate Q-ratio estimates employed data items from both the national income and product accounts and from the flow of funds accounts in order to arrive at the ratio of the market values of corporate debt and equity to the replacement cost of assets. As a proxy for asset replacement cost, an estimate of net depreciable assets and inventories repriced for the effects of inflation, was used. These data items are not easily reconcilable with items in the balance sheet of an individual firm however.

A simple balance sheet method is presented in Dwyer (1979) to calculate estimates of Q-ratios for individual firms using the formula:

$$Q = \frac{MVE + FVD}{RC} \qquad (13\text{-}21)$$

where MVE = market value of equity, including convertible preferred, if any
MVE = RC – FVD
RC = replacement cost of "net assets"
FVD = face value of debt, straight preferred, and investment tax credits

"Net assets" is total assets at replacement cost less current liabilities other than debt, and less deferred credits other than the investment tax credit. For the replacement cost of assets, either trended original cost or the actual replacement cost data required by the SEC in 10K reports can be used.

It is important to note that the face value of debt and preferred, rather than their market values, is used in calculating the numerator of the Q-ratio. This is due to the particular nature of the regulatory process. To determine a utility's overall allowed rate of return, the embedded cost of debt and preferred stock is used. As a result, ratepayers bear the gains and losses associated with the use of senior capital raised in the past. Utility's shareholders neither benefit nor lose by the change in the market prices of the senior capital brought about by changes in interest rates. Accordingly, the use of the market values of senior capital is not appropriate when computing utility Q-ratios.

Based on the latter qualification, a just and reasonable price for a public utility's stock should be determined by subtracting the book value rather than the market value of senior capital from the replacement cost of assets. Litzenberger (1979) articulates the final regulatory standard implied by the Q-ratio as follows. A fair and reasonable stock price should result in a ratio Q_r of the market value of the utility's equity to the value of its equity at adjusted replacement cost that is equal to the Q-ratio for a comparable group of unregulated firms. The value of the utility's equity at adjusted replacement cost is in turn defined as the historical book value of its equity plus the difference between its net plant and equipment at replacement cost and at historical cost.

Implementation

Two excellent examples of the Q-ratio methodology applied in actual regulatory proceedings are contained in Litzenberger (1979) and Dwyer (1979). The general procedure for applying the Q-ratio approach to the determination of equity cost consists of 4 steps:

Step 1: Obtain a sample of comparable risk unregulated companies, using the risk filter techniques described in earlier chapters.

Step 2: Calculate the Q-ratio for each company in the sample, as per Equation 13-21, using the replacement costs of their net plant and equipment and inventories contained in their 10K reports and the market value of their publicly traded debt and equity securities.

Step 3: Calculate the target P/B ratio that would result in a Q_r ratio equal to the equity ratio for the comparable group of unregulated firms. The numerator of the target P/B ratio is the value of the specified utility's equity at replacement cost calculated using replacement cost data.

Step 4: Use transformation Equation 13-9 to convert the utility's cost of equity capital into a fair return on equity.

EXAMPLE

The following example is adapted from Litzenberger. The cost of equity capital for Eastern Power Co. derived from the DCF, Risk Premium, and CAPM methodologies is 15%, consisting of a 5% growth and a 10% expected dividend yield. For reasons of consistency, the same group of unregulated comparable risk firms used in the execution of the DCF method is retained for computing the reference Q-ratio. The average Q-ratio for this group of risk-equivalent companies is 0.85, computed from the application of Equation 13-15 to each company. To estimate the target P/B ratio, the value of common equity at adjusted replacement cost is first estimated from the information contained in the current annual report:

VALUE OF EASTERN POWER CO'S EQUITY
AT ADJUSTED REPLACEMENT COST
(000,000)

Common Equity	$150
Minority Interest Common Equity	$5
Convertible Preferred	$2
Value of Equity at Historical Cost	$157
+	
Difference between Net Plant at Replacement and Historical Cost	$80
Value of Common Equity at Adjusted Replacement Cost	$237

The target P/B ratio for the Eastern Power Co. is calculated as follows:

Value of Equity at Replacement Cost	$237
X	
Comparable risk firms Q-ratio	X 0.80
Target Market Value of Equity	$190
Value of Common Equity at Historical Cost	$157
TARGET P/B RATIO	1.21

Lastly, the cost of equity capital of 15% is translated into the allowed equity return which will produce the target P/B ratio of 1.21, using Equation 13-9:

$$r = P/B\ (K - g) + g$$
$$= 1.21\ (15\% - 5\%) + 5\%$$
$$= \underline{17.1\%}$$

Drawbacks of the Approach

At the practical level, the results of the Q-ratio approach can only be as accurate as the replacement cost data on which it is based, typically derived from 10K reports. The lack of verifiability and the subjective nature of these data are likely deterrents from use of the method. For non-publicly traded companies, the problem of generating suitable replacement cost data is even more formidable; trended original cost proxies could serve instead.

At the conceptual level, despite the convincing logic of the method and despite the economic foundation on which it rests, the basic premise that the P/B ratios of utilities should be more consistent with those prevailing for comparable industrials is controversial. A substantial burden would be imposed on utility ratepayers by implementing the method, while it is questionable whether investors' returns would be ameliorated. A quotation from Kahn (1970, page 52) makes the point:

" ... any attempt of a regulatory commission ... to permit investors the higher return would only be self-defeating. Investors would respond to the higher earnings per share by bidding up the prices of the securities to the point at which new purchases would earn only the old cost of capital on their investments. The only beneficiaries would be those who happened to own the stock at the time the policy change was announced or anticipated."

13.5   COVERAGE RATIOS

To assess the reasonableness of the allowed return on equity, the coverage ratio which results from a given allowed equity return can be computed.

The coverage ratio measures the ability of a firm's earnings to meet its fixed obligations, and is an important determinant of credit worthiness scrutinized by bond rating agencies and by the investment community. The simplest calculation of coverage is the interest coverage based on pretax operating income, calculated as follows:

$$\frac{\textbf{pretax operating income}}{\textbf{interest charges}}$$

The calculation excludes AFUDC, which is a non-cash item, and other income. An equivalent formulation is the traditional and widely used times interest earned ratio (TIE), calculated as:

$$\frac{\textbf{Profit before Taxes + Interest Charges}}{\textbf{Interest Charges}}$$

Another variant is to include AFUDC income and miscellaneous income in the numerator of the ratio. The formula for SEC coverage, which is used in bond prospectuses approved by the SEC, is obtained by including not only AFUDC and miscellaneous income but also the interest component of leasing payments in the numerator, and by including the latter charges in the denominator as part of the financial burden to be covered. Sometimes, depreciation charges are added in the numerator to produce a cash income coverage.

To verify the reasonableness of the allowed equity return, the coverage implied by the latter is calculated, and compared to a benchmark target ratio, such as the median ratio for utilities in a similar bond rating category. Table 13-1 illustrates the calculation of the TIE ratio that would obtain using the utility's projected embedded costs of debt and preferred stock, projected capital structure, and a tax rate of 50%, and a series of allowed return on equity values. The calculations are based on idealized circumstances, and assume that all reported income can be used to meet the coverage requirements, that interest is the only fixed charge to be covered, and that rate base equals total invested capital. The calculation used to calculate TIE is:

$$\text{TIE} = \frac{W_d K_d + W_p K_p / 1 - T + W_e K_e / 1 - T}{W_d K_d} \tag{13-22}$$

where w_d, w_p, and w_e represent the percentage of debt, preferred, and common stock in the capital structure; K_d, K_p, and K_e are the embedded cost of debt and preferred and the cost of common equity; T is the tax rate.

TABLE 13-1 COVERAGE RATIOS AT VARIOUS RETURNS ON COMMON EQUITY

GIVEN CAPITAL STRUCTURE:

Source	% of Capital		% Cost		Weighted Cost
Debt	50%	×	10%	=	5.0%
Preferred	10%	×	12%	=	1.2%
Equity	40%	×	Ke		

Ke	TIE
18.0%	4.36
17.5	4.28
17.0	4.20
16.5	4.12
16.0	4.04
15.5	3.96
14.5	3.88
14.0	3.72

Illustration of calculation where $K_e = 16\%$:

$$\text{TIE} = \frac{.50\ (10.0)\ +\ .10\ (12.0)/1-.50\ +\ .40\ (16.0)/1-.50}{.50(10.0)}$$

$$= 4.04$$

To estimate the cost of equity for publicly owned utilities subject to rate regulation, including several water utilities and municipally-owned electric utilities, there are two approaches. One approach is the "stand alone" approach, whereby the cost of equity of comparable privately-owned utilities is applied, based on cost of equity estimates for private companies of equivalent bond and stock ratings. The rationale for this method is that, from the point of view of efficient economic pricing, the rate of return on equity for publicly-owned utilities should essentially be the same, on a risk-adjusted basis, as the rate of return on equity for privately-owned utilities. Otherwise, the ratepayers-owners of publicly-owned utilities would be better off if all earnings were paid out to them in the form of lower taxes so that they could reinvest the savings in other enterprises of similar risk. Moreover, the standards of *Hope* and *Bluefield* were articulated without reference to the ownership of the utility, so that the use of capital attraction and financial integrity standards as a starting point for analyzing the fair return to publicly-owned utilities is consistent with *Hope* and *Bluefield*.

Another approach is to set the allowed return on equity so as to produce a coverage ratio which will allow the utility to maintain its integrity and to attract capital on reasonable terms. The coverage ratios of other publicly-owned utilities or of non-regulated entities of the same quality can be used as benchmarks. Copan (1983) provides a good description of coverage ratios as measures of publicly-owned firms' revenue requirements.

Part Three

The Weighted Cost of Capital

CHAPTER 14

WEIGHTED AVERAGE COST OF CAPITAL AND CAPITAL STRUCTURE

The focus of previous chapters has resided narrowly on the cost of equity, since this is by far the most controversial element in the determination of cost of capital. These next two chapters examine the effects of financial leverage, that is the presence of debt, on the cost of equity. The consequences of relaxing the assumption made thus far of a constant debt/equity mix are investigated.

Traditionally, the allowed rate of return in regulatory hearings is calculated as the weighted average of the cost of each individual components of the capital structure weighted by its book value. This is illustrated in Table 14-1, where the capital structure, expressed as per cent of book value, consists of 50% debt, 10% preferred stock, and 40% common stock, with individual cost rates of 10%, 12%, and 16% respectively.

TABLE 14-1   ILLUSTRATION OF COST OF CAPITAL CALCULATION

Source	% Of Capital	% Cost	Weighted Cost	Tax Factor*	Capital Cost Including Tax
Debt	50% ×	10% =	5.0% ×	1.00 =	5.0%
Preferred	10% ×	12% =	1.2% ×	2.00 =	2.4%
Equity	40% ×	16% =	6.4% ×	2.00 =	12.8%
	100%		12.6%		20.2%

* The tax factor is 1/1-tax rate; assuming a 50% corporate tax rate, 1/1-0.50 = 1/0.50 = 2.00

The estimated allowed rate of return of 12.6% is then applied to the book value of the rate base to determine the total revenue requirements needed to service the capital employed by the utility. Knowledge of the 12.6%

allowed rate of return on total capital is not enough to determine the total cost of servicing capital to the ratepayers however. Assuming a 50% tax rate, to provide a $1 return to the bondholders, the utility requires only $1 of revenue. But it takes $2 of revenue to provide a $1 return to the preferred and common equity holders because the utility must pay corporate income taxes. In the above example, if the rate base is $100 and the tax rate 50%, to provide a return of $5 on the bondholders' $50 investment, the utility requires $5 of pre-tax revenues; but to provide a return of $1.20 + $6.40 = $7.60 to the equity holders' $60 investment, the regulatory commission must allow a profit before taxes of 2 x $7.60 = $15.20. From the ratepayers' viewpoint, the total cost to service capital and taxes is $5 + $15.20 = $20.20, or 20.2%.

It should be noted that an alternate and equivalent computational procedure shown in Table 14-2 is to express the cost of debt directly on an after-tax basis, and to multiply the resulting weighted average cost of capital by the tax factor to obtain directly the cost of capital including taxes. In the above example, the after-tax cost of debt is $10\%(1 - T) = 10\%(1 - .50) = 5\%$, where T is the tax rate. The weighted cost of debt is then 2.5%, for a total weighted average cost of capital of 10.1%, instead of the 12.6% shown above. The pre-tax cost of capital is then simply the post-tax figure of 10.1% multiplied by the tax factor of 2, or 20.2%, the same figure obtained with the first procedure.

TABLE 14-2 ILLUSTRATION OF COST OF CAPITAL CALCULATION: ALTERNATE VERSION

Source	% of Capital		% After-tax Cost		Weighted Cost
Debt	50%	×	10%(1–.50)	=	2.5%
Preferred	10%	×	12%	=	1.2%
Equity	40%	×	16%	=	6.4%
	100%				10.1%

More generally, if K_d and K_e are the costs of debt and equity, and w_d and w_e are respectively the weights of debt and equity to the total value of capital, the weighted average cost of capital, K, can be expressed as:

$$K = K_d w_d + K_e w_e \qquad (14\text{-}1)$$

Traditional weighted average cost of capital computation employs book-value weights attached to measures of cost of each component of the capital structure at the time of the rate proceeding. The return on common equity is a current cost rate, calculated using any one of several techniques described thus far, such as DCF, Risk Premium, CAPM, and Comparable Earnings. The other rates are "embedded" costs, that is, total interest and preferred dividend costs divided by the book value of debt and preferred stock respectively. They are not market-based costs. The dollar cost of debt capital is viewed narrowly as the explicitly-stated contractual obligation to pay interest during the life of the bond and to pay the principal amount at maturity. This accounting approach to debt cost stands in contrast to the economic approach which views the cost of debt as the yield to maturity required by bondholders, related to the net proceeds of the issue. Moreover, the implicit "risk cost" of debt by way of the increased financial risk borne by shareholders as a result of introducing senior capital is not reflected in the debt cost component but rather in the equity component of the weighted cost of capital. Similar arguments apply to the cost of preferred stock, traditionally defined as the weighted average of the indicated dividend rate for each issue divided by its net proceeds.

Several major issues regarding the weighted average cost of capital arise in regulatory proceedings, corresponding to each term of Equation 14-1, and are the subject of these next two chapters. Section 1 of this chapter rationalizes the use of book value weights rather than market value weights in the computation of the weighted average cost of capital. The next four sections explore the effect of capital structure on cost of capital and the existence of an optimal set of weights, that is, an optimal financing mix of debt and equity which would minimize the utility's cost of capital and thus minimize ratepayer burden. The underlying theory and empirical evidence are described. The next chapter presents some illustrative examples and the practical implications of capital structure theory for regulatory purposes. The notion of double-levered capital structures, the consequences of including or excluding certain components of capital in the weighted average calculation, the treatment of zero-cost items of capital, and the consistency of the rate base and invested capital are discussed in the next chapter also.

14.1 BOOK VERSUS MARKET VALUE[1]

In the context of rate making for regulated utilities, it is universal practice to employ a hybrid computation consisting of embedded costs of debt and a market-based cost of equity with costs of debt and equity both weighted at their respective book values in the determination of the weighted average cost of capital. Letting K_{em} stand for the market-based cost of equity, K_d for the embedded costs of debt at the coupon rate, and D/C,

E/C for the ratios of debt and equity at book value to the total book value of capital, the traditional computation of weighted capital cost, K, is expressed as:

$$K = K_d D/C + K_{em} E/C \qquad (14\text{-}2)$$

Despite its wide acceptance in practice, the curious mixture of book and market values and costs in Equation 14-2 requires some rationalization.

The rationalization of using embedded cost of debt is that the award of a rate of return on rate base to cover market yield on debt would only result in windfall gains or losses to shareholders. That is, if market yields exceed embedded costs, rate coverage of the difference would not accrue to the bondholders, but rather to the shareholders, because of the contractual fixity of bondholders' claims. Any excess of market over book costs of debt falls upon the shareholders, and conversely. By allowing the utility to earn its actual embedded cost and equity earnings equal to the cost of equity times the equity book value, regulators prevent shareholders from windfall gains and losses when interest rates change. Hence, book value weights inflict no harm on bondholders beyond that produced by variability of market price when current yield deviates from the coupon rate. Paradoxically, while the allowed return can be set to make market value equal to book value in the case of equity, there is no obvious way to achieve the same result in the case of fixed-return bonds.

The usage of book value weights is defended on several grounds. First, the relationship of debt and equity at book value is an expression of the utility's long-term capital structure policy. If incremental funds are raised in proportions such that a target debt/equity ratio in book value terms is maintained, the earnings requirements to cover capital costs must be computed using the actual weights in which funds are raised, that is, book value weights. Second, book value proportions are stable. Hence, their presentation to regulatory authority avoids the vagaries introduced by variability of market values. Lastly, if regulation performs adequately, the book value and market value of equity will be driven toward equality.

The use of market value weights is defended on the countering observation that the reflection of capital structure in historical cost values of debt and equity is blemished over long periods by price level changes. Hence, relative proportions at book value are not free of distortion.

One seemingly potent argument in favor of market value weights is that if cost of capital is not formulated in terms of current market costs, there is no assurance that the commitment of funds to investment projects by utilities will earn a rate sufficient to cover these costs. Presumably, the latter is a socially desirable goal of regulation, if the competitive result is to be emulated.

It can be shown however that if the regulatory authority adds the cost of the additional capital required by new investment projects into the allowed rate of return, and if there is no regulatory lag, the utility will realize an appropriate compensatory return on incremental investment. For example, let K' be the incremental market cost of capital for a new project requiring an investment of I dollars. Regulatory authority typically would not calculate K' as a separate return. But if the cost of capital is calculated as a weighted average of the embedded cost of debt and an estimated cost of equity, the incremental cost of capital for the additional asset will add K' I dollars to the overall revenue requirements. In effect, then, if the regulatory commission incorporates the cost of additional capital into the allowed rate of return, the utility will realize K' on incremental investment, other things equal. If there is regulatory lag however, a utility's rate of return on new projects will deviate from the current capital costs. The only way to avoid this is through an arbitrary return adjustment, similar to an attrition allowance.

In summary, the rationalization of the use of book quantities instead of the more economically correct market quantities is not unreasonable for purposes of setting rates.

14.2   THE EFFECT OF CAPITAL STRUCTURE ON COST OF CAPITAL

This section describes the effects of capital structure changes on the cost of capital in an informal intuitive manner. The existence of an optimal capital structure is shown based on reasonable behavior postulates on the part of bondholders and equity holders. The next section outlines the formal theoretical justifications.

Chapter 3 described in detail the distinction between business risk and financial risk. Business risk refers to the variability of operating profits inherent in the nature of the business in which the company is engaged, regardless of its financial structure. This variability is largely induced by the external forces of supply and demand for the firm's products. Financial risk refers to the additional variability of earnings induced by the employment of fixed cost financing such as debt and preferred stock. A fundamental concept in financial theory, demonstrated in Chapter 3, is that the risk of the earnings to common shareholders increases as the financial leverage rises. As a company increases the relative amount of debt capital in its capital structure, total fixed charges increase, and the probability of failing to meet the growing fixed charge burden increases also. The residual earnings available to common stockholders become increasingly volatile and riskier as the firm increases its financial leverage, causing shareholders to require a higher return on equity.

The relationship between capital structure and the cost of capital is developed graphically in Figure 14-1. The horizontal axis is the debt ratio, D/C, assuming that no other form of senior capital exists. The graph depicts the return requirements of bondholders and shareholders in response to a change in capital structure as the firm progressively substitutes debt for equity capital.

The required return on debt is relatively flat from a debt ratio of zero up to a critical debt ratio value, say 50%. Beyond that point, an increase in debt ratio has an upward influence on bond returns as debt holders perceive a significant increase in financial risk. The actual value of the critical threshold can be determined by examining the debt ratio of utilities with the highest quality bonds (AAA). Any reduction in debt ratio below the critical point would not yield significant reductions in interest costs. The security of the bondholders' investment is not subtantially improved by additional reductions in the debt ratio. Beyond the critical point, bond returns increase

Figure 14-1

THE RELATIONSHIP BETWEEN CAPITAL STRUCTURE
AND THE COST OF CAPITAL

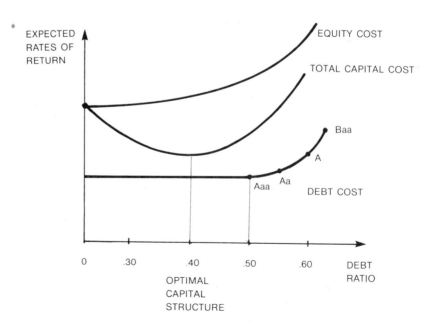

in a manner consistent with the quality gradient observed for utility bond yields and debt ratios. The points on the bond graph in Figure 14-1 correspond to the actual bond yields and debt ratios for electric utilities rated AAA, AA, A, and BAA at a moment in time. Access to debt financing is likely to be severely curbed beyond the BAA rating level.

The curve depicting the behavior of shareholders as the debt ratio is increased is developed as follows. At a zero debt ratio, the return on equity coincides with the return on total capital since the firm is all-equity financed at that point. Beyond that point, with each successive increase in the debt ratio, equity returns rise moderately at first in response to increasing financial risk to the point where the bond ratings begin to deteriorate. As the debt ratio reaches dangerous levels where the solvency of the firm is endangered, shareholders' required returns rise sharply.

The relationship between the average cost of capital and capital structure emerges directly from the assumed behavior of bond returns and equity returns. This is also shown on Figure 14-1. At zero debt ratio, the cost of capital is coincident with the cost of equity. With each successive substitution of low-cost debt for high-cost equity, the average cost of capital declines as the weight of low-cost debt in the average increases. A low point is reached where the cost advantage of debt is exactly offset by the increased cost of equity. Beyond that point, the cost disadvantage of equity outweighs the cost advantage of debt, and the weighted cost of capital rises accordingly.

The most salient characteristic of the graph is the U-shaped nature of the cost of capital curve, pointing to the existence of an optimal capital structure whereby the cost of capital is minimized. Despite the rise of both debt and equity costs with increases in the debt ratio, the weighted average cost of capital reaches a minimum. Beyond this point, the low-cost and tax advantages of debt are outweighed by the increased equity costs. This occurs just before the point where bond ratings start deteriorating, and the cost of capital increases rapidly at higher debt ratios.

Utilities should strive for a capital structure which minimizes the composite capital cost, including taxes. Hypothetical capital structures are sometimes used by regulatory commissions to determine a fair allowed return if a utility is deemed to have deviated significantly from the optimum. A hypothetical capital structure may lower the cost of capital, which in turn may translate into lower rates for consumers as long as by using more debt, the cost and tax benefits of debt outweigh the increased equity costs.

Finding the optimal structure is easier said than done, however. The graphical relationships of Figure 14-1 are difficult to measure accurately. About the only relationship which can be charted with some confidence is the bond return graph. Observed bond yields and attendant debt ratios for comparable companies can be employed to develop such a graph. The equity return graph is difficult to construct precisely. As is evident from the previous chapters, the cost of equity is difficult enough to estimate at a given capital structure, let alone for a whole range of alternative capital structures. Nevertheless, reasonable procedures for deriving the cost of capital curve can be devised as the examples of the next chapter will demonstrate. But first the formal theory underlying the existence of an optimal capital structure will be outlined.

14.3 AN OVERVIEW OF CAPITAL STRUCTURE THEORY

No Tax Version

Assuming perfectly functioning capital markets and the absence of corporate taxes, Modigliani-Miller (1966) have argued that the value of a corporation, hence its cost of capital, is independent of capital structure. Financing decisions are irrelevant under these assumptions. The value of a firm is determined by the left-hand side of its balance sheet, that is, by the earning power of its assets. How the stream of operating income generated by the assets is apportioned among the bondholders and shareholders is irrelevant. By analogy, the value of a pie (operating income) should not depend on the manner in which it is sliced. Modigliani-Miller provide an arbitrage proof of this proposition, whereby two identical firms with differing capital structures must have the same value if riskless profit opportunities are to be avoided. Figure 14-2 shows how the overall cost of capital, hence revenue requirements, are unaffected by the debt ratio under this theory.

If the weighted average cost of capital remains unchanged with leverage, it follows that the required return on equity resulting from the added risk of leverage completely offsets the low-cost advantage of debt. Otherwise, the weighted average cost of capital could not remain constant. In other words, the total cost of capital remains unchanged regardless of the capital structure because the increase in required earnings resulting from greater leverage is exactly offset by the subtitution of lower cost debt for higher cost of equity. This is shown in Figure 14-2. The exact relationship between leverage and the cost of equity is linear and is expressed as:

$$K_e = p + (p - i)\ B/S \tag{14-3}$$

where p is the cost of equity for an all-equity firm, B/S is the market value leverage ratio, and 'i' is the current rate of interest. Equation 14-3 is easily derived by solving for K_e in the following equation:

Figure 14-2

THE EFFECTS OF LEVERAGE ON THE COST
OF CAPITAL: NO TAX

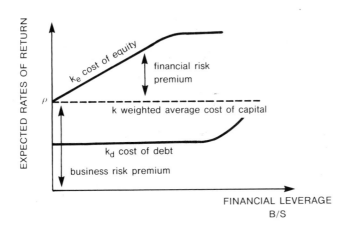

$$K = i\ B/V + K_e\ S/V \qquad (14\text{-}4)$$

which is the straightforward definition of the weighted average cost of
capital, using market value weights and returns, and by substituting 'p' for
'K'. The cost of capital for an all-equity financed firm, 'p', and the cost of
capital of a levered firm, K, are identical under Modigliani-Miller's proposition.

The accounting analog to Equation 14-3, using actual returns instead
of expected returns is:

$$r = R + (R - i)\ D/E \qquad (14\text{-}5)$$

where r = return on book value of equity, R = operating rate of return on
assets, i = interest rate on aggregate debt, D = book value of all interest-
bearing debt, E = book value of equity, T = tax rate. This result is derived
in Appendix 14-A.

The major implication of either Equation 14-3 or Equation 14-3, is
that two firms with different debt ratios will have different equity costs, even
though they have the same business risk and the same overall cost of capital.
This is shown on Figure 14-3 where firm A and firm B have debt ratios of

$(B/S)_a$ and $(B/S)_b$ and equity costs of K_a and K_b respectively, and yet have the same overall cost of capital K.

Introducing Corporate Income Tax

Modigliani-Miller admit that their initial thesis ignores the tax deductibility of interest payments on debt. Recognizing the income tax savings of interest payments, their argument implies a continued reduction in the cost of capital as the debt ratio is increased. Therefore, the firm's optimal capital structure is 100% debt. This is shown in Figure 14-4, where the cost of capital, thus revenue requirements, decline with each relative increment of debt capital. The value of the firm increases with the debt ratio because of the added value of the tax savings generated by debt financing. As the firm substitutes debt for equity capital, the fraction of operating income diverted to the tax authority becomes smaller, and the fraction accruing to shareholders becomes correspondingly larger. Adding debt thus enhances the value of the firm and reduces the overall cost of capital and ratepayer burden. The linear relationship between the overall cost of capital and debt ratio shown on Figure 14-4 derived from the tax-adjusted Modigliani-Miller theory can be expressed as:

Figure 14-3

THE RELATIONSHIP BETWEEN COST OF EQUITY
AND LEVERAGE

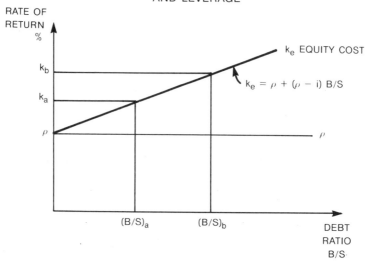

$$K = p (1 - TB/C)$$ (14-6)

where K is the overall cost of capital for a levered firm, p is the cost of capital for an all-equity firm, T is the corporate income tax rate, and B/C is the debt to total capital ratio expressed in market value terms.

The implied relationship between the cost of equity and leverage remains linear as in Equations 14-3 and 14-5, but the rate of increase (slope) is lessened by the tax advantage of debt. Equations 14-3 and 14-5 become respectively:

$$K_e = p + (p - i)(1 - T)B/S$$ (14-7)

and

$$r = [R + (R - i) D/E] (1 - T)$$ (14-8)

As in the no-tax case, Equation 14-7 is easily derived by solving for K_e in the following equation:

Figure 14-4

THE EFFECTS OF LEVERAGE ON THE COST OF
CAPITAL: WITH TAX

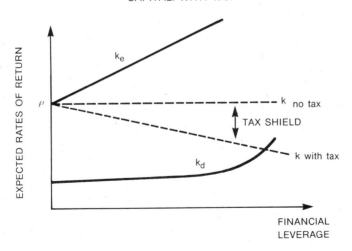

$$K = i(1 - T)B/V + K_eS/V \qquad (14\text{-}9)$$

which is the straightforward definition of the after-tax weighted average cost of capital, using market value weights and returns, and by substituting 'p' for 'K'.[2] The accounting analog in Equation 14-8 is derived in Appendix 14-A.

Miller (1977) has recently presented an alternative capital structure theory which maintains that the value of debt tax shields disappears when both personal and corporate income taxes are considered. Even though interest income is not taxed at the firm level, it is taxed at the personal level. Equity income is taxed at the firm level but may largely avoid personal taxes if it comes in the form of capital gains. The implication of the Miller model is that there exists an optimal debt ratio for the aggregate of corporations, but that for any single tax-paying firm debt policy does not matter if the total supply of debt is to suit investors' need. The reason there is no tax advantage to issuing more debt is that such tax advantage has already been priced.

The Miller model takes us back to the original Modigliani-Miller position whereby no tax advantage whatsoever to debt financing exists and no optimal capital structure exists. Recent empirical evidence and extensions to the Miller model suggest that Miller's conclusion is controversial. Some tax advantage to the use of debt exists, although it may be less than implied in the Miller-Modigliani thesis with tax.

Other Factors

Clearly, the conclusion of an all-debt capital structure suggested by the Miller-Modigliani cum-tax thesis is unrealistic, a situation easily verified not to exist. Therefore, the low-cost advantage and tax benefits of leverage must be offset by some disadvantage varying directly with leverage.

One of the offsetting disadvantages of leverage is the cost of financial distress. Financial distress costs may include direct and indirect bankruptcy costs. Short of bankruptcy, they may include the costs of writing, monitoring, and enforcing debt contracts to avoid the natural conflicts of interest between bondholders and stockholders of firms with high debt ratios. As the firm increases its debt ratio, it increases the value of the tax shield but it also increases the costs of financial distress. See Cheng & Kim (1979) for a recent review of the relevant literature. Beyond some point, the additional tax shield is outweighed by the additional cost of financial distress. Corporate taxes together with debt-related bankruptcy costs and agency costs lead to a U-shaped relationship between cost of capital and leverage, and an optimal capital structure (see Figure 14-5).

Figure 14-5

THE EFFECTS OF LEVERAGE ON THE COST OF CAPITAL:
WITH TAX AND BANKRUPTCY COSTS

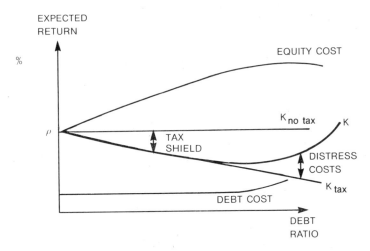

Even if the costs of financial distress are negligible, other explanations for the existence of an optimal capital structure have been proposed. For example, Jensen & Meckling (1976) suggest that an optimal capital structure exists, given increasing agency costs with higher equity ratios on the one hand and higher debt ratios on the other. The firm will select an optimum combination of debt and equity so as to minimize total agency costs.

Several authors have argued that although both regulated and unregulated firms benefit from debt via a lower cost of capital, regulated firms benefit less because a utility's operating income is decreased by the amount of tax savings from debt, unlike unregulated firms. For an excellent review of the applicability of capital structure theory to public utilities, the interested reader is directed to Patterson (1983B). In the regulatory process, taxes are treated as an operating expense in the calculation of revenue requirements. If a utility issues more debt, the attendant tax savings will be passed on to ratepayers in the form of lower rates. Utility shareholders do not obtain the tax benefits of debt financing. If the tax advantage of debt is invalidated by the mechanics of the regulatory process, it would appear that the original Modigliani-Miller capital structure theory without taxes is applicable to utilities. Equation 14-3 rather than Equation 14-7 would be the correct formulation of equity costs.

This is not the complete story however. Because the regulated price changes with leverage, the demand for utility services is likely to be altered. Hence, the precise relationship between cost of capital and capital structure for a regulated firm cannot be derived without specifying exactly its demand and supply curve, as demonstrated by Jaffee & Mandelker (1976). Under plausible assumptions of demand behavior, Jaffee & Mandelker have shown that the value of levered firm under regulation is understated in the Modigliani-Miller no-tax framework, that is, the cost of capital is overstated. In the context of Figures 14-2 and 14-3, the cost of capital line for a regulated firm probably lies between the no-tax scenario and the with-tax scenario for an unregulated firm. In other words, there is still some tax advantage to debt financing, but its magnitude is less than that predicted by the Miller-Modigliani thesis. The slope of the cost of equity equation lies between that predicted in the no-tax case (Equation 14-3) and that predicted in the with-tax case (Equation 14-7). The precise impact also depends on the exact manner in which regulators pass through the tax savings from debt financing unto ratepayers. The demand effects would differ depending on whether the regulator lowers service rates or eliminates certain fixed charges.

14.4   EMPIRICAL EVIDENCE ON CAPITAL STRUCTURE

Several researchers have studied the empirical relationship between the cost of capital, capital-structure changes, and the value of the firm's securities. Comprehensive and rigorous empirical studies of the relationship between cost of capital and leverage for public utilities, summarized in Patterson (1983B), include Modigliani & Miller (1966), Rao & Litzenberger (1971), and Masulis (1980, 1982). Copeland & Weston (1983) also provide a summary of the empirical evidence. Although it is not easy in such tests to hold all other relevant factors constant, the evidence partially supports the existence of a tax benefit from leverage and that leverage increases firm value. The evidence also strongly favors a positive relationship between leverage and the cost of equity, which is consistent with the Modigliani-Miller propositions. However, there is still some controversy over the acceptance of the linear formulation in Equations 14-3 and 14-6. Some investigators believe the relationship is curvilinear, others believe its is linear but has a slope less than $(r - i)$.

In a recent study of public utility capital structures, Patterson (1983B) concludes that firm value rises with leverage and revenue requirements decline at low level of leverage, and confirms the existence of a cost-minimizing capital structure. Whether this optimal capital structure also minimizes revenue requirements depends on the effectiveness of regulation in passing interest tax savings through to ratepayers. Patterson also finds that utilities tend to operate at a debt ratio slightly less than the optimal level, in the interest of flexibility and maintaining borrowing reserves.

Notes

[1] This section draws on Andrews in Morin & Andrews (1983).

[2] These relationships can be easily extended to allow for the presence of preferred stock. Letting 'd' represent the dividend rate on preferred stock, and P/S the market value ratio of preferred stock to common equity, Equation 14-7 becomes:

$$K_e \; = \; p \; + \; (p - i) \; (1 - T)B/S \; + \; (p - d)P/S$$

APPENDIX 14-A

Derivation of Return on the Book Value of Equity

We need to formulate an expression that will identify component variables influencing the final result: $\dfrac{\textbf{Post-tax net income}}{\textbf{Book value of equity}} = r$ as a decimal or percent.

The stream of income available to securities in the aggregate is earnings before interest and tax (EBIT) or pre-tax net operating income (before financial charges). Necessarily, this is the source of all income to financial claims. Adopt R as the rate of return of this income stream relative to assets net of zero-rate debt, A: $R = \dfrac{\textbf{EBIT}}{A}$ as a decimal or percent. Also, adopt other symbols as follows:

t = marginal income tax rate
i = interest rate on aggregate debt
D = book value of all interest-bearing debt
E = book value of equity

Basically, we need only substitute these variables into the expressions appearing first above and simplify

$$r = \frac{\textbf{Post-tax net income}}{\textbf{Book value of equity}} = \frac{[R \cdot A - i \cdot D](1 - t)}{E}$$

Since assets $A = E + D$ we can substitute and simplify:

$$r = \frac{[R(E + D) - iD](1 - t)}{E}$$

$$r = [R + (R \cdot D/E) - (i \cdot D/E)](1 - t)$$
$$r = [R + (R - 1)D/E](1 - t)$$

The final expression says that, r, the return on book value of equity is directly proportional to the overall pre-tax financial return on assets plus a differential (premium) of this rate over the interest rate (rate spread) levered by the debt/equity ratio, D/E. The term $(1 - t)$ multiplied times the pre-tax values reduces them to post-tax equivalents.

For simplicity, especially in graphing, the above expression may be translated to a form more readily recognizable as a linear equation:

$$r = R(1 - t) + (R - i)(D/E)(1 - t)$$

The debt/equity ratio and post-tax equivalent expression are constants and their product is the slope of the function.

SOURCE: ANDREWS (1983)

CHAPTER 15

CAPITAL STRUCTURE ISSUES

The first section of this chapter presents some practical applications of capital structure theory for regulated utilities. The next section examines the interrelationship between the rate base and invested capital, and the consequences of including or excluding certain components of capital in the weighted average cost calculation. The double-leverage controversy is discussed in the last section.

15.1 PRACTICAL IMPLICATIONS

Several practical implications and applications for regulatory finance emerge from the capital structure concepts expounded in the previous chapter.

Anticipated Capital Structure Changes

Consideration should be given to changes in the leverage rate when estimating the cost of equity. Suppose that an unexpected change in the debt ratio from d_1 to d_2 is to be effected as per Figure 15-1. If the cost of equity is estimated from past data based on the debt ratio d_1, an estimate of K_1 is obtained. But this understates the true cost of equity of K_2 based on the new debt ratio d_2.

EXAMPLE

Eastern Power Company's cost of equity is estimated at 16% based on the company's existing capital structure, which consists of 35% debt and 65% equity in market values terms. The current borrowing rate is 12%, and the corporate income tax rate is 46%. The management of Eastern Power Co., perhaps at the urging of the regulatory commission, has decided to alter its capital structure to 40% debt and 60% equity. The revised cost of equity can be obtained by solving Equation 14-7 using the revised debt ratio:

Figure 15-1

ANTICIPATED CAPITAL STRUCTURE CHANGES
AND THE COST OF EQUITY

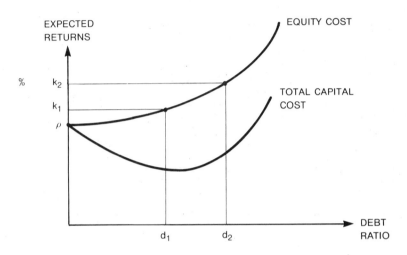

$$K_e = p + (p-i)(1-T)B/S \qquad (15\text{-}1)$$

But in order to solve for K_e, the cost of capital for an all-equity financed firm, 'p', is required. This can be done by solving the above equation for 'p' under the old capital structure, and inserting the resulting 'p' in the same equation under the new capital structure[1]:

$$16\% = p + (p-.12)(1-.46).35/.65$$

from which $p = 15.1\%$. Inserting the latter value of p in the equation and using the new capital structure, the revised cost of equity is obtained:

$$K_e = .151 + (.151-.12)(1-.46).40/.60$$
$$= .1622 = 16.22\%$$

In using Equation 15-1, the market value of equity is easily obtained by multiplying the current stock price by the number of shares outstanding.

The market value of debt is obtained by applying orthodox bond valuation formulas.

One of the assumptions underlying the DCF model discussed in Chapter 5 is the expected constancy of the debt ratio. The reason for this assumption should be evident from this example. The future dividends per share which drive the DCF model depend on expected earnings per share which in turn depend on the expected debt ratio. As long as the debt ratio has been constant historically and is expected to be maintained in the future, the DCF model is salvaged. But if a change in debt ratio is expected, the cost of equity obtained from the DCF model must be altered based on the expected debt ratio, using the procedure outlined in the example.

Two caveats are in order here. First, to the extent that the regulatory process inactivates the tax advantage of debt by passing on the savings to ratepayers, the no-tax equivalent of Equation 15-1 found in Equation 14-3 should be used instead. Replicating the calculations of the previous numerical example using the latter equation instead, a revised cost of equity of 16.33% is obtained, which is not significantly different from the 16.22% number obtained using the tax-adjusted form of the model. More generally, given the extreme nature of the no tax effect assumption, the revised cost of equity probably lies between the two polar values obtained from the two formulations.

Second, while both Equations 15-1 and 14-3 require the use of market value capital structure, the use of book values is preferable because the equity return obtained is in fact applied to the book value of the equity by the regulator. If the stock is trading at or near book value, no problem arises. But if the stock is trading away from book value, the use of market values will lead to distorted cost of equity estimates. The problem is largely academic since, in practice, book value capital structures do not often deviate significantly from market value capital structures.

Comparable Groups

A measurement problem similar to that of the previous numerical example can arise when using the cost of equity capital of other companies as a check against estimates based on the market data for the utility itself. If the group of comparable companies has been carefully designed using adequate risk filters for both business risk and capital structure differences, this will not be a problem. But if substantial capital structure differences exist between the utility and the reference companies, all else being constant, the same remedial correction as in the above example is necessary, using Equation 15-1 and the average capital structure of the reference group to compute the cost of capital for an all-equity firm, and the subject utility's own capital structure to compute its cost of capital using the same equation in reverse.

Levered Betas

One approach to estimating the cost of equity for a non-publicly traded utility or for a utility subsidiary is to compute an industry beta, based on the betas of companies in similar lines of business, and use this beta proxy in the CAPM or in one of its variants. The difficulty with this approach is that although the reference companies may have the same business risk, they may have different capital structures.

Observed betas reflect both business risk and financial risk. Hence, when a group of companies are considered comparable in every way except for financial structure, their betas are not directly comparable. Hamada (1972) suggests a technique for adjusting betas for capital structure differences, based on CAPM theory. The core idea is contained in the following relationship:

observed BETA = business risk BETA + financial risk premium

$$B_l = B_u [1 + (1-T)D/E] \qquad (15\text{-}2)$$

where B_l is the observed levered beta of a company, B_u is the unlevered beta of the same company with no debt in its capital structure, D/E is the ratio of debt to equity, and T the corporate income tax rate.[2]

The following example demonstrates a two-step procedure for estimating the impact of a change in capital structure on a utility's beta. First, the "unlevered" beta of each company in the reference group is estimated and averaged so that the resulting group beta is purged of financial risk and is reflective of business risk only. Second, the business risk beta is relevered, or "recapitalized" to reflect the utility's own capital structure.

EXAMPLE

The General Gas Company, a regulated pipeline distributor of natural gas, is a subsidiary of a holding company engaged in several business ventures, both regulated and unregulated. The utility's capital structure consists of 45% debt and 55% equity. The companies presented in Table 15-1 below are considered comparable in terms of business risk. The second and third columns of the table show the published beta and capital structure for each company, obtained from Value Line as of the end of 1982. The fourth columnn computes the unlevered beta for each company, by solving Equation 15-2 for B_u using each company's D/E. A 50% tax rate is assumed, and book values are assumed equal to market values. The average unlevered beta for the industry is 0.60, and reflects the business risk of the gas distribution industry and hence of General Gas Company. To estimate the levered beta associated with General Gas Company's own capital structure, Equation 15-2 is solved for B_l, using the unlevered beta for the industry and the new D/E as follows:

$$B_l = B_u[1 + (1-T)\ D/E]$$
$$= 0.60 + (1-.50)\ .45/.55$$
$$= \underline{1.01}$$

The estimated beta for the new debt ratio is then used in the CAPM or in an extended form of the model such as the Empirical CAPM to estimate the cost of equity capital consistent with General Gas Company's own debt ratio.

TABLE 15-1 THE COMPUTATION OF UNLEVERED BETAS

GENERAL GAS COMPANY

MARKET DATA

Company	Estimated Beta	Debt Ratio	Unlevered Beta
Diversified Energy Inc.	0.45	36.5%	0.35
Piedmont Natural Gas Co.	0.50	44.3%	0.36
Laclede Gas	0.65	40.1%	0.49
Consolidated Natural Gas	0.85	37.7%	0.65
Nicor Incorp.	0.90	44.5%	0.64
KN Energy Inc.	0.95	46.1%	0.67
Columbia Gas	0.95	49.6%	0.64
Mountain Fuel	1.05	45.5%	0.74
Entex Inc	1.20	50.1%	0.80
Northwest Energy Co.	1.30	64.1%	0.69
AVERAGE	0.88	45.9%	0.60

Hypothetical Capital Structures

Another implication of leverage theory is that cost of capital estimates based on a utility's current market data and capital structure expected by investors cannot be applied to any other capital structure without the adjustment described in previous examples. Regulators frequently assign hypothetical capital structures to utility companies for purposes of revenue requirements computation. This procedure is appropriate only if the cost of equity estimated from current investor expectations is revised to take into account the new capital structure prescribed by the regulator. Otherwise, the cost of equity estimate is inconsistent with the new capital structure. A similar problem arises in the double leverage approach to computing equity costs. If a cost of equity estimate based on a given capital structure is not modified to account for the double levered capital structure used by the regulator to determine the allowed return, a distorted measure of capital cost results. The double leverage approach is discussed in a later section.

Finding the Optimal Capital Structure

It should be stressed from the start that no exact method is available to derive a utility's capital structure. A great deal of judgment is required. The following example is to be regarded as illustrative of the approach only, and not as a precise recipe for finding the optimal capital structure. To derive a utility's capital structure as in Figure 14-1, one can proceed along the following lines.

EXAMPLE

The management of National Electric Co. is of the opinion that the cost of debt is a function of the debt ratio, and that this function is reflected in the schedule shown in the first and second columns of Table 15-2. The second column shows the after-tax cost of debt, assuming a tax rate of 50%. In an actual situation, such a schedule could be derived from the actual bond yields and debt ratios for utility bonds in different quality rating groups averaged over a number of years.[3]

The utility's management also believes that the company's cost of equity can be expressed as the sum of the risk-free rate, R_f, a premium for business risk, 'b', and a premium for financial risk, 'f', as follows:

$$K_e = R_f + b + f \qquad (15\text{-}3)$$

The risk-free rate, as measured by the yield on long-term Treasury bonds, is currently 10%. The premium for business risk demanded by utility investors is estimated at 4%. The premium for financial risk is an increasing function of the debt ratio; the premium rises slowly at first, and then accelerates rapidly as the debt ratio reaches prohibitive levels. The behavior of the premium for financial risk is assumed to be proportional to the square of the debt ratio, and the proportionality constant is 0.20[4]. Substituting in Equation 15-3, the cost of equity function can be expressed as:

$$K_e = 10\% + 4\% + 0.20 \ (D/E)^2$$
$$K_e = 14\% + 0.20 \ (D/E)^2$$

This function is shown as a schedule of equity cost for various debt ratios in the third column of Table 15-2.

The weighted average cost of capital for each level of debt ratio is calculated by adding the cost of debt and the cost of equity corresponding to each debt ratio, weighted by their relative proportions. This calculation appears in the fourth column of Table 15-2 . The cost of capital, plotted on the graph of Figure 15-2 reaches a minimum at a debt ratio of 40%. National Electric Company's optimal capital structure is thus 40% debt and 60% equity. Once again, this result is derived from purely hypothetical cost curves, which, however, rest on reasonable assumptions.

TABLE 15-2 THE RELATIONSHIP BETWEEN LEVERAGE AND COST OF CAPITAL

DEBT RATIO	AFTER-TAX COST OF DEBT	EQUITY COST	COMPOSITE CAPITAL COST
0%	5.00%	14.00%	14.00%
10%	5.00%	14.15%	13.24%
20%	5.00%	14.60%	12.68%
30%	5.00%	15.35%	12.25%
40%	6.00%	16.40%	12.24%
50%	7.00%	17.75%	12.38%
60%	9.00%	19.40%	13.16%
70%	12.00%	21.35%	14.81%

The Decomposition of Return on Book Equity

Equation 15-4, reproduced below from Equation 14-8 in the last chapter, expresses the book return on equity as a function of several underlying explanatory variables, and contains useful analytical properties.

$$r = [R + (R-i) \ D/E](1-T) \qquad (15\text{-}4)$$

The expression formally links book equity returns with leverage. Specifically, the equity return is proportional to the utility's rate of return on

Figure 15-2

OPTIMAL CAPITAL STRUCTURE:
AN ILLUSTRATION

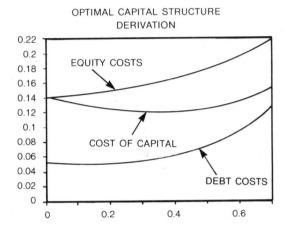

OPTIMAL CAPITAL STRUCTURE
DERIVATION

assets plus a premium equal to the excess of the asset rate over the debt rate levered by the book value debt/equity ratio net of tax effects. It is highly instructive to apply the expression to a given utility on an historical basis in order to quantify the driving forces behind equity returns and explain the behavior and trends of such returns.

EXAMPLE

Table 15-3, drawn from Andrews (1982), shows the decomposition of book return on equity into its constituent parts for South Central Bell for the 1978-1982 period, and provides an analysis of the direction and magnitude of the factors which drive equity returns. For example, the significant rise in realized equity returns in 1982 is largely the result of a widening spread between the asset rate of return and debt cost. Table 15-4 shows a sample calculation for the year 1982.

TABLE 15-3 DISAGGREGATION OF BOOK RETURN ON EQUITY:

Application to South Central Bell Data for 1982

(Dollars in Millions)

Earnings after tax	$ 624
Federal and state income tax	440
Interest expense	278
EBIT = Earnings before interest and income tax	$1,342

Assets net of zero-rate debt = A	= $7,621
EBIT/Net assets = R	= $1,342/$7,621 = .176
Interest-bearing debt = D	= $2,994
Interest expense	= $ 278
Average interest rate = i	= $278/$2,994 = .093
Common equity = E	= $4,628
Debt/Equity = D/E	= .647

Effective tax rate = Tax/Earnings before tax = t
= $440/$1,064 = .414 or 41.4%

Return on equity = r = [R + (R − i)D/E] (1 − t)
= [.176 + (.176 − .093).647](1 − .414)
= [.176 + (.083 × .647)](.586)
= [.176 + .054](.586)
= .135 or 13.5%
or
r = R(1 − t) + (R − i)(D/E)(1 − t)
= .103 + .379(R − i)

SOURCE: ANDREWS (1982)

TABLE 15-4 COMPUTATION OF RETURN ON EQUITY 1978–82 SOUTH CENTRAL BELL

	1982	1981	1980	1979	1978
R(EBIT/A)	.176	.167	.154	.140	.143
i	.093	.095	.088	.081	.076
(R − i)	.083	.072	.066	.059	.067
× D/E	.647	.651	.673	.657	.660
+ R	.176	.167	.154	.140	.143
× (1 − t)	.586	.581	.590	.598	.557
= r	.135	.124	.117	.107	.108

SOURCE: ANDREWS (1982)

15.2 IMPLICATIONS FOR REGULATION

. The major thrust of this chapter is that an estimate of cost of capital on the basis of an observed capital structure is erroneous if the capital structure is expected to change. As a practical matter, the effect of capital structure on total weighted average cost of capital is likely to be minor over the range of capital structures usually found in the utility industry. If one subscribes to the majority view that the cost of capital curve is U-shaped, the error committed by assuming a constant debt/equity ratio is likely to be small, given the flatness of the curve over the range of capital structure normally employed by utilities. Even if one subscribes to the Modigliani-Miller view that cost of capital is a declining function of leverage over a wide range of debt ratios, the magnitude of the error is still likely to be small, especially when compared to the range of reasonableness of cost of capital estimates in regulatory hearings. It is hard not to concur with Myers (1972) that it is fairly safe to estimate a utility's cost of capital on the assumption of a constant debt ratio, unless a major rapid shift in capital structure is contemplated. Similar arguments can be made for a change in dividend policy.

As far as the regulation of capital structure is concerned, the acceptability of a given capital structure is difficult to quantify precisely. The debt and equity cost relationships necessary to derive the optimal capital structure are difficult to establish with any degree of precision. Yet, it is the responsibility of regulators to ensure that a utility's capital structure should reflect a proper balance between investors' interest and ratepayers' interests, and should be an efficient minimum-cost one. Given the analytical constraints, the acceptability of a utility's capital structure should be governed by a general guideline drawn from the capital structure principles enunciated in this chapter. Such a guideline would ensure that a utility should increase the relative amount of debt it employs to the point where the increased returns required by bond and equity investors exceed the total cost savings derived from substituting low-cost tax-free debt for high-cost taxable capital. It is also important that a reasonable safety margin against possible shifts in capital market conditions, and investor risk attitudes be allowed. If the guideline is violated, revenue requirements should be calculated based on the appropriate capital structure.

15.3 RATE BASE AND CAPITAL STRUCTURE INTERRELATIONSHIP

The content of this section draws heavily from Andrews in Andrews & Morin (1983). The meaning and functioning of a utility's weighted cost of capital is interrelated with its companion rate of return on rate base. If the regulator applies the cost of capital to a rate base which deviates from total capital, then to the extent that rate base deviates from total capital, if authorized returns are achieved, dollar earnings available for common equity will exceed or fall short of the dollars necessary to satisfy the claims of shareholders. For example, if the cost of equity is 15% on book equity of $10 million, the dollars necessary are $1.50 million. If that rate of return is applied to an equity component of $9 million, the result would be equity earnings of $1.35 million, or $0.15 million less than that expected to be achieved by comparable risk investments. In general, if there is a discrepancy between the total capital investment, on the one hand, and the total rate base on the other, the fair return on common equity will not be achieved. The dollars available to service equity capital will deviate from the number of dollars required to provide the earnings that investors require as compensation for the risk capital invested in the utility. Shareholders act as the residual bearers of the gain or loss consequences of rate base-invested capital discrepancies.

More formally, once the utility's weighted average cost of capital, K, attaching to investor capital, C, is determined, the total dollar returns required to service capital are K times C, or KC. If the regulator applies the cost of capital to the rate base, W, and if the rate base equals invested capital, then the net utility income produced to service capital will be K times W, or KW. Since the earnings permitted on assets are equal to the earnings necessary to service the capital put up by investors, then KW equals KC. But what if the allowed return on the rate base does not equal K? If the regulator allows a return of 'y', which differs from K, the earnings available to investors are yW. The earnings will equal the requirement of returns to capital so that yW = KC only if the regulator permits it. The allowed return on rate base will then be y = KC/W. Clearly, if the rate base W equals the capital C actually supplied by investors, then y = K.

If the rate base does not equal invested capital, then y cannot equal K. If y is set equal to K but the rate base is less than capital, then yW < KC, meaning that return on capital realized by the utility will be lower than its cost. The integrity of the invested equity capital will not be maintained.

In practice, it is rarely true that the rate base and total capital are equal. For example, CWIP assets excluded from rate base without the AFUDC offset, or asset investments excluded from the rate base because such investments are not deemed "used and useful" and/or "prudent" by the regulator clearly violate the equality of rate base and invested capital. A more subtle example is the case of the working capital allowance. To see this, let's define capital as total financing sources which equals net fixed assets plus net working capital viewed in the usual accounting balance sheet sense. The working capital allowance incorporated into rate base in most jurisdictions bears little resemblance to the traditional accounting meaning of net working capital. If capital is equal to a total composed in part of net working capital, and if the working capital component of the rate base equals net working capital only by chance, then rate base and capital can only be equal by coincidence.

Short-term Debt[5]

Interest-rate bearing short-term debt is frequently an issue in some jurisdictions. The omission of short-term debt from the debt component of weighted cost of capital calculation is sometimes rationalized by the traditional practice of using short-term debt, bank borrowing and commercial paper, as interim financing during construction periods. Since this can be an expensive omission in periods of high short-term interest rates, the inclusion of short-term debt in rate filings has become more frequent.

The omission of short-term debt from the capital structure, or more generally of any component of capital, results in imputation of the resulting weighted average to the omitted element. This result is predicated on the key assumption that the rate base is not reduced by the amount of such funds sources.

To see this, consider the following example. As shown in Table 15-5 below, a utility has a capital structure consisting of equal proportions of debt and equity of $50 each with attaching costs of 10% and 20% respectively to give a weighted cost of 15%. By contrast, the table also shows the calculated weighted cost of capital with another $50 of short-term debt included at an imputed weighted cost of 15%.

TABLE 15-5 SHORT-TERM DEBT AND THE WEIGHTED COST OF CAPITAL

	WEIGHT			WEIGHTED COST	
	Case A	Case B	Cost	Case A	Case B
Debt	.5	.333	.10	.05	.033
Short-term debt	–	.333	.15	–	.050
Equity	.5	.333	.20	.10	.067
TOTAL WEIGHTED COST:				.15	.15

In Case A, dollar earnings total .15 x \$100 = \$15, enough to service the \$5 claim of bondholders and the \$10 claim of shareholders. In Case B, dollar earnings total .15 x \$150 = \$22.50, from which \$5 and \$10 will cover the claims of bondholders and shareholders respectively, and the remaining \$7.50 is available to service the \$50 of short-term capital at a return rate of \$7.50/\$50 = 15%, which is the weighted average cost of capital.

Exclusion of the short-term debt capital from the weighted average calculation is equivalent to assignment of the average otherwise computed if the rate base is defined equal to total capital. This result obtains because of the behavior of the weights attaching to the sources of funds when short-term debt is included or excluded. Inclusion of the short-term debt in the calculation will dilute the proportionate weights of other funds sources. However, attachment of the overall weighted cost to the short-term component adds exactly the costs of the diluted sources for a net difference of zero. This result is proven formally by Andrews (1983), and depends on the independence of the rate base definition. If the rate base is reduced by the amount of the short-term debt, equivalency of result no longer holds.

This last point is demonstrated more formally in Andrews (1983) as follows. Assuming that a weighted average cost of K applies to three rate-bearing components of capital, C_1, C_2, and C_3. The coverage of capital costs is provided by a rate base, W, equal to $C_1 + C_2 + C_3$. The rate base earns at the rate y, thus,

$$yW = K (C_1 + C_2 + C_3)$$

If C_2 is excluded from capital, the missing coverage is KC_2. However, if the rate base is not altered, earnings will exceed $K(C_1 + C_3)$ by the amount $yC_2 = KC_2$. If the rate base is reduced by something less than C_2, partial coverage of C_2 will result. The main point is that these results only hold if the rate base W equals invested capital, $C_1 + C_2 + C_3$.

Zero-cost Capital Components

Zero-cost components of capital arise from (1) the deferred income taxes accumulated from reporting of acceleration for tax purposes as opposed to straight-line book depreciation reported externally in utility financial statements, and (2) deferred credits to income tax associated with investment tax credits. Most jurisdictions permit normalized or deferred recognition of at least one of these means of tax reduction, as opposed to immediate recognition (flow-through) of the tax savings for rate-making purposes. The 1982 tax law amendments have greatly reinforced this practice. The reader is referred to Howe & Rasmussen (1982) for a thorough statement of utility tax issues.

Most regulatory commissions consider deferred tax credits to be a part of the capital structure, but allow a zero rate of return on that capital component, on the grounds that deferred taxes are equivalent to an interest free loan from the government and hence have no cost to the utility. An equivalent treatment is to subtract the zero-cost source of financing from the rate base.

To see this, consider the following example. As shown in Table 15-6 below, a utility has a capital structure consisting of equal proportions of debt and equity of $50 each with attaching costs of 10% and 20% respectively to give a weighted cost of 15%. By contrast, the table also shows the calculated weighted cost of capital with another $50 of deferred tax financing included at a zero-cost rate.

TABLE 15-6 ZERO-COST COMPONENTS AND THE WEIGHTED COST OF CAPITAL

	WEIGHT			WEIGHTED COST	
	Case A	Case B	Cost	Case A	Case B
Debt	.5	.333	.10	.05	.033
Deferred taxes	–	.333	.00	–	.000
Equity	.5	.333	.20	.10	.067
TOTAL WEIGHTED COST:				.15	.10

One alternative treatment (Case B) is to include deferred taxes as a component of capital and find the allowed return as the weighted average of capital, including zero-cost capital sources. The weighted average cost of capital is 10% using this method. Applied to a rate base of $150 which includes deferred taxes, dollar earnings of .10 x $150 = $15 are produced, enough to service the claims of both bondholders, .10 x $50 = $5, and shareholders, .20 x $50 = $10.

Coverage of exactly the same dollar total of capital cost results from subtraction of the zero-rate capital from the rate base and the capital structure (Case A). The weighted average cost of capital is 15%, if deferred tax capital is excluded from the computation. Applied to a rate base of $150 – $50 = $100, dollar earnings of .15 x $100 = $15 are produced, the same dollar total of capital cost achievable under the first method. Note however that the two allowed rates cannot be equal (15% versus 10%). The divergence will be even greater if the rate base does not equal invested capital.

As a result of new tax laws, some deferred tax credits must be allowed a rate of return. The impact on capital costs can be seen by referring back to the short-term debt example in Table 15-5, and substituting deferred tax of $50 for short-term debt. Exclusion of deferred tax from the weighted average is equivalent to assignment of the average otherwise computed, as long as the rate base is defined to include total capital. It is noteworthy that if the return on the deferred credits is captured by the shareholders, the return on equity is in effect increased.

15.4   INTERCORPORATE OWNERSHIP AND DOUBLE LEVERAGE

Determining the cost of capital for a utility operating company owned by a holding company is a controversial capital structure issue. Intercorporate ownership opens the possibility of leveraging the common equity of one corporate entity at two or even more corporate levels. If a parent corporation issues its own debt and if a wholly owned subsidiary also builds debt over the base of equity invested by the parent, leveraging takes place twice on the single layer of the parent's publicly held equity. A parent company and a single subsidiary can thus create double leverage; even more extensive leveraging can occur through the existence of parent-subsidiary horizontal and vertical networks of subsidiaries. The situation is common among utilities with clusters of subsidiaries and their parents.

The expression double leverage stems from the situation where first there is leverage on the earnings for the operating company's common stock, and then additional leverage for the holding company's common stock to the extent that the holding company obtains part of the funds invested in the subsidiary's common stock from debt sources. The situation is prevalent among telecommunications and water utilities. The issue does not arise for electric and gas companies which are subsidiaries of holding companies; the Public Utility Holding Company Act applying to such companies are severely limited in the amount of borrowing they may undertake. Telecommunications utilities are not governed by this act.

Several alternative methods to determine the operating company's cost of capital are possible. Consider the following numerical example. An operating company's capital structure consists of equal proportions of debt and equity, with attaching costs of 10% and 20% respectively. The company is a wholly owned subsidiary of a parent company whose own source of capital is 25% debt and 75% equity. It is assumed that the cost of debt to the parent is also 10%, and that a reasonable return to parent stockholders is 15%. The situation is summarized in Table 15-7 below:

**TABLE 15-7 OPERATING AND PARENT COMPANY
COST OF CAPITAL**

OPERATING COMPANY

	Amount	Weight	Cost	Weighted Cost
Debt	$50	.50	.10	.05
Equity	$50	.50	.20	.10
	$100			
			Total Cost	.15

PARENT COMPANY

	Weight	Cost	Weighted Cost
Debt	.25	.10	.0250
Equity	.75	.15	.1125
		Total Cost	.1375

Independent Company Approach

One way to proceed is simply to ignore the parent-subsidiary relationship, and treat the operating company's cost of capital in the usual way as the weighted average cost of capital using the operating company's own capital structure and cost rates. In this approach, often labeled the "stand alone" or "subsidiary approach", the subsidiary is viewed as an independent operating company, and its cost of equity is inferred as the cost of equity of comparable risk firms. The methodology rests on the basic premise that the required return on an investment depends on its risk, rather than on the parent's financing costs.

In the example, the weighted cost is 15%. The allowed return of 20% on equity is derived from the techniques described in previous chapters, perhaps from a DCF analysis of comparable utility groups, or from a Risk Premium analysis based on the operating company's debt yield. The equity return reflects the risk to which the equity capital is exposed and the opportunity return foregone by the company's shareholders in investments of similar risk. The identity of the shareholders is immaterial in determining the equity return.

Double Leverage Approach

Another approach is the double leverage methodology. This method has several variants. One treatment, shown in Table 15-8, traces the operating company's equity capital of $50 to its source, namely the parent's debt and equity capital. The cost of equity to the operating company is simply the overall weighted average of capital to the parent, since the equity capital was in fact raised by the parent through a mixture of debt and equity. The parent's composite capital cost is imputed to the subsidiary's equity.

TABLE 15-8 OPERATING COMPANY COST OF CAPITAL: DOUBLE LEVERAGE CONCEPT

	Amount	Weight	Cost	Weighted Cost
Debt - subsidiary	$50.00	.500	.10	.0500
Equity - provided by parent:				
Debt-parent (25%)	$12.50	.125	.10	.0125
Equity-parent (75%)	$37.50	.375	.15	.0562
		Weighted Cost		.1187

Advocates of the double leverage approach argue that the utility subsidiary only requires a 11.87% return on total capital rather than the 13.75% indicated in the previous calculation. Although the parent invested $50 in the company, it used leverage itself in raising its capital, so that the true cost of capital to the subsidiary is the cost of its own debt capital, plus the proportionate cost of its parent's debt and equity capital. Moreover, if the parent was allowed a 20% return on its $50 equity investment in the subsidiary, unreasonably high returns would be extracted by the parent's shareholders from ratepayers. In the example, gross dollar earnings of .20 x $50 = $10 would accrue to the parent company's shareholders; but since 25% of that $50, or $12.50, was borrowed at an interest rate of 10%, $1.25 must be subtracted from the gross earnings of $10 to produce net equity earnings of $8.75 on an equity investment of $37.50. That is a 23.33% return on equity. The theoretical and conceptual fallacies of this reasoning will be discussed shortly.

Modified Double Leverage Approach

One refinement to the double leverage method is to recognize that the parent's weighted cost of capital should only be imputed to the portion of equity actually contributed by the parent. The subsidiary's retained earnings should be removed from the double leverage imputation since none of the subsidiary's retained earnings are traceable to the capital raised by the parent. This will associate proportionately the components of parent capital and their respective costs with that part of subsidiary equity ostensibly financed in this way. The revised calculation with retained earnings removed is shown in Table 15-9. It is assumed that $40 of the $50 of subsidiary equity capital was contributed by the parent, and the remaining $10 is the subsidary's own retained earnings, and the latter continues to be allowed a 20% return.

TABLE 15-9 OPERATING COMPANY COST OF CAPITAL: MODIFIED DOUBLE LEVERAGE

	Amount	Weight	Cost	Weighted Cost
Debt - subsidiary	$50	.50	.10	.050
Retained Earnings - subsidiary	$10	.10	.20	.020
Equity - provided by parent:				
Debt - parent (25%)	$10	.10	.10	.010
Equity-parent (75%)	$30	.30	.15	.045
			Weighted Cost	.125

One procedural flaw in the above double leverage computation is the failure to recognize that the debt ratio of the operating company has increased from 50% to 60%. Hence both debt and equity cost rates should be higher as a result of the increased financial risk. The 20% return on equity should be adjusted upward in recognition of the increased financial risk.

Consolidated Approach

Another method of computing the subsidiary's cost of capital uses consolidated data of the parent and subsidiary companies on the grounds that the holding company and its units are financed as an integrated whole, based on systemside financing objectives. The cost rates for debt and preferred capital are system-wide averages, and the cost of equity is determined by traditional methods. Prior to divestiture, the Bell System supported the use of a consolidated capital structure rather than a double-levered capital structure. Where the parent conducts all the financing for the subsidiaries as in the Columbia Gas System, the use of a consolidated capital structure is dictated by the lack of alternatives.

A few points regarding consolidated capital structures are in order. First, the debt of the consolidated company is the sum of the holding company's debt and the subsidiary's debt. Hence, the consolidated cost of debt is a weighted cost of parent and subsidiary debt.

Second, the cost of equity of the holding company is identical to that of the consolidated entity. This is because the value of the parent holding company's stock expressly recognizes subsidiary income to parent investment if accounted on an equity basis. Accounting on the equity basis treats subsidiary net income as income to the parent's equity investment whether such income is received as dividends or not. The parent's retained earnings necessarily reflect this. Accordingly, the cost of equity associated with market valuation of holding company equity is also the cost of equity figure for the consolidated network.

Third, a consolidated capital structure is equivalent to a double-levered capital structure when all the parent's subsidiaries have the same amounts of leverage.

Lastly, some analysts contend that assignment of the consolidated weighted cost to the equity cost of the subsidiary is equivalent to imputation of the holding company's equity cost. This can only be true in the highly unlikely event that the costs of consolidated debt and equity are exactly equal, or, if they are unequal, that the differences in weights between the consolidated and the subsidiary capital structure exactly offset the differences in weights. This is proven formally in Andrews (1983).

Critique of Double Leverage

Adherents to the double leverage calculation argue that the true cost of capital to a utility subsidiary is the weighted cost of its own debt and the weighted cost of the parent's debt and equity funding. Moreover, unless the subsidiary's equity is assigned the parent's weighted cost of capital, parent shareholders will reap abnormally high returns. Although persuasive on the surface, these arguments conceal serious conceptual and practical problems. Moreover, the validity of double leverage rests on questionable assumptions.

Theoretical Issues

The double leverage approach contradicts the core of the cost of capital concept. Financial theory clearly establishes that the cost of equity is the risk-adjusted opportunity cost to the investors, and not the cost of the specific capital sources employed by investors. The true cost of capital depends on the use to which the capital is put, and not on its source. What the *Hope* and *Bluefield* doctrines have made clear is that the relevant considerations in calculating a company's cost of capital are the alternatives available to investors and the returns and risks associated with those alternatives. The specific source of funding an investment and the cost of the funds to the investor are irrelevant considerations.

For example, if an individual investor borrows money at the bank at an after-tax cost of 8% and invests the funds in a speculative oil exploration venture, the required return on the investment is not the 8% cost, but rather the return foregone in speculative projects of similar risk, say 20%. Yet, under the double leverage approach, the individual's fair return on this risky venture would be 8%, which is the cost of the capital sources, and not 20% which is the required return on investments of similar risk. Carrying the example a step further, if the individual investor had inherited the money instead of borrowing at the bank, the double leverage approach would assign a fair return equal to the cost of obtaining the capital, namely 0%. This result is clearly illogical. The cost of capital is governed by the risk to which to the capital is exposed and not by whether the funds were obtained from bondholders or common shareholders, and at what cost.

Just as individual investors require different returns from different assets in managing their personal affairs, why should regulation cause parent companies making investment decisions on behalf on their shareholders to act any differently? Obviously, in a diversified holding company such as Tenneco or GTE engaged through affiliates in many diverse activities, the cost of capital for each activity varies with the risks and prospects of each. Yet, the double leverage calculation would assign the same return to each activity, based on the parent's cost of capital. Investors do recognize that different subsidiaries are exposed to different risks, as evidenced by the different bond ratings and cost rates of operating subsidiaries. The same argument carries over to common equity; if the cost rate for debt is different because the risk is different, the cost rate for common equity is also different, and the double leverage adjustment should not obscure this fact.

The double leverage concept is also at odds with the opportunity cost concept of economics. According to this principle of economics, the cost of any resource is the cost of an alternative foregone. The cost of investing funds in an operating utility subsidiary is the return foregone on investments of similar risk. If the fair risk-adjusted return assigned by the market on utility investments is 15%, and the regulator assigns a return less than 15% because of a double leverage calculation, there is no incentive or defensible reason for a parent holding company to invest in that utility.

Carrying the double leverage standard to its logical conclusion leads to unreasonable prescriptions. If the common shares of a utility subsidiary were held by both a parent holding company and by individual investors, the equity contributed by the parent would have one cost under the double leverage computation while the equity contributed by the public would have another. Or does double leverage require tracing the source of funds used by each individual investor so that its cost can be computed by applying double leverage to each individual investor? No, equity is equity irrespective of its source, and the cost of that equity is governed by its use, by the risk to which it is exposed. If a utility subsidiary with a double leverage cost of equity of 12% were sold to another company with a higher cost of capital of say 15%, would regulation alter the return accordingly just because of the change in ownership? If so, the same utility with the same assets and providing the same service under the new management would have a higher cost of service to ratepayers because of the transfer of ownership.

Clearly, if a utility subsidiary were allowed an equity return equal to the parent's weighted cost of capital while the same utility were allowed a fair, presumably higher, return were it not part of a holding company complex, an irresistible incentive to dissolve the holding company structure would exist in favor of the one-company operating utility format. The attendant benefits of scale economies and diversification would then be lost to the ratepayers.

Fairness and Capital Attraction

The double leverage approach is highly discriminatory, and violates the doctrine of fairness. If a utility is not part of a holding company structure, the cost of equity is computed using one method, say the DCF method, while otherwise the cost of equity is computed using the double leverage adjustment. Estimating equity costs by one procedure for publicly-held utilities and by another for utilities owned by a holding company is inconsistent with financial theory and discriminates against the holding company form of ownership. Two utilities identical in all respects but for their ownership format should have the same set of rates. Yet, this would not be the case under the double leverage adjustment.

The capital attraction standard may also be impaired under the double leverage calculation. This is because a utility subsidiary must compete on its own in the market for debt capital, and therefore must earn an appropriate return on equity to support its credit rating. Imputing the parent's weighted cost to the utility's equity capital may result in inadequate equity returns and less favorable coverage, hence impairing the utility subsidiary's ability to attract debt capital under favorable terms.

Assumptions

Several assumptions underlying the double leverage standard are questionable. One assumption which was already alluded to in the previous numerical illustrations is the traceability of the subsidiary's equity capital to its parent. None of the retained earnings can be traced to the capital raised by the parent. Some analysts salvage the double leverage approach by assigning one cost rate to retained earnings and another to the common equity capital raised by the parent, with the curious result, that equity has two cost rates. The traceability issue goes further. If a parent company issues bonds or preferred stock to acquire an operating subsidiary, the traceability assumption is broken. Corporate reorganizations and mergers further invalidate the traceability assumption.

By virtue of using the parent's weighted cost as the equity cost rate for the subsidiary, another questionable assumption is that the the parent capital is invested in subsidiaries which all have the same risks. Lastly, the double leverage procedure makes the unlikely assumption that the parent holding company invest its funds in each subsidiary proportionately to each subsidiary's debt-equity ratio.

Following an analysis of descriptive examples and a general theoretical examination, Pettway & Jordan (1983) found no valid support of the double leverage approach, and conclude that the independent company approach should be employed in rate cases.

In summary, the double leverage adjustment has serious conceptual and practical limitations and violates basic notions of finance, economics, and fairness. The assumptions which underlie its use are questionable, if not unrealistic.

Notes
[1] An alternate methodology to find cost of an all-equity financed firm, p, is to use Equation 14-6:

$$K = p(1 - TB/C)$$

Knowing the tax rate, T, and the weighted cost of capital, K, at the firm's existing capital structure, B/C, the equation can be solved for p.

[2] Equation 15-2 can be modified to account for the presence of preferred stock as follows:

$$B_l = B_u[1 + (1-T)D/E + P/E]$$

where P/E is the preferred stock/common equity ratio.

[3] Knowing any three points on the curved portion of the bond graph, a quadratic function can be fitted to approximate the shape of the graph.

[4] Empirical evidence on the shape of the equity graph can be found in Robichek, Higgins, and Kinsman (1973).

[5] This section is adapted from Andrews (1983).

INDEX

BIBLIOGRAPHY

Andrews, V. L. (1983) *Determining Cost of Capital for Regulated Industries*, Public Utilities Reports Inc. & The Management Exchange Inc., Washington, D.C. (with R. A. Morin).

Andrews, V. L. (1982) *South Central Bell Telephone Co.*, Prepared Testimony, Alabama Public Service Commission, Docket # 8847.

Archer, S. H. (1981) 'The Regulatory Effects of Cost of Capital in Electric Utilities.' *Public Utilities Fortnightly*, Feb. 26, 1981.

Arnott, R. (1980) 'Cluster Analysis and Stock Price Co-movement.' *Financial Analysts Journal*, Nov.-Dec. 1980.

Arzac, E.R. and Marcus, M. (1981) 'Flotation Cost Allowance in Rate of Return Regulation: A Note.' *Journal of Finance* 36 (December 1981), 1199-1202.

Averch, H.A. and Johnson, L. (1962) 'Behavior of the Firm under Regulatory Constraint.' *American Economic Review*, 52, 6 (1962), 1053-1069.

Banz, R.W. (1981) 'The Relationship Between Return and Market Value of Common Stocks,' *Journal of Financial Economics*, March 1981, 3-18.

Basu, S. (1977) 'Investment Performance of Common Stocks in Relation to Their Price-Earnings Ratios: A Test of The Efficient Markets Hypothesis,' *Journal of Finance*, June 1977, 663-682.

Beaver, W. H., Kettler, P. and Scholes, M. (1970) 'The Association Between Market Determined and Accounting Determined Risk Measures,' *Accounting Review*, 45, October 1970, 654-82.

Berndt, E.R. (1979) 'Utility Bond Rates and Tax Normalization,' *Journal of Finance*, 34(5), Dec. 1979, 1211-1220.

Black, F., Jensen, M.C., and Scholes, M. (1972) 'The Capital Asset Pricing Model: Some Empirical Tests,' reprinted in M.C. Jensen, ed., *Studies in the Theory of Capital Markets*. Praeger, N. Y., 1972, 79-124.

Blume, M.E. (1975) 'Betas and Their Regression Tendencies,' *Journal of Finance*, 30(3), June 1975, 785-96.

Blume, M.E. and Friend, I. (1978) *The Changing Role of the Individual Investor*, Twentieth Century Report, Wiley & Sons, 1978.

Bowyer, J.W. and Yawitz, J.B. (1980) 'The Effect of New Equity Issues on Utility Stock Prices,' *Public Utilities Fortnightly*, May 22, 1980, 25-28.

Brealey, R. and Myers S. (1984) *Principles of Corporate Finance*, McGraw-Hill, 1984, 2nd edition.

Breenan, M. (1973) 'Taxes, Market Valuation and Corporate Financial Policy,' *National Tax Journal*, 23, 417-427.

Brennan, J. (1982) 'Does Utility Long-term Debt Really Cost More than Common Equity?' *Public Utilities Fortnightly*, Feb. 18, 1982.

Brigham, E.F. (1979) 'The Changing Investment Risk of Public Utilities,' Public Utility Research Center Working Paper 2-79, University of Florida.

Brigham, E.F. (1979A) *Georgia Power Co.*, Prepared Rebuttal Testimony, Federal Energy Regulatory Commission, Docket # ER79-88.

Brigham, E.F. (1982) *Pennsylvania Electric Company*, Prepared Testimony, Pennsylvania Public Utility Commission, Docket # R-822250.

Brigham, E.F. (1982A) *Financial Management Theory and Practice*, The Dryden Press, 3rd ed.

Brigham, E.F. (1983) *Pennsylvania Electric Company*, Rebuttal Testimony, Pennsylvania Public Utility Commission, Docket # R-822250.

Brigham, E.F. and Crum R.L. (1977) 'On the Use of the CAPM in Public Utility Rate Cases,' *Financial Management,* Summer 1977, 7-15.

Brigham, E.F., Shome, D.K., and Bankston, T.A. (1979) 'An Econometric Model for Estimating the Cost of Capital for a Public Utility,' Public Utility Research Center Working Paper, University of Florida, May 1979.

Brigham, E.F. and Shome, D.K. (1982) 'Equity Risk Premiums in the 1980's,' Institute for Study of Regulation, Washington, D.C. 1982.

Brown, L.D. and Rozeff, M.S. (1978) 'The Superiority of Analyst Forecasts as Measures of Expectations: Evidence from Earnings,' *Journal of Finance,* March 1978.

Carleton, W.T. (1980) *Southern Bell,* Prepared Testimony, North Carolina Utilities Commission, Docket # P-55, Sub 784.

Chandrasekaran, R. and Dukes, W.P. (1981) 'Risk Variables Affecting Rate of Return of Public Utilities,' *Public Utilities Fortnightly,* 32, Feb. 26, 1981.

Chartoff, J., Mayo, G.W., and Smith, W.A. (1982) 'The Case Against the Use of the CAPM in Public Utility Ratemaking,' *Energy Law Journal,* 54(3), August 1978, 348-61.

Chen, N.F. (1981) 'Arbitrage Asset Pricing: Theory and Evidence,' Unpublished PhD Thesis, UCLA, Graduate School of Management, 1981.

Chen, N.F. (1983) 'Tests of the Arbitrage Asset Pricing Model,' *Journal of Finance,* December 1983.

Chen, A.H. and Kim, E.H. (1979) 'Theories of Corporate Debt Policy: A Synthesis,' *Journal of Finance,* May 1979, 371-84.

Cohen, J.B., Zinbarg, E.D. and Zeikel, A. (1977) *Investment Analysis and Portfolio Management,* 3rd ed., Richard D. Irwin, 1977.

Copan, J.A. (1983) 'Debt Coverage as a Measure of a Firm's Revenue Requirements,' *Public Utilities Fortnightly,* 112(4), Aug 18, 1983, 27-33.

Copeland, B.L. (1979) 'The Cost of Equity Capital: A Model for Regulatory Review,' In *Issues in Public Utility Regulation,* ed. H.M. Trebing, East Lansing: Michigan State University, 1979, 342-66.

Copeland, T.E. and Weston, F. (1983) *Financial Theory and Corporate Policy,* 2nd ed., Addison-Wesley, 1983.

Davidson, W.N. and Chandy, P.R. (1983) 'The Regulatory Environment for Public Utilities: Indications of the Importance of Political Process,' *Financial Analysts Journal,* Nov.-Dec. 1983, 50-53

Davis, B.E. and Sparrow, F.T. (1972) 'Valuation Models in Regulation,' *Bell Journal of Economics and Management Science,* 3(2), Autumn 1972, 544-67.

Dubin, J.A. and Navarro, P. (1983) 'The Effect of Rate Suppression on Utilities' Cost of Capital,' *Public Utilities Fortnightly,* March 31, 1983, 18-22.

Dukes, W.P. and Chandy, R.P. (1983) 'Rate of Return and Risk for Public Utilities,' *Public Utilities Fortnightly,* Sept. 1, 1983, 35-41.

Dwyer, V.A. (1979) *American Telephone and Telegraph Co.,* Prepared Testimony, Federal Communications Commission, Docket # CC 79-63.

Economic Report of the President, January 1978, 1979, 1980.

Efron, B. and Morris, C. (1975) 'Data Analysis Using Stein's Estimator and Its Generalizations,' *Journal of the American Statistical Association,* 70, June 1975, 311-19.

Elton, E.J. and Gruber, M.J. (1981) *Modern Portfolio Theory and Investment Analysis,* New York: Wiley & Sons, 1981.

Fama, E.F. (1975) 'Short-term Interest Rates as Predictors of Inflation,' *American Economic Review,* June 1975, 269-82.

Farrel, J.L. (1974) 'Analyzing Covariation of Returns to Determine Homogeneous Stock Groupings,' *Journal of Business,* 47(2), April 1974, 186-207.

Fisher, I. (1907) *The Rate of Interest,* American Economic Association, 1907.

Fisher, M. and McGowan, J.J. (1981) 'On the Misuse of Accounting Rates of Return to Infer Monopoly Profits,' Boston, Mass.: Charles River Associates, mimeo.

Fitzpatrick, D.B. and Stitzel, T.E. (1978) 'Capitalizing an Allowance for Funds Used during Construction: The Impact on Earnings Quality,' *Public Utilities Fortnightly*, 101(2), Jan. 19, 1978, 18-22.

Fogler, H.R. (1982) 'Common Sense on CAPM, APT, and Correlated Residuals,' *Journal of Portfolio Management*, Summer 1982.

Francis, J.C. (1975) 'Skewness and Investors' Decisions,' *Journal of Financial and Quantitative Analysis*, March 1975.

Francis, J.C. (1976) *Investments Analysis and Management*, 2nd ed., McGraw-Hill, 1976.

Friend, I. (1983) *The Bell Telephone Company of Pennsylvania*, Prepared Testimony, Pennsylvania Public Utility Commission, Docket # 2316.

Friend, I. and Blume M.E. (1975) 'The Demand for Risky Assets,' *American Economic Review*, December 1975, 900-922.

Friend, I., Westerfield, R. and Granito, M. (1978) 'New Evidence on the Capital Asset Pricing Model,' *Journal of Finance* 23(3), 903-916.

Fuller, R.J. and Kerr, W. (1981) 'Estimating the Divisional Cost of Capital: An Analysis of the Pure-play Technique,' *Journal of Finance*, Dec. 1981, 997-1009.

Garfield, P.J. and Lovejoy, W. (1964) *Public Utility Economics*, Englewood Cliffs, N.J.: Prentice-Hall, 1964.

Gehr, A. (1975) 'Some Tests of the Arbitrage Pricing Theory,' *Journal of the Midwest Finance Association*, 1975, 91-105.

Gordon, M.J. (1974) *The Cost of Capital to a Public Utility*, East Lansing, Michigan: Michigan State University, 1974.

Gordon, M.J. (1977) 'Rate of Return Regulation in the Current Economic Environment,' In *Adapting Regulation to Shortages, Curtailments and Inflation*, ed. J.L. O'Donnell, East Lansing: Michigan State University, 1977, 15-28.

Gordon, M.J. and Halpern, P. (1974) 'The Cost of Capital to a Division of a Firm,' *Journal of Finance*, 29, September 1974, 1153-63.

Hadaway, S.C., Heidebrecht, B.L. and Nash, J.L. (1982) 'A Cost-Benefit Analysis of Alternative Bond Ratings Among Electric Utility Companies in Texas,' Public Utility Commission of Texas, Economic Research Division, Dec. 1982.

Hagin, R.L. (1979) *Modern Portfolio Theory*, Homewood, Ill: Dow Jones-Irwin. 1979.

Halpern, P. (1973) *Determining the Cost of Equity for Regulated Utilities*, University of Toronto, 1973, submitted to the Telecommunications Cost Inquiry, CRTC, 1973.

Hamada, R.S. (1972) 'The Effect of the Firm's Capital Structure on the Systematic Risk of Common Stocks,' *Journal of Finance*, May 1972, 435-52.

Harrington, D.R. (1980) 'The Changing Use of the Capital Asset Pricing Model in Utility Regulation.' *Public Utilities Fortnightly*, Aug. 14, 1980, 28-30.

Hickman, W.B. (1958) *Corporate Bond Quality and Investor Experience*, Princeton, N.J.: Princeton University Press.

Holland, D.M. and Myers, S.C. (1979) 'Trends in Corporate Profitability and Capital Costs,' in *The Nation's Capital Needs: Three Studies*, Ed. Robert Lindsay, New York: Committee for Economic Development.

Homer S. and Leibowitz, M.L. (1972) *Inside the Yield Book: New Tools for Bond Market Strategy*, Englewood Cliffs, N.J.: Prentice-Hall, Inc. 1972.

Howe, K.M. (1984) 'Flotation Cost Allowance for the Regulated Firm: A Comparison of Alternatives,' *Journal of Finance*, March 1984.

Howe, K.M. and Rasmussen, E.F. (1982) *Public Utility Economics and Finance*, Englewood Cliffs, N.J.: Prentice-Hall, Inc., 1982.

Hyman, L.S. (1983) *America's Electric Utilities: Past, Present and Future*, Arlington, Va.: Public Utilities Reports, Inc., 1982.

Ibbotson, R.G. and Sinquefield, R.A. (1982) *Stocks, Bonds, Bills, and Inflation: The Past and the Future*, Charlottesville, Va.: Financial Analysts Research Foundation, 1982 edition, Monograph # 15.

Jaffee, J.F. and Mandelker, G. (1976) 'The Value of the Firm under Regulation,' *Journal of Finance*, May 1976, 701-13.

Jensen, M.C. (1972) 'Capital Markets: Theory and Evidence,' *The Bell Journal of Economics and Management Science*, Autumn 1972, 357-98.

Jensen, M.C. and Meckling, W. (1976) 'Theory of the Firm: Managerial Behavior, Agency Costs, and Ownership Structure,' *Journal of Financial Economics*, Oct. 1976, 305-60.

Kahn, A.E. (1970) *The Economics of Regulation*, Vol. 1. New York: Wiley, 1970.

King, B. (1966) 'Market and Industry Factors,' *Journal of Business*, Jan. 1966, 139-91.

Kolb, R.W. and Gay, G.D. (1982) 'Immunizing Bond Portfolios with Interest Rate Futures,' *Financial Management*, Summer 1982, 81-9.

Kolb, R.W., Morin, R.A. and Gay, G.D. (1983) 'Hedging Regulatory Lag with Futures Contracts,' *Journal of Finance*, May 1983.

Kolbe, A.L. and Read, J.A. (1983) 'Missing Assets and the Systematic Risk of Public Utility Shares,' Boston, Mass.: Charles River Associates, May 1983.

Kraus, A. and Litzenberger, R.H. (1976) 'Skewness Preference and the Valuation of Risk Assets,' *Journal of Finance* 31(4) 1085-99.

Lerner, E.M. (1973) 'What are the Real Double Leverage Problems?' *Public Utilities Fortnightly*, June 7, 1973, 18-23.

Lerner, E.M. and Breen, W.J. (1981) 'The Changing Significance of AFUDC for Public Utilities,' *Public Utilities Fortnightly*, 107(1), Jan. 1, 1981, 17-25.

Levy, R.A. (1971) 'On the Short-term Stationarity of Beta Coefficients,' *Financial Analysts Journal*, 27(6), Nov.-Dec. 1971, 55-62.

Levy, R.E. (1978) 'Fair Return on Equity for Public Utilities,' *Business Economics*, Sept. 1978, 46-57.

Lintner, J. and Glauber, R. (1967) 'Higgledy Pidggledy Growth in America?' paper presented to the Seminar on the Analysis of Security Prices, University of Chicago, May 1967.

Little, I.M. (1962) 'Higgledy Pidggledy Growth,' *Institute of Statistics*, Oxford, Nov. 1962.

Litzenberger, R.H. (1979) *Southern Bell*, Prepared Testimony, Florida Public Service Commission, 1979.

Litzenberger, R.H. and Ramaswamy, K. (1979) 'The Effect of Personal Taxes and Dividends on Capital Asset Prices: Theory and Empirical Evidence,' *Journal of Financial Economics*, June 1979, 163-196.

Litzenberger, R.H., Ramaswamy, K. and Sosin, H. (1980) 'On the CAPM Approach to the Estimation of a Public Utility's Cost of Equity Capital,' *Journal of Finance* 35, May 1980, 369-83.

Logue, D.E. and Jarrow, R.A. (1978) 'Negotiations versus Competitive Bidding in the Sale of Securities by Public Utilities,' *Financial Management* 7, Autumn 1978, 31-9.

Lusztig, P. and Schwab, B. (1977) *Managerial Finance in a Canadian Setting*, 2nd ed., Toronto, Ontario: Butterworths, 1977.

Malkiel, B.G. (1979) 'The Capital Formation Problem in the United States,' *Journal of Finance*, May 1979, 291-306.

Malko, J.R. and Enholm, G.B. (1983) 'Applying CAPM in a Utility Rate Case: Current Issues and Future Directions,' Forthcoming in *Electric Ratemaking*,

1984.

Markowitz, H.M. (1952) 'Portfolio Selection,' *Journal of Finance* 7(1), March 1952, 77-91. Reprinted in Lorie, J. and Brealey, R. ed., *Modern Developments in Investment Management: A Book of Readings,* 2d ed., Hinsdale, Ill.: Dryden Press, 1978, 310-24.

Masulis, R. (1980) 'The Effects of Capital Structure Change on Security Prices: A Study of Exchange Offers,' *Journal of Financial Economics,* June 1980, 139-178.

Masulis, R. (1982) 'The Impact of Capital Structure Change on Firm Value, Some Estimates,' *Journal of Finance,* forthcoming.

McEnally, R.W. (1980) 'How to Neutralize Reinvestment Rate Risk,' *Journal of Portfolio Management,* Spring 1980.

Melicher, R.W. (1974) 'Financial Factors which Influence Beta Variations within an Homogeneous Industry Environment,' *Journal of Financial and Quantitative Analysis* 9, March 1974, 231-41.

Melicher, R.W. (1979) 'Risk Measurement and Rate of Return under Regulation,' In *Issues in Public Utility Regulation,* ed. H.M. Trebing, East Lansing: Michigan State University, 1979, 325-341.

Miller, M.H. (1977) 'Debt and Taxes,' *Journal of Finance,* May 1977, 261-297.

Modigliani, F. and Miller, M.H. (1958) 'The Cost of Capital, Corporation Finance and the Theory of Investment,' *American Economic Review,* 48, June 1958, 261-97.

Modigliani, F. and Miller, M.H. (1966) 'Some Estimates on The Cost of Capital to the Electric Utility Industry 1954-57,' *American Economic Review,* June 1966, 333-48.

Molodovsky, N. (1974) *Investment Values in a Dynamic World: Collected Papers of Nicholas Molodovsky,* Homewood, Ill.: Richard D. Irwin, Inc., 1974.

Morin, R.A. (1976) 'Capital Asset Pricing Theory: The Canadian Experience,' Unpublished doctoral dissertation, Philadelphia Pa.: Wharton School of Finance.

Morin, R.A. (1981) 'Market Line Theory and the Canadian Equity Market,' *Journal of Business Administration* 12(1), Capital Markets in Canada, ed. M.J. Brennan, Fall 1980, 57-76.

Morin, R.A. (1981A), *Georgia Power Company,* Prepared Testimony, Federal Energy Regulatory Commission, Docket # ER 81-730.

Morin, R.A. (1982) *Metropolitan Edison Co.,* Prepared Testimony, Pennsylvania Public Utility Commission, Docket # R-822249.

Morin, R.A. (1983) *Georgia Power Company,* Prepared Testimony, Georgia Public Service Commission, Docket # 3397-U.

Morin, R.A. (1983A) *Determining Cost of Capital for Regulated Industries,* Public Utilities Reports, Inc. & The Manaement Exchange, Inc., Washington, D.C. (with V.L. Andrews).

Morin, R.A. (1983B) "Hedging Regulatory Lag with Futures Contracts,' *Journal of Finance,* May 1983, (with R. Kolb and G. Gay).

Morin, R.A. (1983C) *Southern Bell,* Prepared Testimony, North Carolina Utilities Commission, Docket # P-55-816.

Morris, R.B. (1980) 'The Effect of Tax Flow Through on the Cost of Public Utility Debt,' *Public Utilities Fortnightly,* Nov. 6, 1980, 22-24.

Mullins, D.W. (1982) 'Does the Capital Asset Pricing Model Work?' *Harvard Business Review,* Jan.-Feb. 1982, 105-14.

Murphy, J.E. (1966) 'Relative Growth in Earnings per Share — Past and Future,' *Financial Analysts Journal,* Nov.-Dec. 1966.

Myers, S.C. (1971) *American Telephone and Telegraph Co.,* Prepared Testimony, F.C.C. Docket # 19129.

Myers, S.C. (1972) 'The Application of Finance Theory to Public Utility Rate Case,' *The Bell Journal of Economics and Management Science* 3(1), 1972, 58-97.

Myers, S.C. (1977) 'The Relation Between Real and Financial Measures of Risk and Return,' in *Risk and Return on Finance*, Vol. 1, ed. I. Friend and Bicksler, J.L., Cambridge, Mass.: Ballinger, 1977.

Nathan, R.R. (1983) *Southern Bell*, Prepared Testimony, Georgia Public Service Commission, Docket # 3396-U.

Navarro, P. (1983) 'How Wall Street Ranks the Public Utility Commissions,' *Financial Analysts Journal*, Nov.-Dec. 1983, 46-9.

Patterson, C.S. (1973) *Methods for the Estimation of the Cost of Common Equity Capital*,' Bell Canada, 1973.

Patterson, C.S. (1983) 'Flotation Cost Allowance in Rate of Return Regulation: Comment,' *Journal of Finance* 38(4), Sept. 1983, 1335-8.

Patterson, C.S. (1983A) 'Dilution Compensation versus Dilution Prevention: Some Clarifications,' *Public Utilities Fortnightly*, Nov. 10, 1983, 49-51.

Patterson, C.S. (1983B) 'The Effects of Leverage on the Revenue Requirements of Public Utilities,' *Financial Management* 12(3), Autumn 1983, 29-39.

Pettway, R.H. and Jordan, B.D. (1983) 'Diversification, Double Leverage, and the Cost of Capital,' *Journal of Financial Research* 6(4), Winter 1983, 289-300.

Phillips, C.F. (1969) *The Economics of Regulation*, 2nd ed. Homewood, Ill: Irwin, 1969.

Pogue, G.A. (1979) *Williams Pipe Line Co.*, Prepared Testimony, Federal Energy Regulatory Commission, Docket # OR79-1.

Rao, C. and Litzenberger, R. (1971) 'Leverage and the Cost of Capital in a Less Developed Market: Comment,' *Journal of Finance*, June 1971, 777-85.

Reilly, F.K. (1979) *Investment Analysis and Portfolio Management*, Hinsdale, Ill.: The Dryden Press, 1979.

Reinganum, M.R. (1981) 'The Arbitrage Pricing Theory: Some Empirical Results,' *Journal of Finance*, May 1981, 313-21.

Reinganum, M.R. (1981A) 'Misspecification of Capital Asset Pricing: Empirical Anomalies Based on Earnings Yields and Market Values,' *Journal of Financial Economics*, March 1981, 19-46.

Rhyne, R.G. (1982) *Southern Bell*, Prepared Testimony, South Carolina Public Service Commission, Docket # 82-294-C.

Richter, P.H. (1982) 'The Ever-present Need for an Underpricing Allowance,' *Public Utilities Fortnightly*, Feb. 18, 1982, 58-61.

Richter, P.H. (1982A) 'The Correct Transformation Equations — A Rebuttal to 'Flotation Cost Allowance in Rate of Return Regulation: A Note,' ' Working Paper, Treasury Dept., AT&T, 1982.

Robichek, A.A. (1978) 'Regulation and Modern Finance Theory,' *Journal of Finance* 33(3), June 1978, 693-705.

Robichek, A.A. *et al.* (1973) 'The Effect of Leverage on the Cost of Equity Capital of Electric Utility Firms,' Journal of Finance 28(2), May 1973, 353-67.

Roll, R. (1977) 'A Critique of the Asset Pricing Theory's Tests,' *Journal of Financial Economics*, March 1977, 129-176.

Roll, R. (1981) 'A Possible Explanation of the Small Firm Effect, *Journal of Finance*, Sept. 1981, 879-88.

Roll, R. and Ross, S. (1980) 'An Empirical Investigation of the Arbitrage Pricing Theory,' *Journal of Finance*, Dec. 1980, 1073-1103.

Roll, R. and Ross S. (1983) 'Regulation, the Capital Asset Pricing Model, and the Arbitrage Pricing Theory,' *Public Utilities Fortnightly*, May 26, 1983, 22-8.

Rosenberg, V. and Guy, J. (1976) 'Prediction of Beta from Investment Fundamentals,' *Financial Anc'ysts Journal*, 32(4), Jul.-Aug. 1976, 62-70.

Rosenberg, V. and Marathe, V. (1975) 'The Prediction of Investment Risk: Systematic and Residual Risk,' Proceedings of the Seminar on the Analysis of Security Prices, University of Chicago, 20(1), Nov. 1975.

Rosenberg, V. and McKibben, W. (1973) 'The Prediction of Systematic Risk in Common Stocks,' Journal of Financial and Quantitative Analysis 8(3), March 1973, 317-33.

Ross, S. (1976) 'The Arbitrage Theory of Capital Asset Pricing,' Journal of Economic Theory, Dec. 1976, 341-60.

Ross, S. (1978) 'The Current Status of the Capital Asset Pricing Model,' Journal of Finance 23(3), 885-902.

Rubinstein, M.E. (1973) 'A Mean-Variance Synthesis of Corporate Financial Theory,' Journal of Financial Economics, March 1973, 167-82.

Schwendiman, C.J. and Pinches, G.E. (1975) 'An Analysis of Alternative Measures of Investment Risk,' Journal of Finance 30, March 1975, 193-200.

Shanken, J. (1982) 'The Arbitrage Pricing Theory: Is It Testable?' Journal of Finance, Dec. 1982, 1129-40.

Sharpe, W.F. (1981) Investments, 2nd ed., Englewood Cliffs, N.J.: Prentice-Hall 1981.

Solomon, E. (1970) 'Alternative Rate of Return Concepts and Their Implications for Utility Regulation,' The Bell Journal of Economics and Management Science 1(1), Spring 1970, 65-81.

Solomon, E. and Laya, J.E. (1967) 'Measurement of Company Profitability: Some Systematic Errors in the Accounting Rate of Return,' in Financial Research and Management Decisions, A.A. Robichek, ed., N.Y.: Wiley & Sons, 1967.

Standard & Poor's (1982) Credit Overview: Corporate and International Ratings, Standard & Poor's Corp., N.Y. 1982.

Stanley, Lewellen, and Schlarbaum (1981) 'Further Evidence on the Value of Professional Investment Research,' Journal of Financial Research, Spring 1981.

Tobin, J. and Brainard, W.C. (1971) 'Pitfalls in Financial Medel Building,' American Economic Review 58(2), May 1968, 104; Tobin, J., Essays in Economics, Vol. 1: Macroeconomics, Chicago: Markham Publishing Co., 1971, 322-38.

Touche Ross Co. (1982) 'Proxy Disclosures and Stockholder Attitudes,' May 1982.

Trout, R.R. (1979) 'The Regulatory Factor and Electric Utility Common Stock Investment Value,' Public Utilities Fortnightly, Nov. 22, 1979.

Vander Weide, J.H. (1983) General Telephone Company of Illinois, Prepared Testimony, ICC Docket # 82-0458.

Von Furstenberg, G.M. (1977) 'Corporate Investment: Does Market Valuation Matter in the Aggregate?' Brookings Papers on Economic Activity, No. 2, Spring 1977, 35061.

Wagner, W.H. and Lau, S.C. (1971) 'The Effect of Diversification on Risk,' Financial Analysts Journal 27(6), Nov.-Dec. 1971, 48-57.

Wakeman, L.M. (1978) 'Bond Rating Agencies and Capital Markets,' Working Paper, UCLA Graduate School of Management, 1982.

Weinstein, M.I. (1978) 'The Seasoning Process of New Corporate Bond Issues,' Journal of Finance, Dec. 1978, 1343-54.

Westmoreland, G. (1979) 'Electric Utilities' Accounting for CWIP: The Effects of Alternative Methods on the Financial Statements, Utility Rates and Market-to-Book Ratio,' PhD dissertation, University of Florida, 1979.

Williams, J.B. (1938) The Theory of Investment Value, Cambridge, Mass.: Harvard University Press, 1938. Reprinted in Lorie, J. and Brealey, R., ed. Modern Developments in Investment Management: A Book of Readings, 2d ed., Hinsdale, Ill.: Dryden Press, 1978, 471-91.